THE LIBRARY OF HOLOCAU.

My Lost World
A Survivor's Tale

The Library of Holocaust Testimonies

My Lost World by Sara Rosen
From Dachau to Dunkirk by Fred Pelican
Breathe Deeply, My Son by Henry Wermuth
My Private War by Jacob Gerstenfeld-Maltiel
A Cat Called Adolf by Trude Levi
An End to Childhood by Miriam Akavia
A Child Alone by Martha Blend
I Light a Candle by Gena Turgel
My Heart in a Suitcase by Anne L. Fox

My Lost World
A Survivor's Tale

SARA ROSEN

VALLENTINE MITCHELL
LONDON • PORTLAND, OR

First published in 1993 in Great Britain by
VALLENTINE MITCHELL & CO. LTD.
Newbury House, 900 Eastern Avenue,
London IG2 7HH, England

and in the United States of America by
VALLENTINE MITCHELL
c/o ISBS,
5804 N.E. Hassalo Street, Portland, Oregon 97213-3644

Copyright © 1993 Sara Rosen
First published 1993
Reprinted 1996

British Library Cataloguing in Publication Data
Rosen, Sara
  My Lost World: A Survivor's Tale
  (The Library of Holocaust Testimonies Series)
  I. Title   II. Series
  940.5318092

ISBN 0-85303-254-8

Library of Congress Cataloging-in-Publication Data
Rosen, Sara.
    My Lost World: A Survivor's Tale / Sara Rosen.
      p.   cm.— (The Library of Holocaust Testimonies)
    ISBN 0-85303-254-8
    1. Rosen, Sara. 2. Jews—Poland—Biography. 3. Holocaust, Jewish
  (1939–1956)—Poland—Personal Narratives. 4. Poland—Biography.
  I. Title. II. Series.
  DS135.P63R66   1993
  940.53'18'092—dc20
  [B]   92-18032
                                                          CIP

Typeset by Regent Typesetting, London

Printed and bound in the United Kingdom by
Watkiss Studios Limited, Holme Court, Biggleswade, Beds.

Contents

The Library of Holocaust Testimonies
  Martin Gilbert   ix
Introduction
  Antony Polonsky   xi
Acknowledgements   xiii
Preface   xv

PART ONE   THE FAMILY

1. As it was   3
2. The Landerers   9
3. The Weinbergers   28
4. Tradition   52
      Shabbat at home   54
5. Holidays   62
      Sukkoth and Simhat Torah   62
      Hanukkah   65
      Purim   68
      Passover   72
      Shabuoth   75
      Rosh Hashanah and Yom Kippur   76

PART TWO   OCCUPATION

6.   The end of childhood   83
7.   The Occupation begins   90
8.   Midwinter nightmares   97
9.   Black Friday   104
10. Wedrowka   110
11. Ghetto Tarnow   116
12. Letters   125
13. The Weinbergers in Nowy Sacz   143
14. Action in Tarnow   147
15. Escape and return   153
16. "Dus Pintale Yid"   166
17. Faithful friend   169
18. Disappearances   173
19. Ghetto Bochnia   177
20. The little action in Bochnia   181
21. The Baudienst   184
22. The people from Wisnicz: A Bochnia memory   189
23. Arbeitslager   195
24. Joseph and Szaye Horowitz   202
25. Escape. On Ilona's road   208
26. Over the border   218
27. In Hungary   229
28. Among Hungarian peasants   236
29. Back in Budapest   244
30. Over another border   252
31. In Romania   263
32. At long last free   269

PART THREE   NEW LIFE BEGINS

33. Tel Aviv   277
34. No home to go back to   287
35. Eulogy   292

The Library of Holocaust Testimonies

It is greatly to the credit of Frank Cass that this series of survivors' testimonies is being published in Britain. The need for such a series has long been apparent here, where many survivors made their homes.

Since the end of the war in 1945 the terrible events of the Nazi destruction of European Jewry have cast a pall over our time. Six million Jews were murdered within a short period; the few survivors have had to carry in their memories whatever remains of the knowledge of Jewish life in more than a dozen countries, in several thousand towns, in tens of thousands of villages, and in innumerable families. The precious gift of recollection has been the sole memorial for millions of people whose lives were suddenly and brutally cut off.

For many years, individual survivors have published their testimonies. But many more have been reluctant to do so, often because they could not believe that they would find a publisher for their efforts.

In my own work over the past two decades, I have been approached by many survivors who had set down their memories in writing, but who did not know how to have them published. I realized what a considerable emotional strain the writing down of such hellish memories had been. I also realized, as I read many dozens of such accounts, how important each account was, in its own way, in recounting aspects of the story that had not been told before, and adding to our understanding of the wide range of human suffering, struggle and aspiration.

With so many people and so many places involved, including many hundreds of camps, it was inevitable that the historians and students of the Holocaust should find it difficult at times to grasp the scale and range of the events. The publication of memoirs is therefore an indispensable part of the extension of knowledge, and of public awareness of the crimes that had been committed against a whole people.

Martin Gilbert
Merton College
Oxford

Introduction

The Nazi mass murder of the Jews caused the destruction of a whole civilization of East European Jewry with its rich and many sided culture, its vitality, its remarkable creativity in the religious and secular fields, in Hebrew, Yiddish and the languages of the surrounding peoples and in all fields of human endeavour. This devastating act of barbarity was accomplished through the murder of six million men, women and children. It has often been justly observed that whereas the death of one individual is a tragedy, the death of ten thousand becomes a statistic. The great value of books like Sara Rosen's is that they give a human face to the Jewish tragedy, they provide the physiognomy of the faceless, and give form and content to the so cruelly wiped out nameless multitude.

Sara Rosen was born into a prosperous Jewish family in Krakow which enjoyed comfortable relations with the surrounding Polish environment but was still deeply rooted in Jewish tradition and Jewish past. The stability of Jewish life in pre-1939 Eastern Europe has sometimes been idealised and its warmth and cohesiveness given a romantic glow. Yet the picture Sara Rosen paints is convincing and it was the strength of her family ties which enabled her parents, her siblings and herself to summon up the fortitude to deal with the ordeal of Nazi rule. They did not face this ordeal together. Her father and two brothers managed to flee to the Soviet Union from where they wrote guarded and self-censored letters attempting to reassure Sara and her mother and sister of their welfare, while the Landerer women sent to their menfolk equally cheerful and reassuring letters. Some of these her father managed to salvage and they form a moving part of this book. From Russia, their father and one brother eventually made their way to *Eretz Israel*. The other brother went to Belgium together with his wife, a girl from Mielec he met in Siberia. The mother with her two daughters were first moved to a ghetto in Tarnow, from where Sara and her mother escaped to ghetto Bochnia, while Lela, the older girl, perished in Tarnow. Hoping to elude deportation to death camps the women were fleeing from ghetto to ghetto, until in the summer of 1943 Sara and her mother escaped from Poland to Hungary. After the German occupation of Hungary, Sara and her mother fled to Romania where they became liberated by the Red Army. In December of 1944 they left Europe and after a most perilous journey arrived in Palestine in January 1945.

The Landerer family were among the fortunate few who managed by luck and good fortune to survive the *Shoah* with the loss of only one of its members. But Sara Rosen is very conscious of the fact that her fate was exceptional and was not shared by most of her extended family or by the bulk of her fellow Jews in Poland. She concludes her moving and heart-warming account with an attempt to summon up those of her family who did not survive. This obligation to remember is one we all share. It is only by remembering and by giving form to the nameless dead that we can experience the pain of mourning. Only a real understanding, intellectual and emotional, of what we have lost will enable us to start to rebuild something of what was destroyed. To that attempt at rebuilding, Sara Rosen's book is a small but significant contribution.

Antony Polonsky
Brandeis University

Preface

This is a story of one person, one life, one family, one escape and at the same time this is a story of millions of people, their lives and families.

This is a story of one youngster who escaped and of many others who perished.

This is a story of a world that used to be and was wiped out, a story of people and their way of life, as it was and could never be restored.

This is a story of the largest Jewish community in the world, which is no more.

This is a story of a country that will never be the same again for us, the remnants of Polish Jewry.

This is a story of one survivor, and this is a story of all survivors.

Sara Rosen

Acknowledgements

Before I close my manuscript I pause for a moment to acknowledge all those without whom this book would have never come to be. It took me ten years to write – the reader will understand why.

The first to encourage me was Professor William Mara from Fordham University whose faith in my ability made me go on with my work.

My son Mickey, my first unofficial reader, for his constructive criticism that made me see my mistakes.

To Rachel, my daughter and my friend, whose unbounded enthusiasm helped me to go on in spite of the emotional upheaval my remembrances caused.

Mr Moshe Sheinbaum from Shengold Publishing, a good friend, whose guidance helped me bring the manuscript to its present form.

To Professor Lucjan Dobroszycki whose constant encouragement and laudatory appraisal of my work reinforced my often sagging spirit.

To Mr Frank Cass of Vallentine Mitchell and Mr Ben Helfgott of the Yad Vashem Society in London for bestowing on me the honor of accepting my manuscript for the inauguration of the Library of Holocaust Testimonies.

To Professor Antony Polonsky, for his unselfish interest and readiness to be always of help.

To one of the best friends I ever had even though I haven't met him yet, Raphael "Felek" Scharf, who so generously gave of his time, took care of myriad of details that go with publishing a manuscript, and therefore should be considered as the godfather of my book.

And my husband Joe for his patience and understanding, and for just being there whenever I needed him.

To my precious family and my dear friends, Thank you all!

Sara Rosen

The clouds are gathering ...

Polały się łzy me czyste, rzęsiste
Za moją młodość chumurną i durną
Za moje dzieciństwo sielskie, anielskie
Za mój wiek męski, wiek klęski –
Polaly się łzy me czyste ...

Adam Mickiewicz

Tears were gushing, my tears abundant and clear
For my youth lofty and dull
For my childhood bucolic, angelic
For my age of manhood, age of defeat
Tears were gushing, my tears ...

(translated by S.R.)

Part One • The family

1 · *As it was*

My own Odyssey starts with the story of my own beginnings: the family. We were Landerers, Horowitzes, Anisfelds, Rottenstreichs, Goldwassers, and Balkens, aunts and uncles, first, second, and third cousins, grandparents, people related by marriage, a vast network of Polish Jews. We lived in Krakow in the part of southern Poland called Galicia, which constituted part of Austrian Kronland between the years 1772 and 1918. Some of us were well off, some weren't, but it didn't matter. We all belonged. Years have gone by since I last saw them, but in my memory they live as they were then, long ago, a happy, sunny time when we were all together. I'm a mature woman now, but I see them through the eyes of a happy, pampered, and protected child.

Belonging to our kind of family meant having all goals and ambitions spelled out clearly. Generation after generation of young people held onto family tradition, thus fulfilling the expectations of their elders. Each person was a single link in a great, strong chain of love, binding and holding us all together.

Our family was typical of well-established Hassidic families in Galicia. Closely knit, relying upon one another for advice, moral and material support, we felt pride and security in our large numbers and numerous connections, which formed a protective shield around each member.

A large family provided drama and excitement throughout the year, days of joy intertwined with days of sorrow. Three times death knocked at our doors during the period I remember and three times my serene childhood was disturbed by uncomprehensible events that reduced the adults into frightened weepers. The first tragedy to hit the Landerer family was the death of my cousin Pepcia. She became ill very suddenly, and we heard the strange word "meningitis." My

3

mother went to the hospital every day, but Mother was always expected to take over in all the family's emergencies, so we thought little of that, even when she would return late in the evening, subdued and remote. It wasn't until Father came home from an afternoon at the sick girl's bedside and broke down and cried that we became frightened.

Pepcia's life slipped away while her family stood by helpless. I was about ten years old then. Pepcia was one of the kids in the family and suddenly she wasn't anymore. She was younger than I and not my particular pal, so I did not miss her greatly. After her death, my standing among my friends became somewhat elevated; I was the girl whose cousin died. I did not know then that death could leave an unfilled void and never-ending longing.

Then the Horowitz family suffered a loss. One of my mother's younger brothers, Itzek, was found to have cancer. In those days it was a rare disease, and in order to assure for him the best medical care available, he was brought to Krakow from Jaworzno, a few miles away, where he lived. Poor Uncle Itzek, it was as if the lucky star under which most of his siblings seemed to have been born, had hidden behind a cloud at the moment of Itzek's birth. He was not as good looking as his brothers and lacked the exuberance and vitality they projected. He was shy and quiet, attributes not very helpful in trying to eke out a living in the competitive business world of prewar Poland. No matter how the family tried to help him to advance, he never got very far, and now cancer.

Itzek's Horowitz good attributes were acknowledged only after his death. The entire shtetl came to his funeral. I remember mother telling me that the rabbi said in the eulogy: "We are taking farewell of one who followed the footsteps of Abraham, our forefather." When I asked for an explanation, she told me that her brother gave away the one good suit he owned to a poor orphan boy about to be married. "I am married already," he said. "I don't need it."

The brothers and sisters mourned and missed him but because they were not accustomed to see and talk to him every day, his demise did not leave a particular emptiness, especially not in my life. It was only when my Grandfather Horowitz died suddenly, that my little world trembled. He was a figure that everybody looked up to. My own parents, those invulnerable, mighty people (in my concept) assumed

4

an air of greatest humility in the presence of "Tate", as his children called him. I had no personal relationship with him, because his Polish was not very good, but it did not bother me a bit. He was not somebody to relate to as one would to another mere human. The love and respect he generated put him in a special category. He didn't have to say much. "How are you today, good girl or good boy?" was enough to make everyone of his numerous grandchildren ecstatic. Love for Grandfather was a mixture of unquestioning adoration (It was unthinkable that he might ever be wrong) and fear. In spite of his short stature, he was a towering presence in our family. His death left a great void in our lives, as if the crown and glory of the Horowitz clan had been taken away.

I remember more clearly the days of joy. Because the members of our family were all relatively young, there were many occasions for lavish celebrations.

Bar-mitzvah, a boy's rite of passage from childhood to manhood was quietly observed (quite different from the gala event celebrated by most American Jews). On the day of his thirteenth birthday, a boy would put on his phylacteries for the first time in the synagogue. After morning services, because it was customarily done during the morning, pieces of sponge and honey cake were washed down with small sips of spirits. Joyful "L'chayim"s and "Mazel-tovs" resounded in an usually quiet house of prayer, and in no time the men were hurrying off to their daily tasks. The Bar-Mitzvah boy and his friends were permitted to linger in the courtyard, huffing and puffing on the few cigarettes customarily distributed by the Bar-Mitzvah boy. When the last stub was extinguished they returned to their studies. It was a strictly "For men only" affair.

It was only during the *Seuda-Shilshit* (the third Shabat meal) on the following Shabbat, that a boy's entry into the brotherhood of Jewish men became officially acknowledged. As was the custom of long ago, a Bar-Mitzvah boy was expected to deliver a discourse demonstrating his scholarship. No one however, no matter how brilliant the content and delivery, was ever allowed to finish. Out of consideration that many of the thirteen-year-olds were not capable of mastering such a difficult task, the entire assembly would soon break out in a spirited Hassidic song, which signaled the end of the oration. The timing always depended upon the quality of the performance.

5

A boy's third birthday was synonymous with a first haircut. Like a tree, whose fruit must remain untouched during its first three years of growth, was a boy's hair let to go free during his first three years. After the first visit to the barber, the child was usually taken to the heder to get acquainted with his future classmates and teacher. Fistfuls of candies were distributed to everyone present, making it a pleasant occasion.

At four, a boy began to learn the Hebrew alphabet, an event likened by the rabbis to the four-year-old crops that had to be brought as offerings to the Temple in Jerusalem. By their fifth birthday, boys had to be ready to begin the study of the Bible in its original, unabridged text.

A boy's fifth birthday was the partying birthday, the *Seudath Hamesh*. The number *five-hamesh* symbolizes the Five Books of Moses and the age of the child. Those festivities marked the beginning of what all parents hoped would be a life of study and commitment to the Bible, the Talmud, and the values they affirm. It was taken for granted that every child entering heder was fluent in Yiddish the language in which the classes were conducted, and the Bible translated. The children spoke Polish too, and thus from an early age the Jewish boys were subjected to strict intellectual discipline.

Heder was a day school with classes conducted all day long with a recess for lunch. The classes were usually large, a class of forty or fifty being quite normal. Often they were conducted in a belfer's kitchen or family room, where the children were crowded together on narrow benches along a bare, wooden table. Students at different levels of proficiency were dumped together, and harassed belfers conducted classes by methods defying all the rules of modern pedagogy and child psychology. Discipline was maintained by corporal punishment, usually given and taken with a grain of humor. And yet, in spite of all the "wrong" things done to them, the majority of those boys were perfectly well adjusted, and progressed in their studies.

I was too young to remember my own brothers Seudoth Hamesh, but somehow one of my cousin Moshe remains in my memory. My aunt Bala Horowitz was one of the best cooks in the family, and the repast she prepared for that occasion gave full credit to her reputation. The entire family from Krakow and some from out of town, neighbors, and friends crowded their spacious apartment. It seemed as if the entire community were there. Separate tables were set in different rooms for men and women, but as most of the guests were related, they happily intermingled anyway. Only the Grand Rabbi and his entourage remained seated at their table. The high point of this banquet was a little dialogue between the birthday boy and one of his older cousins. Both tykes were put on chairs so that everybody could see them. Moshe was asked a few questions pertaining to his study in the heder. The ritual was repeated at every Seudath Hamesh, usually concluded by a triumphant, friendly exclamation: "Du bist avade a voiler bucher!" (You sure are a terrific guy!) This, emphasized by a supposedly friendly kneep in the bakel (pinch in the cheek) that seemed to me more like a slap, reduced Moshe to tears. Picked up and embraced by strong, loving arms of his father, covered by teary kisses of his mother and aunts, the child soon recovered his composure and went on to enjoy his great day.

But the most exciting of all were the matches. In order to assure that the background of a prospective bride or groom was acceptable to our family standards, a thorough investigation, often going back over generations of long ago was conducted by the numerous relatives. Even when the young people were finally permitted to meet face to face and took a liking to each other, the choice had still to be approved by the majority.

My mother, being one of the oldest of fourteen children, had a very decisive voice, and she was not one to tolerate maudlin romantic notions. And yet she herself had married out of love, an unheard of thing in those times and circles. But my mother always knew what she wanted. She refused all suggested matches, married the man she loved, and lived happily ever after.

Nobody was forced into marriage against his will, but even so, there wasn't much choice. The selection was made by the elders, and the young people had only the option of choosing among acceptable prospects. No one asked what their dreams were, and I assume that sometimes, during youth or childhood, they must have entertained rosy, romantic fancies. But soon enough they were made to understand that life wasn't lived in order that one's romantic dreams might come true. Living a full, happy life meant being able to satisfy all of God's commandments and commitments toward family and community. A woman with a devoted husband, obedient children, and a nice home felt fulfilled. A man was supposed to strive to become a Talmudic scholar, to support his family, and be a respected member of the community. These ambitions, when achieved, formed a pretty solid foundation for marital bliss.

But dreams they all had. A story from Grandmother Landerer's childhood in the tiny village of Zator, high in the Karpathian Mountains circulated in the family. At the time she was growing up, hoop skirts were the vogue. When her sisters got their hoops, she badly wanted a set too, but her mother decided that she was too young for that kind of finery. Grandmother was not one to give up easily. She promptly removed a hoop from a barrel and fastened it into her petticoat.

What dreams about waltzing in great ballrooms and being swept off her feet by dashing cavaliers she must have dreamed! The reality of her life dashed them all. As a young girl she was married to a prosperous widower with six children, and after bearing six more, she herself was widowed at an early age.

But as though to prove that the demands of living under a strict tradition and hardships need not crush the human spirit, she lived a life of ingenuity, inventiveness, vigor, and good humor, until her seventy-fifth year. I'll start my story with Grandmother Landerer.

2 · The Landerers

Grandmother Landerer

A small, dark figure, always in the background, was moving quietly about the house. Her long skirt swished around as she efficiently attended to her daily tasks. Not a stylish person, she never conformed to the perpetually changing mode of women's wear. Her outfits, all made to the same patterns, consisted of a long skirt gathered at the waist and a fitted short jacket with long, narrow sleeves, one row of small buttons down the front and a little round collar around the neck. Black-laced shoes, black stockings, and the eternal wig, seemed to be a part of her. Her dresses were made out of worsted in winter, and a similar looking but lightweight fabric in the summer, always in a dark shade of gray.

We, granddaughters, brought up in the modern way of life, hardly knew her. Every Shabbat and holiday afternoon we visited her dutifully, kissed her hand, and curtsied, as was the custom of the day. In her broken Polish she inquired about our well-being, asked us to sit down with her and offered us her home-baked cookies and sourballs. We didn't like those sour candles or the crumbling cookies, but she always insisted.

"Take it, take it," she used to say with a smile, while pushing a cookie or a candy into a reluctant fist.

That was the contact we had with her. Having been brought up in a culture that revered old age, we paid our tribute to Grandmother out of duty, with little enthusiasm. But she adored us all indiscriminately. We represented the embodiment of her boldest dreams. These progressively brought up granddaughters, speaking impeccable Polish, skiing, skating, swimming, taking piano lessons, always beautifully dressed, must have been a source of unending pride for her. She loved us not for what we were as individuals, because she did

9

not know us as such, but as living proof of her children's success. We were poised and worldly the way she must have wanted to be, but more important, we were hers!

Always an early riser, every Friday she was up before dawn, to be the first one in the fish store, so she could get her pick of the fresh catch. When I was about five years old, I had to undergo an emergency appendix removal. In preantibiotic days, any surgical procedure was dangerous, and my parents decided not to tell her. But news traveled fast in the tightly knit Jewish community of Podgorze, and everybody knew and talked about my operation. Thus the storekeeper, wanting to show an old customer how concerned she was, greeted my grandmother with the words: "Good morning, Mrs. Landerer. Is your granddaughter coming along well after the operation? And when will she be coming home?"

Grandmother was stunned and demanded to see me immediately. All I remember is seeing her early in the morning in my hospital room. I was still sore from the surgery and a little groggy from the night's restless sleep, where a small, dark figure bent over my bed, touched me, gently kissed my hand, and said a few words in Yiddish. She was too agitated to speak Polish. I saw tears in the corners of her eyes, and one of them detached itself and fell on my cheek. Grandma wiped it with her finger and left the room.

At one time my unprepossessing grandmother became a kind of celebrity. Our relatives from another town were stricken by a grave disaster. Their daughter, a beautiful, young girl became a melancholic, what today would probably be diagnosed as a manic-depressive. Mental diseases and psychological disorders were considered a stain upon family reputation, creating a disturbance in life with which very few people could deal. The most famous mental hospital in Poland was located in Kobierzyn, near Krakow, where the heartbroken father took his daughter. After an initial four-week stay needed to evaluate her condition, he was told that his daughter was incurably ill. The medical specialists had no remedy for her sickness. She could remain in the institution for the rest of her life, but she would never improve. The cost of keeping her there was beyond his means, so he was forced to take her home.

One day the stunned father took her to my grandmother and asked her to watch over the stricken girl while he went out. Grandmother was home alone, and good-naturedly invited the girl to stay. A few hours went by, and the anguished father came back to collect his unfortunate daughter. He had just knocked at the door when he heard the girl say in a normal tone, "You are right, Mrs. Landerer." She opened the door herself and addressed her father directly for the first time since she became ill saying "Let us hurry, Father. We might miss the train and Mother would worry." He stared at her in disbelief and then burst out crying.

They returned home to their own town, and the girl resumed normal life. She was never sick again. Some time later she married, emigrated to Palestine, had two children, and for many years worked as a kindergarten teacher.

It was a sensation, a real miracle! Grandma was besieged with questions.

"What did you do?"

"Oh, nothing, nothing?"

"But you must have done *something*. The doctors proclaimed her hopeless, and she walked out of your house as if nothing ever happened to her."

"I just talked to her," Grandma answered quietly. "What do the doctors know? Only what they read in their books. I know what I learned from life."

"But what did you say to her?"

"I just started by saying: Look, Mania, a beautiful, smart girl like you, and what are you doing to your father? He has become an old man in these few months since you have been acting sick."

"What did Mania say to that?"

"At the beginning she seemed not to listen at all, but I just kept talking and talking, because I'd made up my mind not to give up on that girl. One cannot give up on a child. I thought about her mother – I just could not agree that there was no hope. There is always hope in life! And so, I kept on talking about her parents, her life and future, and all that came into my mind. I don't remember anymore what I said. The girl just sat there, and finally I started to run out of breath, and then we heard the knock at the door. Mania got up – and returned to life."

My grandmother, without any knowledge of psychiatry or psychology, without formal education, conducted a marathon therapy ses-

11

sion, fifty years ahead of her time. So strong was her faith and personality that she accomplished in a few hours time what trained physicians failed to do in a month. That small, quiet, always hiding-in-the-background woman who was my grandmother, how many secret powers and gifts did she possess?

Seemingly frail, she was full of vigor and strength. Although she made her home with her daughter Ryfka Balken, she often visited her other children and stayed with them for prolonged periods of time. The winter of 1939 she spent in Krakow, because the Balkens had moved to Sambor then in eastern Poland, now Stary Sambor, U.S.S.R. First she was with her oldest daughter, Haya Goldwasser, later with her youngest son, Haskel. While she stayed there, we found that our grandmother was quite a character. She established herself in Aunt Sala's kitchen. There was an unspoken, unwritten agreement: Sala was a young woman who enjoyed being relieved of the kitchen chores for a while, Grandma was old, and cooking occupied and filled many long hours of her otherwise empty days. Taking care of her family was Grandma's idea of fulfillment in life. The large household she married into and the raising of her own six children hadn't left her much time to be idle, so she was accustomed to being busy – busy always. No arguments could convince her that she needed rest or should take things a bit easier. A bit easier? Not for her?

Koshering of the meat was a long and intricate process, which she didn't trust to anyone but herself. Whatever meat was on the menu for a particular day had first to be submerged in cold water, soaked for half an hour, afterward salted and left in salt for an hour. When the hour was over, the meat was rinsed in cold water and ready for cooking. Every kosher household had a large pail, similar to those used to bathe babies but serving the sole purpose of soaking the meat. When the pail was filled with water to the brim, so that the submerged meat was completely covered, it was very heavy. Much, much too heavy for an old lady, over seventy years of age. But not for Grandma! Left alone in the kitchen for one moment, she used to pick up the pail from the floor and empty it into the sink. With an disarming smile, she used to promise never to do it again – and next day, she would forget her promise.

Once she was taken ill and had to stay in bed for a few days. In order to please her, her granddaughter Dorcia Goldwasser made her a bedjacket out of pink flannel. The little old lady, always dressed in dark gray, was as happy as a child.

"Look how nice this pink color looks on me. Maybe I shouldn't be wearing always such dark colors?" she said, patting the soft fabric with her small hand. It was a rhetorical question, however, because when she got up from her sick bed after a few days, she put on her gray dress and became her old, sprightly self.

To celebrate the recovery, my parents bought her a new outfit. Again, the same style, the same color, only my mother saw to it that the fabric was of the best quality available. The thin wool fell down in soft pleats, the high collar and long sleeves covered her small body completely, camouflaging the vitality it contained.

Somehow, in a totally unconscious way, she liked to preen herself, to dress up, to look nice. Beaming, she showed off the new dress to all, and everybody assured her that, indeed, it was extremely becoming. We said it just to please her. Truthfully, it was hard to see the difference between the old garments and the new one.

She always wore a wig.

According to religious law, a married woman should not be seen with her head uncovered. With the sole exception of that one evening when she received visitors from her sickbed, I never saw her without one, but even then she had a kerchief tied over her head. Big and heavy, those wigs were a real nuisance. They were made out of human hair, which was threaded through tiny holes of a scalp-fitting net. This long and painstaking process was done by hand in many little shops scattered throughout the Jewish neighborhoods.

She was a pious woman for whom the observance of all religious regulations was of major importance. Following tradition, her black hair was shaved off the morning after the wedding ceremony, when she put on her wig for the first time. Since then she kept a careful watch the moment her hair grew a bit, she used to cut it herself with scissors reserved for that purpose.

One day her daughter-in-law Sala, a woman in her early thirties and already gray, heard her called out excitedly: "Sala, come here fast! QUICK!

Grandma was standing in front of a mirror, her scissors in one hand, the other pointing to a spot on her scalp.

13

"Look, I have gray hair already!"

For a long time afterwards often during our long evenings of curfews, this was our favorite anecdote. Poor, poor grandma! Only one of her ten granddaughters and two great-granddaughters lived to see her own hair getting gray.

Wolf Landerer

The sudden death of my grandfather, Bernard Landerer, from Makow Podhalanski abruptly ended my Father's childhood. A mere child, twelve years old at that time, he took up the yoke of providing for his mother and his five siblings. My grandmother Feiga was Bernard's second wife and there were older siblings, the children of the first wife.

Gela, the oldest of the unmarried half-sisters, a high spirited young woman, emigrated to the United States, where she married, and the younger sisters, Lena and Hana, followed soon after. After hard beginnings, so typical of all emigrants, they put down roots in the new country. Gela, who changed her name to Gussie, raised a large family – five sons and two daughters, who established an immensely successful chain of movie theaters.

Keen business acumen combined with the ability to deal with people, drive, and ambition, was characteristic of all Landerers, and they evidently took it to America with them.

At the time his nephews the Brandts were building their movie empire in the United States, my father was working his way up in the business world in Poland, and his stature in the Jewish community was rising steadily. Wolf Landerer's life was a Polish edition of a Horatio Alger story.

I remember Father telling me about his first business venture. The butchering of animals was regulated by the government, which put a tax on every head of cattle slaughtered. My father, hardly out of school at that time, received a license to collect the tax for every animal slaughtered in the entire district of Makow Podhalanski.

The transformation of the twelve-year-old boy into a legitimate tax collector was seen by the slaughterers and cattle dealers as a joke. Because of the nature of the slaughtering process, which includes transportation of noisy animals, the stench emanating from the

Sara Rosen's father, Wolf Landerer

entrails of the slaughtered beasts, and the generally messy procedure, the slaughterhouses were located in open fields, far away from the town. Confident that by switching the time of their operations from regular hours to after dark, they could dodge the burdensome impost undetected, some of the slaughterers changed their working schedule. That didn't fool my father for long. While other boys his age were safely tucked under the warm quilts, he, accompanied by a policeman, was traversing the countryside under the cover of darkness, collecting his dues.

Having a direct approach to slaughterhouses all over the county, he started buying and reselling hides, and before long he abandoned the troublesome franchise. By the time he married at the age of twenty-eight, he had been in the leather business for sixteen years and was already a man of substantial means. By the late 1930's, he was recognized as one of Poland's foremost experts in the tanning and marketing of hides and had established an export-import business with an international reputation.

After my parents were married in the year 1919, they settled in Krakow, a major commercial and cultural city with a large Jewish community. We, the four Landerer children, were born in a succession of apartments in the section of town called Podgorze, and when I was two years old, the family moved to the house on Bonifraterska Street in the heart of the Jewish section, Kazimierz. My parents' dream house, built according to their specifications was a modern structure, four stories high.

At that time my father had, in addition to his export business, a large retail store, where the entire family – or so it seemed – plus some very needy friends were employed: my father's brothers and brothers-in-law, Szymon Balken and Alter Goldwasser, mother's brother-in-law Meir-Haim, Uncle Joseph Horowitz, and even Joseph's father-in-law, Schmerl Balken.

The store took up the entire ground floor and was connected with the basement by a spiral staircase. A special lift to unload the hides from the trucks and transfer them into the basement was installed under the sidewalk. It was the first – or at any case, one of the first – contraption of that kind in Krakow.

Our apartment took up the entire second floor. My parents did not spare money or effort in order to create the house of their dreams. In the Jewish section, where most of the buildings were old and in run-down condition, it stood out. For many years it served as a model; even architects used to come and marvel at our movable glass wall connecting two rooms, the lattice metal doors at the ovens, the ultramodern bathroom, and the small sink hidden in the wall of the bedroom. Because ritual demanded that hands be washed right after rising from a night's sleep, a small sink was inconspicuously installed in my parents' bedroom. We had a sink in the dining room as well, because hands have to be washed before every meal.

There were six large rooms in the apartment, five facing the street, one – the smallest, our nursery – facing the courtyard. The spacious kitchen, pantry, the maids' room and bathroom, all faced the back-yard. The largest and most imposing room in the house, pompously called the Salon, was not furnished. It contained some pieces of furniture, probably discards from the old apartment, but certainly not of the kind one would expect of Mother's salon. We, children delighted in the empty space, where we played tennis and could perform a string of cartwheels without bumping into anything. "All the children in my class say that we are rich, and how come the room is not furnished?" I remember asking Mother once.

She smiled a wistfull smile. "The truth is that I almost had the room furnished. One of Father's business associates was moving and wanted us to buy a magnificent Oriental rug and antique furniture. I fell in love with them all, and in my imagination I had all that beauty arranged in my empty room. But when I asked your father if we could afford it, he said that yes, he certainly had the money – except that he had promised to give a dowry to two poor orphan girls, and he would hate to disappoint those children. Since we were still young and our future looked only bright, he assured me that one day he would buy me even more beautiful things."

"I can imagine what you answered."

"Giving charity with a large hand was the only personal luxury your father indulged in. I could not stand in his way."

This was my mother. No wonder that, with a wife like her, Father was counted among the biggest *Baalei Zedaka* (charitable men) not only in Krakow but in all of Galicia, even when he was still quite young. His reputation was justly earned.

Father's mastery of the Polish language was so unusual for a

Hassidic Jew in Poland that it singled him out favourable both among his Polish business associates and acquaintances and various government officials. He never hesitated to use his prestige or connections in order to help someone in trouble. Whether it was a license for a poor vendor in Krakow, a punishment for anti Semites harassing Jews in Zakopane, or a reprieve for a poor coal merchant in Jaworzno who was threatened by a creditor with an arrest on the eve of Passover, Father always accomplished what he set out to do. Thus, before he knew how it all came to be, he found himself an unofficial intermediary between the Hassidic community and the local government. Together with Rabbi Hirsh Ajzenstadt, another Orthodox Jew with an impeccable mastery of the Polish language, he used to represent the Orthodox segment of Jewish population whenever the need arose.

As Father's reputation in the international market of hides grew, he was offered the position of representative of Argolanda, a Dutch firm in Rotterdam, for all Poland. Argolanda was a part of a large conglomerate whose chief stockholder was Van der Vorm, a member of the Dutch royal family. All personal dealings with Argolanda and the entire correspondence were conducted in German. All letters, statements, memoranda, were written by Father, with Mother acting as his sole critic and adviser. Argolanda's director, a Mr. Schroeder, became Father's friend and was entertained in our house during his visits to Poland. He was especially partial to Mother's famous almond cake, the fluden, and never failed to take some home for his wife.

Shortly before the war Argolanda begun to exert pressure on Father to move to the Netherlands and become part of their operations there. I remember mother's reaction as clearly as if it were yesterday.

"What are you saying, Wolf? I should move to Holland? Can you imagine a life without seeing Dincia with the children, Blimcia, Josiu and Haim every day?"

In spite of lack of formal education my father was one of the best informed people I ever met. He had mastered five languages. His command of Polish, English and Yiddish was remarkable, and he was well versed in biblical Hebrew. His English was self-taught. I still remember Father poring over sheets of Langenscheidt's self-teaching method every free moment he had, and those were few. As he had no one to practice on, his knowledge of this language remained limited to reading and writing.

No success could satisfy my father's hunger for knowledge and quest for education, which went on his entire life. The self-educated man par excellence, he nevertheless wanted scholarly guidance in his Judaic studies. He solved this problem by inviting a brilliant Talmudic scholar, Reb Haim Siniwer, a scion of a great rabbinical dynasty of Sieniawa, to study with him. The man's only assets were his vast knowledge of Talmud and his aristocratic pedigree, neither of which could be put to practical use. But father, who voluntarily subsidized the family anyhow, asked Reb Haim to our house, and whenever Father could free himself, they studied together. According to Father, it was one of his most successful partnerships, with equal distribution of profits. My father had the good lessons, and Reb Haim earned a living in the most honourable way.

At war's outbreak Father was only forty eight years old – a wealthy man, a prominent personality, beloved and respected by all who knew him, and yet the most modest and unassuming of all. Surrounded by adoring wife and children who worshiped him, devoted family and countless friends, he was looking forward to the future with anticipation and hope. Fate ruled otherwise.

Six years later, Wolf Landerer's life was in shambles. All his possessions were lost, and the man whose life's moving force was love for his family found himself a bereaved father, son, brother, brother-in-law, and uncle. In spite of the tragic losses, his faith remained unshaken. He never questioned, was never bitter, and with his indomitable spirit and youthful vitality he painstakingly attempted to rebuild his life. But the lucky streak had left him. When a fatal illness took his life at the age of sixty seven years, he was full of projects and plans for the future. Tragically, his dreams never came true. On September 27, 1958, my father's pure soul left his suffering body and returned to his beloved Creator.

He was buried in the old cemetery in Bnei-Brak. May his soul find eternal peace.

Avroom Landerer

By contrast with the oldest Landerer brother my successful father, the second brother, Avroom, was the family's tragic hero. Good fortune and failure, happiness and misery interchanged in his life as in a Greek

18

tragedy. Avroom was the family comedian, the practical joker, but he was also the one who had had the most to mourn over.

Avroom and his wife Cilla had three children: Gusta, Pepcia, and Israel. Gusta was a lovely child – until the first of long line tragedies struck this young family. At the age of seven Gusta contracted scarlet fever, and it destroyed the hearing in one of her ears. The stricken child rebelled against her fate and became a discipline problem that plagued the family for years.

The parents found comfort in their second daughter, Pepcia. Beautiful, bright, and easygoing, lovely face framed by a mass of golden curls contrasting with large, brown eyes, she was called the Shirley Temple of Podgorze, and the delight she brought to her parents was boundless. Pepcia was followed by the hoped-for son, Israel, nicknamed Lulek.

I have already told you of her death. At the age of nine she was stricken with meningitis. One afternoon she returned from play in the park, complaining of a headache. Ten days later she was dead.

Avroom and Cilla never got over the loss. Looking for escape from memories, Avroom begun to neglect his business and his family. The major part of his days was spent in Cafe Royal where a good game of cards was always going on. He became like a man possessed. His business deteriorated. His wife and children suffered from his neglect. Soon they had to give up their spacious apartment. The successful, respected business and family man had become a black sheep.

Help came from a most unexpected source. The sisters in America decided to give Avroom a second chance by bringing the whole family to the United States. The hope of a new life, far from bitter memories and failure, restored Avroom's spirit. He abandoned his card-playing cronies and devoted his energies to business once more. The effects were immediately visible. The family moved into a new apartment uptown. The children, especially Gusta, responded to the 'new' father like magic. Gusta's performance in school improved dramatically. A doting father restored her self-esteem, and being nicknamed by her classmates the Future American Millionaire reinforced that feeling. The Prodigal Son returned and was received with open arms by the entire family.

Before embarking, however, the Avrooms had to fill endless forms

19

and fulfill senseless-seeming requirements. A lot of red tape had to be untangled before the magic tickets to The New World, the ship cards had arrived. The emotional good-byes had begun when one of the last routine formalities required by the American embassy was proof that an aspirant for a United States visa had no police record. Detailed examination of Avroom's records revealed that he had two! The old bridge was his catalyst.

When the old wooden bridge linking Krakow with Podgorze began to show signs of wear and tear, the municipality started to charge a toll for crossing it, to raise funds for construction of a new one. The price of a ticket was ten groszy, which in terms of the then exchange rate came to less than one penny. This ordinance was the cause of one of Avroom's crimes."

His first transgression was totally unpremeditated. One day, as he was crossing the bridge, he saw the old, revered Reb Sroolke the Maggid, entering from the opposite direction. An aged, unaccompanied Jew was always a fair game for Polish rednecks. The policeman, stationed at the entrance, wanted to have some fun with this one.

"Your ticket is not good!" he bellowed.

"What, voos?"

"This ticket is not good!"

Old Reb Sroolke, slightly hard of hearing, did not understand the shouting policeman.

"You dirty Jew, you cheating kike, you old leper, your ticket is not good!" spouted the eager law enforcer, at the same time punching and pushing the old man down.

Avroom, approaching from the opposite end of the bridge, ran and threw himself between the brute and the old rabbi. The startled bully released his grip on the old man and seized Avroom. So, because he would not stand by while another Jew, especially an old man, was being abused, he was arrested and fined for assaulting a policeman on duty.

His second offense resulted from a bet. Avroom, the practical joker, made a bet that he could cross the bridge without a ticket. By mischance he was found out, lost his bet, and was booked at the police station. He paid a minor fine, and this silly incident was forgotten by all. The police, however, kept detailed records, and when the time came to examine his references, these "crimes" were unearthed. Before the American embassy in Warsaw could be convinced that this particular candidate for visa was no menace to American society, miles of red tape had to be untangled. By then Hitler's armies were flooding Poland, and it was too late for a new life.

Escaping the German army, the Avroom Landerers reached Przemysl in eastern Poland. By then the Soviets had occupied the eastern half of Poland, and they stopped the Avrooms from going any farther east. But, from all we heard, they were leaving refugee Jews alone, and we had good hope that the Avrooms would weather the war, and when it was over – or there was a lull – they could continue on to the United States.

But then in June 1941, the Germans crossed the Soviet frontier, and we lost contact with Avroom and his family. Ominously, though, we heard that the Wehrmacht had occupied Przemysl and had herded all its Jews into the ghetto – usually a prelude to deportation to labour camps and worse. We heard nothing more from the Avrooms for a good eighteen months.

But that's another story.

David Landerer

In the innocence of my childhood, I never realized that all happy families have secrets. How could I, as sheltered and protected as I was, have guessed that, under the serene surface of ours, dark, murky currents of disappointment and bitterness must have been stirring. As a rule problems were hidden from children, and to me my family presented a unified, happy front. Today I realize that hurt and pain were hidden often under the guise of cheerful smiles.

We were fond of our Uncle David, my father's younger brother, even if we did not see him often. He lived in Przemysl and came to us seldom, but because he looked very much like our father, we assumed that he was almost as great. It was only recently that my brother told me that among the generous, giving, and charitable Landerers David was considered the one who would not hesitate to give the shirt off his back to a poor man.

It was natural for David, the third Landerer son, to enter the leather business in which his brothers Wolf and Avroom were active and doing well. Fast thinking and sharp, honest and hardworking, he traveled about buying hides from agents all over the country. On one of his travels, he met a girl with whom he fell in love. I do not know who she was, but as my mother told me when I was already a grandmother myself, she was from a simple background. At that time the Landerers had worked themselves up, and their own hard times after their father's death were forgotten. The successful businessmen basked in their success, and they would not hear of their "Davidel" marrying beneath their social level. As strange as it may seem to a reader today, David – already a successful businessman in his own right – would not think of defying his mother's and brothers' wishes. A popular matchmaker with contacts in the "best circles" arranged a suitable match. David Landerer married a "right" girl from a "right" family and moved to Przemysl, his bride's hometown. There he established a leather and hides business, and he and his wife had two beautiful children: a girl Sala, the same age as I, and a boy Benek, two years younger.

Behind the facade of orderly life and prosperity, disappointment and deep hurt were hidden. David was not happy. I don't know about Thilla, his "proper" wife, but it is not hard to guess how she felt. With time his business begun to deteriorate, whether as a result of hard times or neglect I don't know. I only know that at Thilla's request, my father sometimes sent him considerable amounts of money for new ventures that somehow never materialized.

"Who knows," Mother said wistfully. "If he had married his first love, would his life have turned out different? He had so much promise, and he was so good."

The following story confirms Mother's opinion. It happened shortly after my parents were married when David was a frequent visitor. It was a gray, wintry morning while the city was still asleep and its streets desolate. A howling wind tore through the narrow alleys. Few men passed by, hurrying to early services. The old bridge connecting Krakow with Podgorze – where Uncle Avroom later tried to save old Reb Sroolke – was deserted, except for a lonely ticket taker huddled in the wooden booth at the entrance.

In the middle of the bridge, a man was bending over the railing. The tails of his long, black coat were flapping in the wind, but he, oblivious to the cold, stared silently at the rapid waters. Suddenly a gentle tap on the shoulder interrupted his reverie. The wind had covered the sound of the stranger's approach, and the intrusion startled the man.

"Reb Yid! What is the matter with you?"

The man, taken unawares, turned his head and looked at the newcomer. Facing him was a young man, dressed in a long, black coat and a black velour hat, as was the custom among the Hassidim in Galicia.

"Young man, go away. Please, leave me alone."

"Oh, no," replied the stranger resolutely. "I will not go away. Not until you tell me what is the matter with you."

"Young man, you don't understand, you can't understand. I must be left alone. Please, go away! Go away!

Repeating "Go away, go away," he turned his head toward the gushing waters and shuddered. The stranger stepped closer, put his hand on the man's shoulder, bent toward his ear, and shouted: "If you tell me what is the matter with you, I will leave you alone!"

"You promise to leave me alone – here, on this bridge."

"If you promise to tell me the truth, then I promise to leave you alone – here, on this bridge!"

"I am from the village Z," the man begun reluctantly. "My wife, may she rest in peace, died young and left me with a little girl. I never remarried because my whole life was devoted to my child. Working day and night, I provided for her, and she grew up to be just like her mother: beautiful, pious, and good. An exemplary Jewish daughter. By the time she had reached marriageable age her reputation spread throughout the entire county. One day a matchmaker from Krakow arrived and proposed the finest match a father might have wished for a daughter: a young scholar from a prominent family. It was more than I ever dared to dream about. But there was a catch. The parents of the prospective groom insisted that the future bride bring a dowry into the marriage. I don't know what possessed me. I acted like a madman. Refined, big-city people, asking for a poor labourer's daughter? The only explanation I had was that her mother's pure soul had interceded for her child in Heaven. Thus, carried away by hope and vanity, I promised a dowry." Here the flow of his narrative was interrupted by a suppressed sob. He wiped his eyes and nose with a soiled handkerchief and went on: "When we set the wedding date, the whole village rejoiced. Even the rabbi himself congratulated me on my good fortune."

"Wonderful! When is the lucky day?"

"Today."

"Today? I don't understand. What are you doing here in Krakow?"

"Yesterday afternoon." the man went on, "the groom's father sent a messenger with a note saying that, if I don't bring the dowry money, there will be no wedding. I came to town right away, hoping to beg him off, to make him wait. Unmoved by my pleas, he threw me out of his house. How can I face my child now?"

The desperate man was talking to himself. "What am I going to say to her? She is getting ready for her wedding, and I, her father, have to put her to shame. Shame! Shame! Shame! I brought shame on my only child! How can I face her now? What should I say to her? I can't go home. I can't, I can't, I can't! Don't you understand? I can't?"

The stranger had been pondering this mournful tale.

"Reb Yid, how large a dowry did you promise?" he asked finally.

"Very, very large. Satan himself must have tempted me, because I could never find a sum as huge as that." Overcome by the enormity of his plight, the man was crying openly.

"How large is large?" asked the young Hassid.

"Two hundred American dollars." cried the wretched man.

"Two hundred dollars ... two hundred dollars ..." echoed the stranger, rummaging in his pockets. "That is a large sum for a poor man. But – smiling shyly, he stepped close to him and pushed a bundle of money into his pocket. "There is the dowry for your daughter. Hurry home! *Mazel tov!*" And he was gone.

It happened so fast that the man thought he was hallucinating. He put his hand into the pocket, and sure enough, it was full of paper money. Opening his large coat in order to protect the precious papers from flying away in the wind, he began to count. No matter in what order he arranged the notes, they always totaled two hundred. The magic number "two hundred."

"What is happening? Who are you?" he asked, looking around.

But there was no answer. The stranger had disappeared. The bridge was empty, not even a shadow to be seen around, just some dry leaves and scraps of paper chasing each other in the wind.

Suddenly, it struck him like lightening: "Elijah the Prophet!"

Wasn't Elijah known as the protector of orphans? The realization that he, a simple, unlearned man, had been chosen as the receiver of divine grace made him shiver. How had he merited it? No, it was not for him. The pure soul of his saintly wife was watching over her child.

The rapid water, which a moment before appeared to be his only refuge on earth, looked menacing and forbidding. Thank God, he was saved from them. His place was not in the depth of the river anymore, nor his grave by the cemetery wall with the suicides. Now he must hurry to be among Jews and to give thanks to the Almighty.

The synagogue closest to the bridge was the one of the Skaviner Ruv on Jozefinska Street. He covered the distance in record time. Weariness from his sleepless night was replaced by elation.

"Skaviner Ruv, where is the Skaviner Ruv?"

"Reb Yid, what is your hurry? What do you want from the rabbi so early in the morning?"

"I must talk to him. I have something very important to tell him."

"What is it? Tell us?"

Hearing the commotion the rabbi entered the sanctuary, and the excited man turned to him. "Rabbi, rabbi,! Elijah the Prophet was in town this morning!"

"Elijah the Prophet?" repeated the men with disbelief. "Have you been drinking so early in the morning? Maybe you should take your temperature?"

Was he feverish? No. Here in his pocket was the most tangible proof of the miracle. Two hundred dollars! The Skaviner Ruv was skeptical. He did not think that his generation merited a visit by Elijah.

"But, Skaviner Ruv, here is the money he gave me."

"How did Elijah look?"

Hastily the man described the youthful stranger, and as he did so, the rabbi smiled. The looks of Elijah were familiar. "Let me make a phone call to my friend, Wolf Landerer, and ask him if his brother David is in town today."

Thus the authenticity of the mysterious stranger was fast established. But no matter how hard the other men tried to convince the village Jew, not even the authority of the celebrated rabbi could change his mind. From that day on he was called "the Jew who saw Elijah the Prophet face to face."

Haskel Landerer

Haskel was ten years younger than Wolf and the baby of the family, two years old at the time of his father's sudden death. Once Wolf had shouldered the support of his mother and siblings, he and Haskel became more like father-protector and child than two brothers. And even though they matured and each eventually established his own business and his own family, Wolf always remained the "big brother" of Haskel in the most positive connotation of that word.

After working for my father for a number of years, Haskel went on to set up a business of his own and was soon a successful merchant in his own right. While he was still quite young, he was made a representative of the largest tannery in Poland, owned by the Margoshes family in Stanislawow, a region in southeastern Poland.

Haskel married Sala Landau, daughter of Berish Landau, a pious Talmudic scholar, and they had two children, Eva and Bubek. As he prospered in the business world, he moved his family from Podgorze uptown into a quiet quarter opposite Wawel, the city's sixteenth-century castle, sometimes called the Acropolis of Poland. The beautiful tree-lined streets of this section were inhabited mostly by professionals: artists, merchants like the Spiras, owners of an exclusive textile store on Grodzka Street, and the Taffets of a renowned family of antique book dealers. There were no Hassidic Jews in that neighborhood, and Haskel, although he observed all Orthodox ways, was very modern in his dress, outlook, and way of life, a free spirit.

He was an expert skier, an amateur photographer, and – a rarity in those days – a daring driver. (Car driving was not considered a pastime for a gentlemen in those days, especially one from a respectable Jewish family; since wages were low in Poland, anyone who could afford a car could afford a chauffeur.) Above all, Haskel had a gift for music.

As a boy he had wanted music lessons, but his mother had refused. Despite this, he taught himself to play both piano and violin, and his ear was so accurate that he could pick up any tune or melody he heard. At the coffeehouse or a family celebration for which a band had been hired, he used to join the musicians and play along, and these professionals encouraged him. A born performer, outgoing and friendly, he always attracted attention and applause. After the playing was over, he used to treat the musicians to a round of drinks and cigarettes, but they would have welcomed him without any reward.

Once, while a renowned Hungarian pianist named Imre Ungar was touring Poland, to sensational acclaim, my cousin Eva reproached Grandmother Landerer for not having let Haskel study music. "Daddy might have been another Imre Ungar," she said, "a great artist."

Grandma intervened. "Never mind, never mind. A man should do what his father did and what his brothers are doing. Better to be a good leather merchant than a not-so-good musician."

Grandmother Landerer could not have foreseen that a day would come when her son's talent would enable him to survive the disasters of our world turned upside down. But that came later.

3 · The Weinbergers

Blimcia

Aunt Blimcia was my mother's older sister, married to Uncle Meir-Haim Weinberger. Blimcia was the dimunitive of Blume, which in Yiddish means "flower," and she was indeed the tender and beautiful ornament of our family. The two sisters looked so much alike that strangers often mistook one for the other, but because of the difference in temperaments, the family always knew who was who. Gentle and emotional Blimcia like the flower she was named after, personified inner beauty, while mother, though good and kind in her own right, was realistic, logical, and cerebral. Whether it was the result of their supplementing each other's traits, or just the unbreakable Horowitz family bond, these two were extremely close, and so were their children. We grew up together like a large group of siblings, always together, even dressed alike.

So many details of our life together are deeply etched in my memory, while many others have been forgotten in the passage of time. The following pages are all that is left to me from people who were my second family.

I remember one day in the park. I had been pumping too vigorously at my scooter and fell off, grazing my knee. I went crying to the bench where Aunt Blimcia was sitting.

"My poor 'ketzale' (kitten) let me see."

Her arm around me, she attended to my slight abrasion with the seriousness and concentration of a brain surgeon performing a complicated operation. The other children stood in a semicircle, staring in awe at the impressive-looking dressing she applied, while Blimcia wiped my tears, combed my hair, brushed the dirt off my dress with her hand. I felt singled out and important, the hurt forgotten. Blimcia had that effect.

All of Blimcia's six lovely children were poor eaters, and this was the cross she had to bear. The call "Mommy, I want to eat!" was music to her ears. Hoping that fresh air and outdoor play would arouse hearty appetites in her noneaters, she always liked to take them all, and us cousins as well, to the park, and she always carried large amounts of food, numerous sandwiches, a large thermos with coffee, fruit. Her large carryall leather bag seemed bottomless. In addition to food, it contained socks to be mended, knitting in progress, and books. It was a standing joke in the family that Blimcia's children swallowed books instead of rolls, because every day, on their way to the park, they passed by the lending library and exchanged books.

Blimcia was beautiful. Not just in the usual sense of physical beauty – even though like most of my mother's family, she was very handsome – but because she was all love, understanding, comfort, and goodness. How does one depict a woman who was the personification of kindness and altruism, and not make her appear like a sugar-plum fairy?

Blimcia was never idle. But in spite of her endless household chores, she was never too busy to listen to anyone who approached her; one of her children, somebody's baby burbling incomprehensible words, the peasant woman who supplied her with produce. The special way she had with people, regardless of their station in life, is best illustrated by her relationship with her laundress and the cook. The age of the laundress, worn out by a lifetime of hard work, was difficult to guess. Slightly limping, her back hunched from years of bending over scrubbing board, her face lined by a myriad of tiny wrinkles, she appeared ancient to us children. Blimcia insisted that everyone address the poor old woman as Pani (Mrs.) Makaronikowa. The woman, not used to respectful treatment, appreciated this deeply, and my aunt became "Auntie Weinberger" to her. Her tales about her "Auntie Weinberger's" wonderful children used to annoy her other customers to no end. Fifty years ago, Polish society was extremely class conscious, and this was possibly the only instance in the entire country of a laundress referring to her patroness as Auntie.

Helcia, the cook, was the exact opposite of the older woman; she was a girl full of joie de vivre and youthful exuberance. Shortly after coming into Blimcia's employment she had an accident. While slicing noodles, Helcia cut off part of her fingernail. Frightened by the sudden gush of blood and feeling guilty at having spoiled the dough, she wept bitterly. Blimcia dressed her finger, calmed her down, and quietly finished the day's work by herself. She understood how lonely Helcia must have been for the mother she did not have and her need for attention. The large dressing on her finger exempted her from part of her duties, which were taken over by my aunt, so the next few days Helcia proudly paraded her bandaged finger and told everybody within earshot about her accident. Her story grew longer and more dramatic with each telling until all us children secretly wished we could cut our fingers, so we too could be wounded heroes.

One day Helcia was stricken with typhus and had to be hospitalized. As soon as she was out of isolation, my aunt – left suddenly without help in her large household – nevertheless insisted on visiting the girl at every allowable time and in between sent to the hospital Helcia's favorite dishes.

An old Jewish tradition dictates that in time of great distress or illness in the family, special charity should be distributed. When Helcia's condition turned critical for a few days, Blimcia secretly ordered *hallahs* and cakes from a local bakery and had them delivered late in the evening to all poor families in the neighborhood. Except for the baker and my mother, from whom her sister had no secrets, no one knew about it. My aunt paid the baker from money she had secretly saved from her household accounts.

My mother could never understand why Blimcia, whose children were notoriously bad eaters, every Friday prepared large amounts of dough, stood for hours over the hot oven, and baked numerous loaves. Under cross-examination Blimcia admitted that she had a list of respected but impoverished families, to whom she sent delicious yeast cake filled with chocolate and raisins every Friday. As long as there was somebody in need of help or attention, she could not rest.

The happy life of the Weinberger family was suddenly interrupted by tragedy. In the spring of 1938, Blimcia was found to have cancer. When I first heard about it, I did not comprehend the gravity of the situation. Illness as I experienced it during childhood and early youth, was a pleasant interlude and break from regular routine, usually bringing lots of attention and loads of presents, followed by a pampered convalescence. Mother, of course, always watched carefully for dreaded symptoms, but we children looked forward to illness, blissfully unaware that it could have anything to do with suffering and death.

One afternoon I returned from school, eager to go shopping with Mother. I rang the doorbell loudly and was surprised when it was opened by Jozia instead of Mother. The door to my father's study was ajar, and the long hallway was filled with sounds of sobbing and weeping, while Jozia informed me gravely, "Pani Blimcia is very ill."

Much later I learned the details. Blimcia accidentally bumped into a door, and as she was taking care of a seemingly insignificant injury, she noticed changes in her underarm. This woman, who never paid much attention to herself, had a frightening premonition and went to the family physician. After a thorough examination the doctor, an old family friend, said to Blimcia, "Tell your brother Josef to call me."

Uncle Josef Horowitz, fearing the news, came to our house to use the phone, so that the family should face together whatever the situation might be. When he cried out: "Doctor, have pity on us! My sister is the mother of six children!" everyone present burst out in tears. My Grandmother Horowitz had died leaving a houseful of little children. This was the fate they feared most. To see the family of their beloved Blimcia on the brink of similar tragedy was more than they could bear.

Particulars are blurred in my memory. Blimcia went to the hospital. A mastectomy was performed by the foremost surgeon in Poland. During her convalescence, her older children came to us, while the younger ones stayed with Aunt Bala and Uncle Josef Horowitz, who lived close to their school. During Blimcia's entire stay in the hospital, Mother stayed at her sister's bedside. In a few weeks time Blimcia recovered enough to return home.

I remember seeing her for the first time since her operation. My vivacious aunt was changed into an old woman. Blimcia – Little Flower – the name did not fit her anymore; the flower had withered. Was it the ghost of her own mother that had sapped her vitality, or just the extent to her sickness? Who knows? She sat in a deep armchair, a loose housecoat covering her mutilated body, wisps of hair sliding out from under the kerchief tied over her head. An open book of Psalms lay on her lap, large horn-rimmed glasses camouflaged her face, her lips soundlessly mouthed the words. Her usually busy hands were idle, the ever-present mending basket forgotten.

I had looked forward to her homecoming with so much joy, hoping to resume life as it had been before. On my way to her house. I imagined our joyful reunion – how I was going to kiss and hug her, tell her how much I missed her. But when I saw her, hunched over and shrunken, I froze. Courage left me, I couldn't utter a single word. This was not my aunt! This woman was old and broken by despair.

Blimcia's wound healed slowly. As the pain subsided, she gradually resumed her normal activities. She found support in the love and devotion of the entire family, but in spite of all the efforts of her husband, children, and the people surrounding her during and after her ordeal, she never regained her old zest for life.

Then came September 1939, and war brought its final incredible solution to all personal problems. In the winter of 1941, the Weinberger family was forced to relocate in Nowy Sacz, about fifty miles southeast of Krakow. The way I want to remember Blimcia is how she looked during the last week of August 1939. They had just returned from Zawoja, where they spent the summer. She looked well and glad to be back home, as she bustled happily around the house; and when she opened her sewing basket and pulled mending out of the bulging bag I knew that the trauma of her sickness was far behind.

Meir-Haim

Meir-Haim, the husband of Blimcia, was a quiet man surrounded by an aura of mystery; this was how we children perceived him. During World War I he was conscripted into the Austrian army and thus became the only member of the large Horowitz family actively engaged in upholding the might and glory of the Austro–Hungarian Empire. It was hard to believe that this slightly portly and quiet man had ever been a soldier. There was little resemblance between the photo of the gallant, trim young warrior in the Weinberger family album and sedate Uncle Meir-Haim.

This is how I remember him: a serious Meir-Haim bent over accounting books in the office or heavy Hebrew volumes at home, or a beaming Meir-Haim, presiding at the head of his family table on

Shabbat and Holidays, the picture of happy domesticity, surrounded by his brood, the youngest on his lap.

The severity of Hassidic garb complemented Meir-Haim's looks, especially so on Shabbat. The *streimel* – broad hat whose flat brim was trimmed with sable – framed his face, blending with his brown beard, at the same time emphasizing a few prematurely graying hairs. His teeth and the thumb of his right hand were slightly yellowed from his perpetual cigarettes. He smiled easily, radiating friendliness and tranquility. The long, black Hassidic coat seemed to add to his height and to the dignity of his bearing. Meir-Haim was adored by his six children; they all looked up to him as perfection personified.

This yeshiva boy from a small town in Galicia, who had been conscripted into the army, turned out to be brilliant with figures and in spite of his lack of formal education, he was made *Rechnungsfeldwebel* (accounts sergeant). As such, he was considered indispensable and kept away from battle. But to his children, and especially to his daughter Reeva, he was a valiant soldier whose path was strewn with glory.

I remember Reeva showing me the heavy fur lining of her father's coat.

"Do you know what kind of fur this is?" she asked.

"No."

"A bear's."

"A bear's?" "It can't be. I never heard of anybody having a bear's fur."

"My daddy has," Reeva answered with a triumphant smile. "He killed the bear in the war!"

This was overwhelming! Absolutely devastating! A real bear's fur-lined coat. Reeva's father not only possessed one but he had single-handedly killed the bear! This masterful stroke of Reeva's established the superiority of Meir-Haim over all the other fathers in the family.

Whether or not the years spent in the service of his Imperial Majesty Kaiser Franz Josef left an imprint upon Meir-Haim's character was difficult to judge. There was no trace of soldierly manner in his behavior or speech. Though his mother tongue was Yiddish, he was fluent in both Polish and German; he seemed like one who had never left his surroundings.

In retrospect I think the military discipline of Meir-Haim's youth left its only traces in his religious observances. Even in a traditionally Orthodox family, Meir-Haim was considered the Very Pious. A pedantic stickler as to details, he demanded that all his children, even while very young, follow religious laws to the letter. He himself cut the girls' nails, to make sure that the cuttings were properly disposed of and that the girls would not get used to having long nails (a habit that in future might interfere with certain religious observances). It was believed that hair begins to grow three days after being cut; therefore, their hair was always cut on specific days, calculated so that it would not start growing back on Shabbat. They were not allowed to use combs on Shabbat, lest they pull out some hair while combing it, for that day they had special brushes – unfortunately not equal to the task of subduing the thick, wavy Weinberger hair. Meir-Haim projected such authority that, even when the girls were growing up and becoming concerned with their appearance, they never questioned his right to impose these rules.

His inflexibility in religious matters was most emphasized during the eight days of Passover. He insisted that his family eat only matzo from a bakery that he approved of. This matzo was handmade and produced under strictest rabbinical supervision, from the moment the wheat was planted until the packaging of the finished product. The employees of that bakery were picked for their piety and scholarship, especially for their familiarity with the Talmudic tractate dealing with the laws of Passover. Scholarship does not a baker make, but that was irrelevant.

As long as the matzo was prepared according to the minutest letter of religious law, Meir-Haim did not care about the taste or aesthetic quality. The boys, always emulating their father, did not complain, but the girls rebelled against the unfamiliar tasting matter.

"What happened, Blimcia?" my mother asked her upset sister.

"The children can't swallow the matzo. They say it looks and tastes like wooden board."

"Let me see and taste it."

Neatly lined up along the living room wall were round packages of matzo, wrapped in brown paper, each weighing five kilo. One look, one bite – and my mother shuddered.

"Blimcia, let Meir-Haim eat it! You buy edible matzo for the girls and keep it in the kitchen."

34

Blimcia refused to listen; she could not bring herself to cross her husband, or undermine his authority. Thus, her notorious noneaters, who always had to be coaxed with chosen tidbits, during Passover longed for a slice of bread.

Meir-Haim, not a demonstrative person, was nevertheless a deeply devoted father. I remember the Yom Kippur when Reeva, who had passed her twelfth birthday, had to fast for the first time for the whole day. Since Blimcia's children were masters in the art of not eating, and Reeva was a healthy child, there was no reason for concern. But Meir-Haim did worry, and several times during the day he spent in the synagogue, he sent out his younger son to inquire about Reeva. After the long day's fast was over, and everyone had returned from the synagogue, his first words were "Reevunia, how did it go?"

Poor Meir-Haim. His peace of mind was disturbed by that one day without food. How could he have foreseen that a few years later his children would suffer months, years of hunger, while he could only stand by helpless?

Iciu and Moniek

My memories of Iciu, the oldest of Blimcia's and Meir-Halm's children, are few and blurred by the passage of time. He was six years older than I, and by the time I was old enough to be included in the games cousins played together, he was a grown boy, no longer interested in childish play. But my parents and other relatives remembered Iciu vividly and often spoke of his promise.

Isaac was always called Iciu. Ordinarily a childhood name was discarded once a boy started heder, but Iciu's name stuck to him. He grew taller than his father and was fair where Meir-Haim was dark, but his kind and gentle nature retained the best aspects of both his parents. From Meir-Haim he inherited his analytic mind and sense of humor, from Blimcia compassion and loving kindness toward everybody. He was at the top of his class in school from kindergarten on, establishing the tradition that the other five were expected to follow. His secular education ended after he completed seventh grade, but he read voraciously and in time became a self-educated man. He was so devoted to Talmudic studies that, even as a youth, he was well-known for his scholarship.

That's about all I know of this older cousin.

But Moniek was different. We were the same age, and I particularly remember him from the summer we were both five. At Rabka, where we spent the warm months, he and I were constant companions. The other children, already conscious of the boy-girl mystery, made fun of us. But we, two, inseparable companions, were oblivious to them. Immersed in endless colloquies, we fantasized, assumed different personalities; and acted out various roles. We played house, collected pebbles at the brook's steep bank, attempted to catch butterflies in our green nets, clumsily imitating the bigger children.

The summer resort Rabka is situated a few hours' ride by car or train from Krakow, and all fathers commuted for the weekends. Waiting for the daddies on Friday afternoons and seeing them off on Sundays became part of the summer ritual. All children were eager to see their fathers, and it became a challenge to spot a father first, to run to him fast, to throw arms around his neck, and to see the contents of his travelling bag. Everyone asked the question children have been asking ever since the first father in history returned home from his first trip: "What did you bring me?"

I remember one Sunday afternoon Moniek and I were left alone in front of the house. The older children were away on a trip, the younger ones asleep in their cribs. Our fathers had just left after lengthy and emotional good-byes. The girls used to shed tears at every parting, and those moments brought drama and color into our lives. By pretending that Moniek was a father going away, and I the mother staying in the country with the children, we decided to prolong this moving scene. The porch became the train station, and we began to give each other instructions, the way we'd heard our parents do:

"Don't let the children stand on the swing."

"Please, remember to water the plants as soon as you enter the house."

This dialogue, like most adult conversations, soon got boring, so we made believe that our train was soon to arrive, and began our final good-byes. Suddenly Moniek leaned to me and kissed me on the cheek.

Surprised by his own impulsive gesture he jumped on "the train," ran away, and hid behind the house.

It was a spontaneous gesture. His childish lips hardly touched my cheek, but it was the first time that one of my boy cousins had kissed me. I was flabbergasted.

"Moniek," I exclaimed gravely, "you committed a sin."

"What sin?"

"You kissed me, and I am a girl."

"Oh no, You're not a girl. You're my cousin."

This simple logic settled the matter, and the incident was promptly forgotten.

This long, happy, carefree summer finally came to an end. In anticipation of our homecoming and the beginning of a new season, the established routine was abandoned. While the adults were busy winding up the households and packing, the children hung out in the backyard and garden. Age differences forgotten, everyone talked about the delights awaiting us in Krakow. Life was one great, happy adventure for the youngsters of the entire clan. We had a very strong sense of belonging. Loved and protected by our large family, we always felt secure. As young as we were, we knew instinctively that, no matter what, the entire family would always rally to help, support, and stand behind.

All cousins were friends, but this particular summer in Rabka was the only period in my life when I was close to Moniek Weinberger. We were two young children living in a fairy-tale world. Unfortunately, we never had a chance to get to know each other after we both grew up. Therefore this cousin, my ideal playmate of a summer of long ago is just a faint shadow in my memory.

We returned to Krakow, and our ways began to part. Being a girl I was allowed to enjoy the bliss of childhood for another year. (In Poland compulsory education started at the age of seven, but having been born in February, I began first grade at the age six and a half.) Moniek started heder, a preparatory school for yeshiva, at the age of four. There he first learned the Hebrew alphabet, then began the study of Bible in Hebrew, translating the biblical language into colloquial Yiddish. He began to avoid me, afraid to be seen socializing with a girl, which could have tarnished his reputation among his heder friends.

At the age of eight he was promoted into Talmud class, where he became immersed in the serious study of this ancient text written in

Aramaic. In addition to the regular elementary school curriculum, he studied the Bible and Talmud, and was proficient in four languages: Yiddish and Polish (used for everyday communication) and Hebrew and Aramaic, (applied in his religious studies).

His attire from our magic summer – short pants, knee socks and sandals, colorful shirts, and "kaszkiet," a cap resembling an American baseball hat – was outgrown and discarded. His outfit now consisted of three-quarter-length charcoal gray caftan, black-striped pants, again three-quarter-length, white shirt, black shoes, and stockings. Ties were absolutely forbidden; they symbolized the decadence of the modern world that the yeshiva opposed. All yeshiva boys and Hassidic men wore, in place of a tie, a little black insert, like a tiny vest in front of the shirt, made out of heavy brocade-like material, it was always black and uniform, and it buttoned behind the collar in the back. The boys got their first pair of long pants when a young man reached marriageable age.

The last summer before the war Moniek suddenly shot up tall. His three-quarter-length pants hardly covered his knees, and his caftan resembled a garment suddenly shrunk in the wash. All this was promptly replaced by clothing a few sizes larger. It was the last outfit of new clothes in Moniek's life, not counting the concentration-camp garb, which came later.

At the beginning of the war, we were both fourteen years old. During the first year, while our families were still in their apartments in Krakow, girls had more mobility than boys. Jewish men avoided the streets as much as possible, because abusing Jews was one of the German soldiers' favorite sports, and this beastly pleasure was shared by many Poles. So I used to be the one to visit the Weinbergers. I remember Moniek – the little cousin who had kissed me during that golden summer ten years earlier – moving quietly about the apartment like one practicing invisibility.

Not enough, as it turned out.

Recha

Recha, the second of the six Weinberger children, was the favorite of the entire clan. Her kind disposition, looks, intelligence were exemplary. One could not help but respond to Recha with affection.

Our mothers wanted their children to grow up side by side, so we always played together. Even during the summer vacations we remained inseparable. Our families used to rent cottages in the same resort, usually with adjoining backyards or within walking distance, and the group of cousins played through many carefree hours.

To fill rainy days or to occupy the long, hot hours of sunny ones, we resorted to games: school, house, cops and robbers, and our favorites, The Witch is Looking and The Coffeehouse is Burning. The leader of the games, elected by acclaim, was usually Recha. Those are my earliest memories of her.

"The Coffeehouse is Burning – let's play The Coffeehouse is Burning!" We were gathered on the lawn shaded by an old linden tree.

"Recha, you be the leader!"

"Why always me? Let someone else be this time!"

"Please, Recha, we want you!"

Being the oldest girl in a large family, Recha was used to dealing with younger children, and they all followed her orders.

"Everybody be seated in a semicircle and tell me what you want to be."

"Recha, I want to be a table!"

"I, Swiss cheese!"

"I, me, sweet cream!"

"A cookie,! Today I am a cookie!" And so it went on.

After The Coffeehouse was all furnished and its pantry well stocked, Recha, seated on a wooden crate, and facing the players seated on the grass, began to tell a story about The Coffeehouse. The moment the narrative mentioned table or Swiss cheese or whatever, the person who had assumed that identity had to clap hands. Often the young listeners, absorbed in the plot, failed to respond when their turn came. Then the narrative stopped, and the leader, looking at the culprit, repeated the sentence in a slower tempo: "I asked for ... the sugar ... again, and there was no sugar." Giggles, winks, nudging usually brought poor Sugar back to reality, and he or she had to deposit a pawn.

The tricky thing about the game was that the denouncement came at the most unexpected moment. We would all be sitting, spellbound by a breathtaking story: The travelers, stranded in a broken coach, (in fairy tales they always traveled in coaches) were attacked by cruel highway men. Brave rescuers led them to a large coffeehouse, where they rested, and they were about to depart when suddenly one of them turned back and saw that the hospitable inn was on fire. The moment the words "The Coffeehouse is Burning" were spoken, all were supposed to clap hands and change their seats – and if you weren't prepared, you were caught and had to pay another pawn.

This story had a myriad of variations, each more fascinating than the other, depending on who was telling it. Recha's stories, while exciting and interesting, were never scary, and she never made fun, not even when Sugar clapped hands at mention of Tea.

The redeeming of the pawns was the greatest fun. First, we parted with our hair clasps handkerchiefs, and aprons. When the going got tough, we had to surrender sandals, socks, and other items of clothing (decency permitting). Taking turns, each of the players had to close eyes, while Recha hid the pawn behind her back and asked: "What should the owner of this object do to get it back?" This was the tricky part because one never knew if the object was his pawn or someone else's. Daring spirits used to come up with dangerous suggestions: "Sneak into the kitchen and bring us cake ... Run through the (forbidden) meadow!" Gentle Recha's presence usually inspired easier solutions: "Say a poem ... Bring home flowers to your mother."

"One, Two, Three, the Witch is Looking" was the Polish equivalent of Statues. It was an outdoor game involving a leader (the Witch) and the rest of the gang. The Witch, usually one of the older children, turned his back to the group, covered her eyes with both hands, and pronounced the magic formula: "One, Two, Three, the Witch is Looking!" All players attempted to advance before the Witch turned back and then remain unmoving. "Witches" counted so fast that the younger children could hardly manage a single step, and as for remaining immobile, that was almost impossible for a lively youngster. A player caught moving had to go back to the starting line, but the one who ran up to the Witch and tapped her on the shoulder before she uncovered her eyes was the winner and the next Witch. Whenever Recha was the Witch, the game was great fun even for the youngest set. She deliberately counted slowly, thus giving everyone a chance to advance. Her consideration for us younger ones gave us our first sweet taste of success.

Whenever we played house and she was the mother, she was the best. Not even once did she take advantage of a mother's spanking privileges. When we played school, and it was her turn to be the teacher, everybody felt in himself the promise of a genius. All "homework" turned in was graded with high marks, and every "test" was passed with brilliance by the entire class.

Wherever she was, whatever she did, Recha Weinberger always excelled. At the head of her class, she finished elementary school with straight A's and went on to do the same thing at Ognisko Pracy, the high school she attended.

During her second year, the school transferred into a magnificent new building, donated by the Frankel family (so magnificent that it was requisitioned by the Germans the instant they arrived in Krakow). The Frankels had founded the school in the first place, and Elisa Frankel was honorary headmistress, the soul of the institution. She knew every student by name and was involved in every aspect of school activity, and since most of the students were from poor homes and could not afford tuition, her donations literally maintained the school.

At the ribbon-cutting ceremonies, Recha Weinberger represented the student body – one girl among a daisful of Krakow's Jewish intellectual elite. She acquitted herself with the greatest aplomb, as one might expect from my extraordinary cousin, and in 1938 she graduated with top grades.

(Today, the former Ognisko Pracy building, now a cold, sterile edifice, houses government offices; there is not so much as a small plaque or inscription to identify it as originally founded, built, and maintained by Jews for the education of Jewish girls).

Immediately after her graduation, Recha began to put her expertise to practical use. Working out of her home as a designer of lingerie, she soon had a thriving little business launched. At the same time, word of her slender beauty, gentle nature, and top-grade skills began to spread through the community, and matchmakers were soon knocking at Meir-Halm's door. He took his time deciding. There would always be suitors for Recha. Let her older brother marry first.

But them came September 1939, and a harsh fate overruled him.

Reeva

As far back as my memory reaches I was always with Reeva. We played together, and whenever there was a crisis in the family, we were shipped to one another's houses. When our cousin Josek Beer, who was studying in a yeshiva in Krakow, became ill with typhus, my mother nursed him to health in our house, and we were sent over to Blimcia. Whenever Blimcia's younger children contacted one of the numerous childhood diseases, her two older girls stayed with us. In order to accommodate those most welcome guests, we had to double up in beds. My sister Lela used to whisper with Recha till late into the night, while I prattled and giggled with Reeva.

The Weinberger family lived in a large apartment house across the bridge in Podgorze, their windows facing the river. Podgorze was and is a lovely quarter, divided from the center of the city by the River Vistula – much like Buda and Pest on the Danube. The Vistula is an important waterway. It starts as a little stream in the Carpathian Mountains, flows throughout the whole length of Poland, passes through Krakow and Warsaw, and finally, it reaches the Baltic Sea. There was always life on the river. One of our favorite pastimes was watching its changing scenes. When the winter was mild and the river only partially frozen, it looked like a narrow, dark stream flowing between icy banks. Polish winters are usually harsh, and the river, frozen most of the time, is blanketed by deep snow. One year a tall snowman, built by anonymous artists, stood a lonely watch.

The mystery of the river unraveled during the spring, when large blocks of ice in different shapes chased each other, sometimes colliding and crushing one another, or piling up in a narrow passage and creating a natural dam, which collapsed finally under its own pressure. From the safety and comfort of the Weinberger's third-floor apartment, we admired the spring thaw, water rising high between steep banks, carrying large blocks of floating ice that hourly acquired different shapes and dimensions. Our imagination changed the ice blocks into racing horses, chariots, or boats, and our joy when one overtook another was as genuine as only children can experience. Noses pressed flat to the cold windowpane, we shouted with growing excitement:

"A boat!."

"No, this is a leviathan!"

"I saw it first, this one is mine!"

After the thaw steamships passed up the river, white puffs of smoke ejected by their tall, black chimneys, trailing after them and slowly dissolving in the breeze. When the weather was mild, we used to stand on the balcony, shouting and waving, trying to attract attention of passengers and crew, but they were too far off to notice us. The Carpathian Mountains abound in forests, and every spring rafts of fresh-cut logs were shipped to the north. Rafts carrying coal from the south to the center of the land were of more year-round character. Their cabins resembled little huts, and often the skipper's whole family lived right on the raft. At times we saw laundry hanging on a line, a woman nursing a baby or a riverman's dog, quite at home afloat. It must have been a harsh and lonely existence, but to us children, it seemed romantic and adventurous. In warm weather people came to the river to cool off, to bathe, to row boats, to swim or dive from the lower supports of the bridge. This spectacle usually coincided with the end of the school year when our families were leaving for the country.

Nature played an important part in our lives. City-bred children, we were fortunate to be growing up in Krakow, a town full of greenery. The passing of the seasons was symbolized by the blooming of different trees. The blossoming chestnut trees were among the first harbingers of spring. Krakow abounds in them, and every spring those venerable, majestic trees brought us the promise of future delights – the gathering of chestnuts in the fall.

When tender leaves replaced the wilted flowers, we knew that lilac time was near. In Poland the lilac blooms in May, and all during that month the city is permeated with its sweet fragrance. An old folk tradition has it that a three-petaled lilac flower brings luck, and thus we were always on the lookout for such a special flower.

After lilac, the acacia trees came into bloom. This meant that instead of going to the park, we spent our afternoons on Krzymionki, a large meadow spread over the hills. Unlike the park, which was equipped with a water pump and kiosks selling refreshments, Krzymionki was unattended, overgrown with grass, wildflowers, and acacia trees. Occasionally an ice-cream vendor came by, but otherwise everybody brought his own equipment; thermos bottles filled with tepid coffee, bags of sandwiches, large blankets to be spread in the shade of the trees. Not as imposing as the chestnuts, the acacias were easier to reach, and we could break off a few flowery twigs. Sucking out the sweet nectar, waving our arms, we pretended to be bees. When the acacia flowers wilted, we knew that summer had arrived.

I could still see us as we were then, Reeva and I, two pint-sized girls. We were compatible and for a long period of our childhood inseparable. Even as a young child Reeva had a feminine softness about her. Her hair was brown with a light, reddish hue, always neatly combed. Her narrow nose was sprinkled with few freckles, which always multiplied during the summer months. We played together, jumped rope, rolled hoops, but mostly we walked the paths in the park, and talked and talked for hours. I was an avid reader, and she an acute observer of the world around her. Reeva did not have great interest in books, but her practical mind was a virtual sponge, soaking up information about the world around us. She loved to listen to my condensed versions of the books I had read and uncritically approved my literary taste. When her turn came to talk, it was always about everyday existence. She used to report to me everything that was going on. Somehow, she always knew what our mothers and others were talking about, and she was well-informed about her numerous neighbors and their families, and children in school. She was my contact with the real world. We confided all our secrets to one another, swearing to guard them to all eternity.

I distinctly remember the day when it was my turn to make a sensational revelation to Reeva. My brother Moshe had come home from heder and called me out of the room. "Lala," he said, "do you want to know what I know?"

"What do you know that I don't know?"

"I know where children come from."

"Everybody knows that."

Both Reeva and I were old enough to reject the myth of the stork, but until this moment I'd never given much thought to other possibilities. Children were desirable miracles, gifts sent straight by the Almighty Himself. My mother, who always knew everything, repeatedly assured me – teasingly – that I was sent as punishment by God, and according to Aunt Blimcia, a girl who always cleaned her plate was a blessing, so every child was God's personal creation.

44

But when my brother said, "If you know it, why don't you tell me?" I was at loss for words. Then Moshe said, "A child comes out of a mother's belly!"

I was flabbergasted. "From a mother's belly? How did you get that warped idea?"

"We read a parable in heder about a woman who was kicked in her belly, and the baby in her died. The rebbe said it was so."

If the rebbe said it was so, then it must have been so. Anyway, who was I to say that it was not so? But how could it be so? Left alone with my doubts, I could hardly wait to go to the park and discuss the matter with Reeva.

With the utmost gravity I informed her that we must go to the farthest corner of the park and find a secluded bench, because I had a big secret to tell her. After making sure that no one was in hearing distance, I moved close and whispered into her ear: "Guess what?"

"What?"

"Guess."

"I don't know."

Reassuring myself again that absolutely no one could hear us, I conveyed to her my newly acquired wisdom. To my amazement she was not shocked at all.

"I knew that," she said nonchalantly.

"You knew? And you never told me? We swore over a million times not to have secrets from each other!"

But my curiosity was stronger than my hurt, and I bombarded her with questions. How is it possible? How does a child see and eat and breathe and hear? How does it get in and out?

Reeva began to explain the mystery of procreation. First she confirmed the original information. Yes, indeed, a baby does come out of a mother's belly. As proof she reminded me that one of our aunts had become very fat, and after the baby came, she returned to her former shape. I could hardly see the connection between the ugly bulge and the beautiful baby, but Reeva, who was very patient for her age, convinced me that it was so. Then she dutifully shared with me all the other information she possessed even the mind-boggling revelation that the children don't grow inside just because the lady eats a lot. This enlightenment was given to her by an older girl in her class, whose family had a maid, who had a sister, who was a midwife.

The authority behind this statement was overwhelming. Still, I could not comprehend.

"Oh, no!" I said, shocked. "My father would never do such a thing. Never!" And Mother? Prudence personified? It was unimaginable.

My mother never appeared to me as a sexual being. In our world parents did not show affection for each other in front of their children, even if they happened to be as much in love as mine were. Reeva's parents were even more reserved; we never even saw them stand close together. We would have been scandalized at the idea that husband and wife slept in one bed. Perhaps uncouth peasants or some poor wretches who did not have another bed, but not people as dignified as our parents!

Rational and sensible Reeva was at loss. She herself had difficulty accepting our newly acquired wisdom, but she was one year older than I and was coming to terms with it.

"Well," she said, "how do you imagine we were born?"

I couldn't think of any alternative explanation. "You mean that a baby and 'pippi' come out the same way?" She shrugged. In order to shake off the hard-to-live-with revelation, we joined a game of ball.

From little bits of information here and there, some eavesdropped conversations, we gradually completed our knowledge about propagation of the human race. As we matured, our tolerance and understanding increased, but still, we could not visualize our mothers as anything but what they appeared; simply our mothers. The housewives. Those stout matrons in their coiffed wigs, their heads mostly covered even while in their negligees, those personifications of chastity. How could they have been anything else but our mommies?

As we advanced in years and progressed in school, Reeva and I began to grow apart. We were in different schools and grades, and each formed new friendships and attachments. After graduating from elementary school, Reeva completed a two-year course in "Ognisko Pracy". There she learned how to design sweaters and operate the knitting machine, and took some general education courses. In retrospect I realize that this was when Reeva's happy childhood ended, and an unsatisfactory adolescence began. She was the third of six children, and there was too much excellence for her to live up to. The girl did not even try to match Iciu and Recha. Both were taller and better looking than she, and thus Reeva, a sweet, lovely creature, felt ugly by comparison. She was a fairly good student, excelled in arts and crafts, but she was not the star of her class that they both had been. She withdrew, became quieter, more remote.

The Weinberger family returned from the mountain resort Zawoja in the last week of August, 1939. Within one week Krakow was occupied by the German army.

One of the first decrees against the Jews was the closing of schools for Jewish children. With her two younger sisters staying home, Reeva was relieved of a large part of her household duties, so she joined the staff of a soup kitchen manned by volunteers. Refugees were arriving daily by trainloads and the Jewish community in Krakow had organized free kitchens to feed them. Reeva's quiet personality, her efficiency and cooperative spirit endeared her to the people at work, and she became one of the most valuable members of the team. The satisfaction she derived from this work, the acknowledgment she received from her coworkers restored her self-esteem. The turmoil and suffering all around her brought out the inner strength she possessed. Calm, efficient and helpful, she remained at her post until the family's last day in Krakow.

Hinda and Dina

Being a parent myself now, I realize that Blimcia and Meir-Haim must have preferred some of their children to others. But to their credit, be it said that such preferences remained well hidden. Meir-Haim was a disciplined individual, not given to emotional manifestations. Exuberant, outgoing Blimcia responded to her children by treating them all exactly the same way, with love, and love and more love.

Hinda was the third daughter and the fifth Weinberger child. She was no more than a year or two younger than me, but somehow, in the secret age-conscious hierarchy of childhood, she was assigned to the "babies," while I, to the great dismay of my sister, was accepted into the older group.

It was my irreplaceable loss. Hinda was brilliant, supposedly the brightest of the lot – and bright they all were. I remember Hinda starting the first grade, a skinny little pixie, all dressed up in a navy-blue sailor dress and a regulation navy-blue beret with the number 1 pinned in front. Her freckles had reappeared from under the fading summer tan, her brown eyes shone excitedly, and her perennial smile indiscretely bared two missing front teeth.

Freckles were her most characteristic feature and in those days freckles on a girl's face were considered a calamity. Shirley Temple was the undisputable ideal, the embodiment of childish beauty, and my cousin Hinda was the exact opposite of Shirley.

She was the last one to worry about her looks. After a few weeks in school, Hinda mastered the art of reading, and read she did. In the second grade she was already reading books intended for students of what would have been junior high. The Weinbergers' roomy apartment was full of couches and armchairs and a large rocking chair, and in each of these a child was perennially curled up with a book.

They lived close to the lending library, which for them was the source of unending delights. It was a private lending library, well equipped, and organized into two departments: adults' reading material in one room, children and adolescents in another.

One day Hinda, at that time no more than ten years old, returned from the library without a book.

"Mommy," she said, "the librarian didn't want to give me a book."

"Why?"

"I don't know. She said my mother should come."

Blimia's consternation was great. The constant supply of reading material was a matter of vital importance in her house, and she went to see the librarian right away. To her astonishment, she was informed that her daughter had already read all books in the junior library, and because their rules forbade giving books from the adult library to minors, Hinda could not be served by them anymore. But no library regulations could stop Hinda from reading! From that day on, her older sisters and cousins brought her books.

Black Peter was a card game rather similar to Old Maid and highly popular with children. The cards had funny symbols and pictures of people that had to be matched, but one card was without a match – the dreaded Black Peter. If a player was dealt this fatal card, the trick was to get rid of it somehow, but this was not as easy as it sounds. At the end of the game, all winners used to surround the one who still had the unmatched card and yell with the might of their collective lungs: "Black Peter, Black Peter!"

By watching the older children play, Hinda picked up the rules of the game and was allowed to join whenever there were not enough players of respectable age. I vividly remember a particular game she participated in, because it ended with my humiliation. She was seated at my right, which meant that I had to choose cards from her hand. With a straight face she arranged her hand in such a way that one card stuck out conspicuously. With a feeling of great superiority, I took the card next to the one sticking out and – it was the Black Peter! I can still see the familiar faces of children standing in front of a humiliated me, pointing fingers, laughing, and yelling: "Black Peter! Black Peter!"

Afterward I asked her how she had pulled the trick, and she explained it clearly:

"You see, I knew you'd think I wanted you to pull out the Black Peter, right?"

"Right."

"So I put this other card in front, as if it were the one I wanted to get rid of, right?"

"Right."

"I knew you'd try to outsmart me and pull another card. Right?"

"Right."

"And this is what you did. Right?"

"Right."

As she was growing up, my precocious cousin became very absentminded. Nobody asked her to do errands because, preoccupied with her thoughts, she was always losing things.

"Hinda, where is your sweater?" ... "Hinda, where is your jumping rope?" ... "Hinda, where is your head?"

A disarming smile, sometimes a silent nod or a shrug of her shoulders were all the answers she gave. Hinda didn't know how things disappeared from her custody, and it didn't bother her much. For a time she became a butt of family jokes, but eventually she was left alone with her thoughts.

Hinda was nicknamed by one of her teachers "Professor Mucha (fly)," because she was skinny, agile, and dark as a fly, and knowledgeable far beyond her age group. When she was in the eighth grade, her school had visitors from the department of education. As usual on such occasions the school prepared a presentation. The year was 1938, and the public opinion in Poland was greatly impressed by

Italy's conquest of Abyssinia. Colonialism, as interpreted by official policy, was an inherent right of all civilized nations, and the patriotic Poles deeply resented the fact that their nation was deprived of a justly deserved asset. Hinda Weinberger, our brilliant, darling pixie, was chosen to prepare a presentation on the theme "We Demand Colonies for Poland!" It was received by a standing ovation, and later Blimcia was told that the important visitors had asked who had composed the brilliant political treatise read by the student. Blimia only shook her head. She never helped any of her children with their homework. She didn't have to.

The youngest of the Weinberger children was Dina. Being the fourth daughter and sixth child made her life quite difficult. All the cute sayings were already pronounced, all clever deeds performed; all that was left for her was to join the gang and follow the good example.

My first recollection of Dina is when she was still a toddler. For some reason her cradle was in the dining room. We were visiting and waiting for them to finish lunch while they were all seated at the table, I was permitted to rock the cradle with the sleeping child. The whole tribe was involved in a lively discussion, and their loud voices woke the baby. She sat up. Looking around and seeing all familiar faces, she smiled broadly. "What should I do with the cradle? Dina is awake!" I asked anxiously. I was only four years old and did not know what to do with a living, moving, and smiling doll.

"Dina, Dinusia, look at me, look here!" they called brightly, as she went sailing high up in the air in the arms of her father, both of them laughing delightedly.

An old joke says that a sixth child has to be good because all the patience had already been exhausted. Caring for Dina did not require any special effort. From the cradle she graduated to the large bed she shared with Hinda, from the pram to a stroller, everything in a matter-of-fact way that became her trademark. Nobody fussed when Dina started school. I remember Recha and Reeva excitedly inspecting Hinda's new school outfit, hugging and kissing her, all the time repeating those hard-to-believe words: "Our schoolgirl, our little student!"

But Dina started school in a hand-me-down outfit and with used books, a younger sister's perennial fate. Her mother, not used to supervising her children's homework, was startled when the mothers of Dina's classmates began to approach her, asked her to persuade Dina to play with their daughters and help with their homework. She became the favorite of teachers and students, and as the indisputable number one in class, very much sought-after company.

At home, in the midst of her siblings and cousins, she slowly developed her own personality and established her individuality. Once, when asked by a woman why she avoided her daughter's company, Dina said: "I am sorry but I cannot play with your daughter."

"Why not?"

"Because she is not sophisticated enough," she replied with a straight face. This, from a seven-year-old!

Dina was slender, graceful, and an excellent gymnast. An easygoing child, she had large, brown eyes and raven-black hair. A happy little girl, always cheerful, laughing, giggling, always surrounded by friends. In September 1939 she was supposed to enter seventh grade.

4 · *Tradition*

It was a world of women. Mothers, aunts, maids, and teachers, always close by. Houses full of familiar aromas of cooking and baking, an atmosphere of warmth and security. A world of love, gossip, story telling, hugs and kisses. Overheard conversations on a variety of topics: health, fashions, movies, theater, and books. Women of all ages were avid moviegoers and enthusiastic admirers of movie stars. In our family there were two camps of fans: those who considered the "heavenly Marlene" the greatest star, and those who favoured the enigmatic Swede, Greta Garbo. Children delighted in the antics of a pair of comedians, Pat and Patachon, and the arrival of Shirley Temple upon the silver screen marked the beginning of a new era in girls' dreams. Everybody wanted to be and look like Shirley.

Parallel to this was the world of men. Fathers, uncles, brothers, cousins, and husbands, whose mode of life was so different that they seemed like inhabitants of another planet. Theirs was a somber, serious, seemingly colourless world.

In our family they were all Hassidim, uniformly dressed in black and charcoal gray. Their hair was invariably cropped short, like an exaggerated crewcut. Only a few strands of hair in front of the ears were permitted to grow long, in order to become earlocks. Their beards, untouched by razor since the sprouting of the first down on adolescent faces, made them all appear much older than they were. Beards, hair, clothing were all worn according to a rigid code that left no allowance for the expression of individual taste. No exciting new combinations of colors, patterns, or fabrics. Styles and fashions did not exist for Hassidim. The strict discipline governing their lives was total. Its goal was the intellectual growth of every individual.

Reading for pleasure was considered a waste of time. The only secular literature openly approved were newspapers and technical writings, dealing with one's particular profession or trade. The young men hungered for secular knowledge, and in our family they were lucky. They had sisters and cousins attending secular schools, and thus their access to forbidden books was easy. Otherwise, those dark-clad, benevolent strangers in our midst were bent over volumes of Talmud, Bible, or the Commentaries. Despite their proficiency in Polish, they spoke mostly Yiddish, while the women preferred to use the Polish language.

This paradox resulted from the educational system. The boys attended Jewish elementary schools, the heder maintained, sup-ported, and staffed by the Jewish community. The heder's teachers were rebbes, with little knowledge of the Polish language and culture. There was a secular department, staffed by needy Jewish students of the university, but secular studies were allowed only a minimum of time, just enough to satisfy the governments' demands for compul-sory education for all children.

Thus, immersed in the teachings of Judaism, separated from the culture of the gentile world which their women were a part, the men-folk lived in a world of work, business, study, and prayer. Theirs was a serious world. Entertainment and sports were considered trivial, not befitting serious Talmudic scholars.

To outsiders, it may appear strange that, a society that attached major importance to religious education of its sons left its daughters almost wholly ignorant of the origins and reasons for religious customs and laws. The answer is to be found in the division of functions and responsibilities. Women were entrusted with tradi-tional preparations for the holidays and the maintenance of high standards of kasruth (the state of being kosher), and this was so overwhelmingly time-and-attention-consuming that there was little energy left for asking questions. The importance of carrying out the Jewish traditions acquired a significance similar in importance to the Ten Commandments. Every detail of Jewish observance had to receive strict attention. This never-changing continuity became a source of strength and hope which gave our people the courage to go on in a hostile world. The vital role women played in the Hassidic community made this possible.

And then there was the belief in the coming of the Messiah. And when he arrived then all knowledge and bookish wisdom would

53

become unnecessary. The predominant belief was that faithful adherence to God's commandments would hasten the Redemption.

Thus the women eagerly fulfilled every obligation religious laws imposed upon them. Just as their mothers had done and their mothers' mothers before them, from the beginning of time – till the coming of Messiah.

Shabbat at Home

I remember when my mother acquired a device called the Shabbat Oven. It was a wooden cabinet the shape of an oversized Icebox, its innards lined with tin and tightly locked. Inside the cabinet, below the shelf for food, two large petroleum lamps kept the food warm. My gadget-loving, superhousewife mother rejoiced in the innovation, and our home became the Mecca for all Shabbat food "connoisseurs."

Each Shabbat was special. Every meal served on that day resembled a small banquet. We had at least ten people at the table: my parents and us, the four children, two "boys," (poor yeshiva students from out of town, one from each of my brothers' classes). We had a Jewish governess, who ate with the family, and most of the time we were joined by out-of-town relatives. Staying in a hotel when one had family in town was unheard of; often we had to double up for the night in order to accommodate guests.

For the Shabbat meal, my mother lighted ten candles in two resplendent candelabras. Every Friday evening we had a "candlelight dinner," except that for us the flicker of the candles, the gleaming silver and china, accentuated by the snow-white damask tablecloth, did not signify high living or elegance but the religious aspects of the day of rest.

On Friday afternoons everybody was home on time, early enough to change into Shabbat finery. Because we were Orthodox, pictures were never taken on Shabbat, even though we were expert photographers with our Kodak-Junior 120 camera. (And even if we had taken photographs of the family gathered at the table, these would have been lost or destroyed, like everything else we possessed.) Nevertheless, I will try to restore from memory the beautiful tableau our family presented. My father, his dark good looks accentuated by his Shabbat attire – the black satin coat and sable-tail "streimel" – sat at the head of the table. At the opposite end was my mother, her hair completely covered by a wig. On Friday, the busy housewife was transformed into a stylish lady, renowned for her good taste and elegance. Both my brothers were yeshiva students and wore caps made out of black velvet and black satin coats like Father's.

The women and the girls were always dressed according to the latest style. We were part of the secular world not only in appearance but in our way of thinking. The boys, dressed in their Hassidic garb, lived in a world apart, which we, the secularly educated sisters, were supposed to understand and share. Today it may seem strange, but this was the way we were brought up, and we accepted our world as the best possible.

This Shabbat table was duplicated in every Orthodox Jewish home, individual circumstances permitting. This day meant more than just an elegant dinner table, time spent in the house of prayer, visiting, or walking in the park. It was the setting apart of a chunk of time, the shutting out of all material problems, total absorption in the sanctity of the day that made it so special. Rejoicing in God's gifts, even the poorest of the men became a king for a day, his wife a queen, his family his kingdom.

Spirits were never served in our house. The wine over which Father said benediction, the silver cup from which everybody took a few sips, and the few drops of liqueur given to the children on a little piece of "hallah," somehow defied any association with the stuff upon which people used to get drunk in the liquor concession on the opposite corner.

Our lives were regulated by a rigid code that included even the menus for Shabbat and holiday meals. No matter how creative and innovative a housewife was, the kind of dishes and the order in which they were served remained unchanged. The Friday night meal always started with the blessing over wine, the Kiddush, recited by Father. All men and boys over Bar-Mitzvah age had their separate cups, and each chanted the blessing in a traditional melody. Female guests had separate cups too; only the wife and children shared Father's cup. Kiddush was followed by the ritual of hand washing and the blessing over the "hallah," and then the first course was served, always fish. Large Polish carp, its insides filled with a savoury mixture of ground fish mixed with bitter almonds, eggs and onions, salt, pepper, and sugar. It was a standing joke in Galicia that the "noshers" from Krakow ate sweet fish. Father seemed to have been the biggest nosher of them all because the fish served in our house was really sweet.

After the fish came chicken soup with needle-thin, homemade noodles and large lima beans, followed by boiled meat, vegetable, and compote. The list of the different compotes served resembles a catalog of Polish fruit. The first harbinger of spring was rhubarb, served as a delicious puree, then strawberries cooked whole in sweet syrup, followed by sour cherries. As the summer progressed, lingonberries appeared on our table, in turn followed by gooseberries. At the end of the summer came blueberries, and with the beginning of the fall season, apples, pears and plums. Pears were the last to ripen, but the blueberries were the most troublesome. The tiniest drop of their juice left a stain, and no matter how much scrubbing went into it, the stubborn stain remained till the blueberry season ended. But they were luscious, easily available, and cheap. No housewife could resist bringing them into her kitchen, where they became transformed into delicious compotes, cold soups, and fillings in cakes, pierogi and blintzes.

The crowning glory of every meal in our house was the cake. Mother never tired of collecting and trying out new recipes, and the varied desserts served were unsurpassable in their taste, elegance, and originality.

Our sweets-loving father always tried to trick out an extra portion from his temperance-preaching wife.

"Let me cut that little piece before it falls off and stains the tablecloth." "It looks to me like someone put some pepper into the cake by mistake. I must taste it before the children start to eat it."

We would roll with laughter, and even Mother, who always extolled moderation – "One should leave the table feeling still slightly hungry . . . To finish everything on the plate is bad manners and bad taste, and hard on the digestion" – had to laugh whenever Father, all smiles, would declare between bites "Marvelous, delicious, sweet, just like our Mamusia!"

No meal in this part of the world could end without tea. After the grace was said, we were free to do what we wanted. On Friday evenings we mostly stayed at home and read. People did not venture out much in the evenings because, according to the law, all house-gates had to be locked at 10 P.M. Around 9:30 the streets were already deserted.

One of the Saturday morning's biggest delights was reading and having late breakfast in bed. Everyday Father was up before dawn, starting his day with recitation of the Psalms followed by morning prayers. On Saturday mornings he used to add the weekly portion of the Bible. He read it aloud, and his singsong voice, carrying throughout the whole house, became a part of Shabbat's joyful solemnity.

The results of Mother's baking skills were most obvious on Saturday mornings. The assortment of coffee cakes included long, brown loaves sprinkled with white confectioner's sugar and filled with chocolate, cinnamon, raisins, and the best of all, poppy seeds. Or crumb cake smelling of fresh butter and tall, two-layered babka, one layer chocolate brown, the other cream-white. A bigger and better selection would be hard to find.

We were still breakfasting when the usual procession of beggars started to arrive. They did not rest on Shabbat – could not afford to. Besides on weekdays they received only a few groszy, while on Saturday they were sure to receive something to eat from every religious household.

One of the beggars who always appeared on Shabbat was a woman who made her rounds with her little daughter. The woman adored her child and carried her on her back most of the time. I was fascinated by that odd pair and used to watch them through the peephole in the door while they, unaware of me, rested on the stairs. Once I opened the door for them and found out to my great surprise that the woman spoke fluent Polish. Most of the beggars did not. They lived in a subculture of their own and communicated in a jargon that was a mixture of Polish, Yiddish, Russian, and other languages, comprising a dialect incomprehensible to the uninitiated. My curiosity got the better of me, and against standing orders not to talk to strangers, I spilled out my questions to her:

"How old is your daughter?" . . .

"What is her name?" . . .

"Why isn't she in school?" . . .

"Where is her daddy?"

At the mention of the child's father, the woman, till then friendly, started to curse, pouring fourth words that I could not understand.

The frightened child begun to cry. I didn't know what to do. Luckily, Jozia heard the commotion, came out of the kitchen with a large piece of cake for the woman, and chased me away.

"Go to your room! You know that your mother does not approve of talking to people from the streets!"

Another Saturday morning habitue was a woman of nondescript age, always dressed in black. Even the sack she carried on her back was of the same color, as was the shawl that covered her head and most of her face, giving the impression that she was all made out of that material. For some reason she was called Meshuggene Kops (crazy head). We children were petrified of her. Legend had it that she had been to America and that she was crazy. Urchins used to tease her and once at a safe distance, yelled: "Meshuggene Kops! Meshuggene Kops!" The wretched woman cursed and threw stones at them, thus worsening her reputation of being violent. In our house she was pitied, and whenever she knocked at the door, she was given a large slice of white hallah, which she devoured on the spot. The aura of her supposed vehemence and the intensity with which she ravished the food frightened us children. When we heard her rasping voice as she talked to the maid, we used to hide in a dark corner and stay huddled till we were reassured that she had left the building. The threat "I will tell Meshuggene Kops on you," or "Meshuggene Kops is coming to take you" made me run for cover more than once.

(After the occupation the homeless and the beggars were the first to be rounded up for deportation. Poor Meshuggene Kops took her secret – or maybe just an overdose of misery – along with her to the crematorium.)

Saturday lunch was another feast. By noon the men were back from the synagogue, and again the family gathered at the dining room table. Kiddush, washing of the hands, and the breaking of the hallah was repeated exactly as on Friday night, but on Saturday the fish gravy was all jellied and could be eaten with a fork. Then came hard-boiled eggs chopped with onions and chicken fat, accompanied by chicken giblet aspic and calves feet aspic with slices of hard-boiled egg seemingly frozen in the jellied dish. But the main attraction of the meal was the procession of delights coming out of mother's *chulent* oven. First and foremost was the famous *chulent* itself. Scholarly opinions about the etymology of the word differ greatly. One school claims that it comes from French chaudeslentilles, (warm lentils), another, claims that it comes from the French *lentement*, (slowly), a reference to its slow cooking. Anyway, it was and still is a most delicious dish. Every town swore by its variations. Krakow's *chulent* was made out of thick barley, chickpeas, and a generous amount of chicken or goose fat. Inside the pot with *chulent* was little *kugel* (literally, ball or bullet, a kind of sweet pudding), made out of noodles, or chicken or goose neck filled with delicious, fat-dripping stuffing. During the slow process of cooking, all the fragrances and tastes blended into a bouquet of flavors, impossible to describe in words. *Chulent* was often accompanied by hot bone soup called "patchei," which after having spent over twenty-four hours in the aforementioned oven, emerged from it dark brown in colour and divine in taste.

Hot dishes were followed by cold roast meats, compote, and cake. From the description of the meals it might appear that all we did on Shabbat was indulge in eating orgies. In reality it wasn't so at all. The portions were small, a tablespoon of *chulent*, a morsel of *kugel*, a few spoonfuls of *patchei*, and so on, everybody tasted a tiny bit of the traditional dishes. These were leisurely meals, lasting a long time. Friday dinners and Saturday lunches were the only times during the week that we, the four Landerer children, could sit at ease with our parents, talk, sing, and enjoy each other's company. Those were most precious, happy, unforgettable hours.

How seriously people took all the religious and traditional codes concerning the sanctity of Shabbat could best be illustrated by a little incident I remember from long ago. One Saturday morning, after Father and the boys had left for the synagogue, we, the female members of the household, were leisurely lingering at our breakfast. Suddenly the doorbell rang. It was out of the ordinary, because Orthodox people did not ring the bell on Shabbat. The caller was a lawyer whose name I don't remember anymore, a partner in one of my Father's enterprises, a secular Jew. This usually suave gentleman, often a guest in our house, was very agitated. Forgoing his usual pleasantries, he asked in a loud voice: "Where is Wolf?" Upon hearing Mother reply that Father was in the synagogue, the man became exasperated and added in an even louder voice:

"Either he conducts business, or he keeps Shabbat!"

In her usual calm and dignified way Mother promised to deliver this most important message to Father and made the lawyer leave. As soon as the door closed after him, she warned everybody present:

"Not a word to Father till I tell him after the Havdalah."

I was frightened. No one had ever spoken to Mother in such a peremptory way. It seemed to me that something horrible must be about to happen to us. At the same time Mother's composure impressed me greatly. I remember saying to her:

"Mommy, you are just like Bruria, the wife of Rabbi Meir."

I did not mean to equate monetary loss with the death of children, but the man's loud, angry voice had made me fear a catastrophe that only Father's immediate intervention could have prevented.

The matter was eventually settled. Something had gone wrong with a large shipment of hides, and unless there was an immediate intervention, the partners were facing a great loss. We learned that a threat of money loss could not cause our father to break the laws of Shabbat.

Shabbat did not fade into oblivion at the end of the day, but like the queen it was compared to in Talmudic parables, it got a royal sendoff. I remember us all as young children, standing at the window and looking for the first stars. As soon as we would count three, we knew that Shabbat was over. On Bochenska Street, across from our house, was a synagogue, and from our window we could see when the great candelabrum was lighted at the end of the evening prayers. A few minutes later Father was back, and everybody gathered around the dining room table for the Havdalah. Father always recited this blessing over an overflowing cup, a symbol for the new week's anticipated blessings. Being the youngest, I usually held the braided candle, reaching as high up as my short arms permitted, so that the future would bring me a very tall groom. The smelling spices were passed around in a turret-shaped silver container, the candle extinguished in the wine that overflowed from the cup – and the new week began.

The only housekeeping chore I ever saw my father perform was the folding of his prayer shawl. While pacing the room and humming traditional melodies, he performed his function, which to me seemed like a mysterious ritual. First the shawl was folded in two, then doubled again and again, until this large piece of fabric, woven out of thin wool and embellished with silver application, was small enough to fit into its special envelope made out of velvet, with Father's name and symbolic designs embroidered in golden threads. When that was done, we knew Shabbat was truly over until next Friday night.

5 · Holidays

Sukkoth and Simhath Torah

During Sukkoth the usual decorum of a holiday was abandoned. Instead of eating in the dining room, we took our meals in the "sukkah." My father had the apartment house built according to his specifications, and in our flat we had a large, permanent sukkah, otherwise unused the rest of the year. There the family took Sukkoth meals. It resembled a screened porch with electric lights, and the heat was provided by a little gas stove. In place of a celling it had wooden scaffolding and during the entire holiday pine branches were spread over it. This was protected by an awning, which could be closed in case of rain. Hardly an exact replica of the abodes our forefathers erected during their wanderings in the Sinal desert, but considering the cold weather at that time of the year in Poland, it was quite an inconvenience and disturbance in the usual way of life. For the children, however, it was one great party!

High on the list was the making of the decorations for the sukkah. While I was still very young, five or six years old at the most, a boy by the name of Mojsie-Simha regularly took his meals with us ("eating days" was part of yeshiva life.) Talmudic scholarship was not among his major virtues. Somehow he always managed to sneak out of the classroom before the end of the lessons and arrive at our house before lunch was served. This miscast scholar was an extremely creative and artistic boy. His fingers could change a page from a newspaper into a funny hat, airplane, or a ship that could sail in the bathtub. According to my critical judgment at that time, there was not a thing in the world that Mojsle-Simha could not make. But in our world it was considered a waste of precious time that should have been spent studying at the yeshiva. Poor Mojsie-Simha longed for approval, but he got it only from me. He basked in my adoration, and it was through his recommendations that I was admitted into the sukkah decorating committee of the Landerer family. Until the arrival of Mojsie-Simha, the committee was monopolized by my oldest brother, Benek. First I was allowed to hand the scissors, then to apply the glue, and finally I became a fully fledged coworker.

During the weeks before Sukkoth, our creativity bloomed to the fullest. In Krakow in those days, there were no models to build or glue together, no party shops with ready-made decorations. Thus we children had a marvellous time using our imagination. I can still see the beetles and butterflies we made from gold-painted walnut shells, the fabulous birds of paradise from eggshells, and melted candles and stiff, shining colored paper. How could one ever forget the various cutouts, the fans glued to the walls, and the chains? There were yards and yards of chains of different colors and shapes hanging from the branches. It was in the making of chains that one graduated, first from being an onlooker to a paper-cutting apprentice, finally becoming a creative master. For the eight days the holiday lasted, the usually empty sukkah became transformed into a special sanctuary.

With time Mojsie-Simha left yeshiva and town to return home to his disappointed family, who had to accept the fact that their son would not become a scholar. We Landerer children were growing up. Decorating the sukkah changed into a mere chore that my brothers were more than willing to relinquish to their unwilling sisters. To have the most beautifully decorated sukkah ceased to be one of our ambitions. We were acquiring other interest in life.

While reminiscing about holidays I cannot bypass the memory of my last Simhath-Torah flag. It was and still is customary for the children to come to the synagogue on Simhath Torah with a flag topped by an apple serving as a candle holder. My brother Moshe brought a flag for me. It had a picture of the Holy Ark with paper doors on it, and behind those doors was an insert with a Hebrew verse. I was beside myself with delight, opening and closing the doors so often that they had to be reinforced with glue. Marching along the foyer, I folded and unfolded the flag, waving it to my reflection in the mirrors of the long hallway, and could hardly wait for the great day when I would take it to the synagogue and march in the big circle with all the children and their fathers.

Finally the great day arrived. On Simhath Torah evening I walked with my father, one of my hands holding his, another proudly carrying the flag. As it was time for the evening services, and since the neighbourhood was predominantly Jewish, many fathers were hurrying with their flag-carrying children to the houses of prayer. Walking with Father, whose dignified good looks attracted attention, always made me happy. But this particular evening my pride was a thousand-fold magnified. Every Jewish man we encountered was greeted by Father with a broad "A guten yontif," (good holiday) and answered with the same. Even though we, his children, considered Father to be an all-knowing person, we never realized that his omniscience included every person in town. Not being able to contain myself anymore, I asked: "Daddy, how come you greet all those people? Do you know them all?"

"Sure I do. Aren't they all Jews?"

As soon as we came into the little Shtibel, I, proudly holding my flag, walked with father to the men's side. On the women's side was my cousin Reeva Weinberger. Reeva, one year older than I, was my constant playmate, but since she was the third of six children, she considered herself a grown-up person, whereas I, the youngest of four, was still regarded as a child. Therefore Reeva stayed with the women, where carrying the flag was considered baby stuff, and when she saw me, she wore – or at least I thought she wore – an ironic smile.

Suddenly, my pride changed into shame, my happiness into misery. I did not want that flag anymore! I did not want to stay with the men and children. This symbol of my pride and joy became transformed into a badge of shamful babyishness. I hated it, but in order not to attract more attention, I had to keep holding it. Looking around I asked myself bitterly "what I, a big girl, was doing among all those babies?" Miserable, embarrassed, close to tears, I held that ridiculous stick in my stiff fingers, wishing for the services to end as soon as possible, and when nobody was looking, I pushed the flag under a bench. And Father, blissfully unaware of the calamity that had befallen his daughter, walked home with a very humiliated child. Finally we reached our apartment, a radiant father and a sulking daughter, minus one flag. As if to add to my misery, Mother declared: "I was right in saying she should not have gone to the evening services. She was so tired she even lost her flag."

That night I cried myself to sleep.

Hanukkah

"Move over."

"Let me have a look. Just one look."

"Attention! The show starts in one minute!"

This was my first backstage experience. We, the pupils of Bella Asher, were presenting a play in honor of Hanukkah.

Both my sister and I were students in secular elementary schools, where religious instruction was taught one hour a week. Jewish children studied with Mr. Helfgott. His name translated means God's Helper, as befitted a teacher of religion. Mr. Helfgott was a talented story teller, and during our religion classes, he used to regale us with tales of Jewish heroes, Talmudic parables, and great Jewish scholars. Under his influence, when I was in the sixth grade, I wrote an essay about Maimonides, which my father proudly showed off to everyone who came to our house. (Father was convinced that his daughters were so talented that it was only proper to expose their genius to all poor schnooks who were not blessed with children like his. Admiring our gifts was the price that had to be paid for doing business with Wolf Landerer.)

In spite of Father's pride in our achievements, however, our Jewish education was lagging behind. This dilemma was solved by Bella Asher.

One afternoon Mother and I set out to inquire about this teacher. The Ashers lived in a large tenement building, not far from us. There was no indication that the dilapidated entrance and dark, wooden stairs led to an institution of learning.

We climbed two flights of stairs and stepped out onto a long balcony overlooking a courtyard. All the apartments facing the courtyard opened off this balcony. Mother knocked at one door, and an elderly, heavyset woman opened it. She was dressed in a dark, loose-fitting dress that reached down to her feet, shod in clumsy, well-worn slippers. A black wig perched on her head, a black, crocheted shawl was wrapped over her shoulders; at the tip of her nose a pair of steel-framed glasses tried to maintain their balance. I steathlly touched the four-leaf clover hidden in a little medallion on my neck, and made a secret wish: Dear Lord, don't let that old woman be the teacher!

God must have heard me, because Mother immediately asked, "Does Bella Asher live here?"

"Yes, yes, please come in". The woman turned toward the room and called: "Bella, Bellusia, come here!"

A tall, young woman, stylishly dressed and good looking, appeared in the doorway, shook hands with Mother, and ushered us in.

In the room behind the kitchen a lesson was in progress. I looked around this strange classroom. Two large beds, their headboards painted with huge flowers, took up most of the space. In between the beds, on a night table covered with a crocheted doily, a crinoline-dressed doll was holding court. A large armoire leaned against the wall, and piled high on both beds were the students' coats.

In this room the enterprising young woman had arranged an assortment of benches and chairs along a long, narrow table. A few girls from my class at school sat at the table, and I was ready to join what seemed like real fun, hoping that Mother, never quite sure if any accommodations were good enough for her children, would be pleased with what she saw.

I need not have worried. After Bella, in her pleasant self assured way, informed Mother that her method of teaching was based upon an innovative pedagogical method, mother enrolled us right away.

Next afternoon my sister and I trekked the unpaved street, and in the dark room behind the Ashers' kitchen, our religious education began. Bella was a natural teacher, and the children responded to her with zeal. Her students did so well that she decided to branch out and started a dance class. Her younger sister Sala became her assistant, and soon a group of girls was happily cavorting on the kitchen floor. Musical accompaniment was provided by the dancers themselves. A girl who could dance should be able to sing too. And sing they all did at the top of their voices.

Still, it was not enough. Bella and her students needed another outlet for their creative powers. It was unanimously agreed that next on the agenda should be a theatrical performance. The story of Hana and her seven sons, the martyrs of the Maccabean revolt, was chosen as suitable for the occasion. Bella's ingenuity supplied all the production required. A friendly neighbor's apartment was transformed into an auditorium. The door leading from one room to another was opened full width, and two white sheets were hung on the door frame to serve as curtain.

Being the youngest I was chosen to play the seventh son, the last of Hana's sons to choose death instead of bowing down to the Greek gods. The rehearsal began right after Sukkoth, and by the time Hannukkah arrived, everybody, including the families of the entire cast, knew the play by heart. The Ashers' apartment was converted into backstage. In order to reach the "stage," we had to run along the entire length of the balcony. I was self-conscious, because my brother's old nightshirt, which transformed me into a Maccabean hero, was a bit short, and I worried lest my underwear show. But our audience was not petty. Every performer was received with enthusiasm. We played to a full house, standing room only.

As the tension mounted, remarks were heard from the audience:

"Look, look, the big brother is my sister Hania."

"Fela, Fela, say no. I will not bow to your gods!"

"Genia, jump already from the roof! Jump and die!"

"See how beautiful my sister died. She looks like a real corpse."

Familiarity with the drama did not diminish our audience's delight. Misty-eyed mothers were watching their children reenacting the courage of heroes of long ago. No one thought that the gruesome scenes innocently portrayed by the children would pale in comparison with what lay ahead of us all.

Hannukkah was another one of the holidays that seemed to have been created in order to delight children. The historical background of Hanukkah was too remote in time and history to have real relevance for us; the suffering and bravery ending in defeat seemed like another fairy tale. But the games and all the fun Hanukkah brought into the home made it appear like one big party.

The lighting of the Hanukkah lights was a joyful ceremony. We had a large silver menorah which, according to custom, was placed by an open door joining two rooms. Olive oil from the Holy Land was used to fill the little containers of the menorah. We liked to watch Father tilting the can of oil, which had a large picture of a camel and Hebrew letters on it, and then pouring oil, enough to burn for at least half an hour. Then he rolled narrow wicks out of cotton and immersed them in the oil already in the menorah. The lighting was preceded by short liturgy and blessing sung to a traditional melody. On the first day one light was lighted, and on every progressive day another was added. Most impressive was the last evening when eight lights burned brightly, and the whole family stood around it singing traditional, happy Hanukkah songs.

But the real fun came after the lighting ceremony. During the eight days of Hanukkah my brothers were dismissed from their classes in yeshiva earlier than usual, so each boy could light his own menorah. Every evening their friends gathered in our house, played card games and spun the dreidel, filling the entire house with their youthful presence.

Another very important feature of Hanukkah was the Hanukkah Gelt. It was perfectly legitimate to ask for money, and no child would miss this opportunity to get rich fast. First parents, then all aunts and uncles, sometimes even close family friends, if they happened to come by, were solicited. When the eight days of Hanukkah were over, every child felt like a little Rothschild.

In the life of the community the Hanukkah Gelt became a kind of supplementary salary for the needy. The teachers, sextons in the synagogues, workers in bathhouses, hospitals, and other institutions maintained by the community expected this addition to their meager earnings. Many poor brides were thus provided with dowries, floundering businesses saved from bankruptcy, cold flats given coal to keep warm during winter.

Hanukkah Gelt was a voluntarily accepted obligation, put on by the community self-imposed code of ethics. The pressure to contribute to help the poor was strong. Unfortunately, due to the anti-Semitic policies of the Polish government, the economic situation of the Jewish community was deteriorating, and support of its poor was becoming more and more difficult. Nevertheless, the act of giving at Hanukkah lightened the heart as the menorah lighted the home.

Purim

We did not need a calendar to know that Purim was near. Grandfather Horowitz, who was a representative of a large brewery, used to send each one of his children a case of beer as a Purim gift. As soon as the wooden crate was delivered, our superintendent Antoni would appear with his toolbox. While his own sons were ashamed and looked down on their laborer father, we admired him. To us his lack of education didn't mean a thing. All the men we knew although quickwitted were clumsy, while Antoni was the only man who was clever with his hands. We, the four Landerer children followed him throughout the apartment and vied for the privilege of carrying his toolbox for him. Four pairs of wide-open eyes watched him expertly pulling nail after nail, lifting the lid, and taking out the first bottle. "Beer! Beer! Beer!" we shouted – as if, to quote Mother, we had never seen a bottle of beer before.

Sipping beer in the morning was not customary in our house, but Mother always opened one bottle and treated Antoni. Each one of us received a few sips of the brew. It tasted good, this beer from my grandfather; it was golden, bubbly, slightly bitter, crowned with white foam that always settled on Antoni's mustache.

The beer-tasting ceremony was followed by established procedure. Mother used to present him with a bottle to take home. First wiping his mouth with his sleeve and clutching the precious bottle under his arm, Antoni used to bow, at the same time trying to get hold of Mother's hand, kiss it, and mumble humbly: "I kiss your hand, gracious, benevolent lady."

"No big matter Antoni. No big matter."

The closest I ever got to one of my secret childhood dreams – namely to find the chocolate house of "Hansel and Gretel" fame – was on Purim in our house. Never, not even for a moment, did I doubt the veracity of this story. It was written in a book, and books, especially the fairy tales, played a very important role during our childhood. They put the supernatural in proper perspective. By making the imaginary world believable, they taught us to accept the unexplainable, at least until we matured enough to know what to ask and to understand the answers.

Going to the market with Mother was always exciting, more so before holidays. I loved walking and watching the life in the busy streets of the Jewish quarter. In the backyards of the old dilapidated houses, children played noisily. The narrow, winding streets were crowded with little shops and stalls and vendors praising their wares loudly. The singsong sounds of learning and prayer from the houses of study mixed with the bustle of life in the Jewish street.

The favorite of all marketing trips was to Broncia – the chicken lady. It was in her store that I found out that chicken, geese, and turkeys have what seemed like yards and yards of intestines over-grown with yellow-golden fat. Broncia's expert fingers used to remove the fat in one move, then pile it on the counter in little mounds. It was very expensive and considered one of the best and most important ingredients of Jewish cuisine. Margarine was poor people's substitute for fat. Olive oil was used as fuel in anniversary lamps and Hanukkah menoras. Supposedly some barbarians also used it in cooking.

From behind her counter Broncia ruled her customers like a medieval lord, demanding total acquiescence.

"Pani Broncia, I want two chickens, my sister is coming."

"No chicken for you. Your brother-in-law does not like chicken. You forgot what was last time?"

"Pani Broncia, what do you have for me today?"

Arguing with Broncia was useless – her decisions were always right. Especially so before Purim, with its traditional turkey dinner. She had a bird ready for each of her steady customers the size fitting exactly the number of portions needed. No wonder that every day of the week housewives swarmed in front of Broncia's stall, while all around her idle competitors cast envious eyes.

Preparations for Purim required trips to specialty stores where mother bought nuts, almonds, raisins, baking chocolate, all the ingredients for her kitchen's alchemy. We children were not allowed into the kitchen, but the exquisite smells emanating from there drew us unresistingly towards this forbidden territory. Sneaking in under the pretext of getting a cup of lemonade or tea, we hoped to get a few licks from the bowls with their marvelous mixtures, which would later emerge as tortes, nougats, and the prince of all, the almond *fludden*. This was a special cake made out of almonds, sugar, choco-late, and homemade cherry jam, prepared only for special cele-brations. But Mother was adamant:

"When Purim comes, everybody will get a share."

Purim was the one day in the Jewish calendar that turned into a carnival. The Purim Spielers, dressed in funny costumes and masks, came all day long, and presented skits and songs. The most popular was a short ditty:

Today is Purim, tomorrow it's gone.
Give me a few groszy and throw me out.

There was a serious side to the fun-filled holiday too – distributing money to those in need. On that day Father was always home, receiving callers, not, as usual, in the study but in the dining room. Dressed in his Shabbat attire, he sat at his usual place at the head of the table covered with white tablecloth. In front of him, instead of china and silver settings, were rows of coins and bills neatly piled together and arranged according to denominations. They were given away as Father saw fit. It was a rule in our family (kept even in the hardest of times during the war) that no person in need should ever be refused. My father, famous all over Galicia for his charity, distributed a small fortune every Purim. The pleasure he took in generosity was marred only by the fact that it was not possible for him to reach and help everyone in need.

His mixture of love and respect for every human being enabled him to treat even the poorest of the poor and the most ignorant of ignoramuses as his equal. I was too young to comprehend it then, but I understand it now. The reason so many of Father's callers left with their heads high was that my father was one of those rare persons capable of giving charity without hurting the receiver's pride.

"Shlah Mones" was another exciting part of Purim tradition. On that day Mother reigned in Father's study, where all day long she received and expedited gifts of luscious delicacies. The children, free from school on that day, didn't know where to be first. Every time the doorbell rang, we raced to the door and loudly announced every arrival: "Shlah Mones! Masks! Somebody to see Daddy!"

The ideal situation would have been to be all places at the same time. At the door to see all Purim Spielers and masks, in the study, where one could try to sneak some of the goodies from behind Mother's back, or in the dining room, taking part in the ritual of giving alms and watching Father receive the poor.

In the late afternoon, after the doorbell finally quieted, we would sit down at the table for the traditional Purim dinner. Then a group of special Purim Spielers always came to entertain us. These were hungry and aspiring actors from the Yiddish Theatre on Bochenska Street; their performances were professional. Theirs was the only group to be invited into the dining room, while others had to stay in the foyer.

The festivities seemed to have no end. After an elaborate dinner the whole Landerer family gathered at Grandmother's. The Landerers were convivial people, and these family gatherings were full of laughter, music, joking, good times and love.

Passover

In our house the preparations for Passover began right after Purim. For one afternoon the top of the kitchen stove was replaced by the special Passover insert, an enormous pot was taken out of the closet, and in it pounds of goose fat were melted into yellow liquid. Blissfully unaware of cholesterol, every housewife prepared jars and jars of fat. Once the jars were tightly sealed and put away, we knew that Passover was under way.

The Passover Cleaning was every housewife's nightmare. In addition to our maid and cook, Mother always hired extra help, and they all proceeded to turn the house upside down.

One of the hardest tasks was the cleaning of the floors. First they had to be scrubbed with steelwool, then washed with benzine, waxed, and polished. My mother, the collector of household gadgets, had an electric floor polisher, but the maids preferred to use the foot brushes. They were experts in balancing on them while sliding forth and back in even, long strokes, thus shining the floor without falling off. I loved watching them do it. Their graceful movements resembled those of an ice skater's or a ballet dancer's and made this hard work appear easy and pleasant. I liked the gaiety of their voices in our usually quiet home, loved listening to their stories and adored their gossip.

The general upheaval of the household included the cleaning of the rugs. This was a man-sized job, usually performed by our superintendent Antoni. They had to be taken off the floors and carried down to the yard. There all the winter dust and, most important, any of the bread crumbs that might have escaped the regular weekly cleaning procedure were mercilessly beaten out with a special carpet beater. Every backyard in Poland had a special scaffold intended for beating carpets and airing bedding. After nine o'clock in the morning, none were permitted on the balconies or windowsills. We had some very large carpets, and Antoni needed help in rolling them up, getting them down, bringing them back again, and spreading them on the floors.

This was only the first stage of the rug-cleaning ritual. Once they were well aired and dust-free, he used to clean them with sauerkraut – as unbelievable as that may sound. Oriental rugs are dyed with natural dyes, and they respond well to the acid of the pickled cabbage. Always joking that, if it was healthy for the rugs, it must be good for him too, Antoni first stuffed a handful into his mouth before kneeling down to clean the carpets. It was fascinating to watch the sauerkraut lose its yellowish color while absorbing the dirt, and at the same time to see the bright colors of the rug emerging from under his fist.

This must have been one of my mother's housekeeping secrets, the other being the recipe for floor wax, the creation of our maid, Jozia. Her concoction had the unusual quality of maintaining the shine of the parquet without darkening the wood. Nowadays floors are stained dark – or, worse, covered with wall-to-wall carpeting – but in those days a dark floor was a proof of sloppy housekeeping.

Window washing was part of the regular household chores. As soon as the temperature went up enough to permit it, the women took down all the curtains, drapes and embroidered bedspreads and tackled the glass. Then the finery was expertly laundered at home. Everything was washed by hand, starched, and ironed. It was fascinating to watch the laundress expertly gliding the hot iron over delicate lace inlaids, embroidery, and ruffles. The iron used was warmed up and kept hot by charcoal, which involved a complicated procedure. First the iron had to be filled with charcoal, then light by match and swung forth and back till the little coals glowed. Because of the flying sparks, this was usually done on the kitchen balcony. My mother owned both an electric and gas iron, but the women felt themselves to be in better command of the old fashioned ones, which they preferred.

Passover meant backbreaking work for every housewife and her help, but for the children it spelled the greatest fun. Everything had to be changed – all dishes, the top of the stove, the insert in the baking oven. Each table top in the house was covered with a specially made exactly fitting wooden cover. Mother always worried lest some forgotten crumb should be left in any of the crevices in the floor, even though the way she maintained her house, this was not possible at any time of the year. Then came new dresses, new shoes, different foods, and the biggest attraction of all, the seder nights.

The first seder I attended signified a short-lived victory over Mother's stern discipline. I was very young, four years old, too young to take part. Having watched the preparations for the evening all day long, I resented being sent to bed because of the late hour. Knowing from lifelong experience that fighting Mother was useless, I accepted her verdict with a broken heart. The commotion in the house, the voices coming from the kitchen and dining room kept me awake, and my wounded pride did not permit me to cry. Determined not to fall asleep, I sat in my bed feeling dejected and forgotten by all. This was the only safe form of protest available to me.

Suddenly, I heard steps – someone was approaching my room. The doorknob was turned, the door opened a bit, and I heard a familiar voice, whispering, "Are you sleeping?" It was Father. He could not start the celebration when he knew how disappointed I was. I whispered back, "No."

"Do you want to come to seder?"

"Yes!"

A minute later I made my triumphant entrance into the dining room in Father's arms. I held my arms around his neck and avoided Mother's eyes. To her credit it must be said that she always knew when she had lost. This time too she ignored the two of us. But my victory was only symbolic. While being carried into the room in Father's arms, I felt an elation probably surpassing Titus' and Napoleon's as they were carried under their triumphal arches. Mine was probably much shorter lived. The irritating thing about Mother's rules was that, in most cases, she was right, and soon my eyes begun to close. When Father carried me back to bed, I was fast asleep.

As the years went by I stayed at the seder longer – first till the afikomen, later till the very end, the song "Had-Gad-Ya." For many years the stealing of the afikomen was the high point of the evening. Father always made it easy to get, but it was not his fault that there were only two sederim and one afikomen each, and four children eager to get them. My brothers were swifter and had the advantage of being seated next to Father, so they usually got it before Lela and I did.

As we grew older, the stealing of the afikomen became just another traditional custom, and the Passover cleaning a bothersome disturbance in our orderly lives. The Landerer children were leaving their childhood behind just as the gruesome war loomed on the horizon.

Shabuoth

I try to recollect this holiday as it appeared to me as a child, but all memory brings back is a house full of flowers and greenery, large cheese and fruit cakes. New summer dresses, white anklets instead of dark knee-socks, and a new large white taffeta bow crowning my head. Unmade beds in my brothers' room, and the boys sleeping during the day.

In my childish concept this holiday was different because Passover had the seder and matzo, Rosh Hashanah the blowing of the shofar, Yom Kippur the fast, Sukkoth the meals taken in the sukkah, but Shabuoth, did not impose any restrictions. For the girls it was time to be happy and enjoy our blessings to the fullest, for the boys to change into sleepyheads.

On Shabuoth Mother's entire collection of flower vases was put to use. In addition to that, my brothers used to decorate the house with green branches. The flowering plants on the balcony, together with the arrangements inside, and our apartment resembled a large garden.

Weeks before the holiday Panna Adela, our dressmaker, began coming into the house. Once she established herself in our room, it became a sewing workshop. The sewing machine was open and buzzing, the table covered with colorful fabrics, the floor unrecognizable under the scraps of paper, threads, and summer materials. Every once in a while we were made to stand on a chair for fittings. This was the most troublesome part of the process of getting new dresses. "The one minute only" I was asked to stand quiet seemed to last longer than an hour.

According to an old custom the first night of this two-day-lasting holiday is devoted to the study of the Torah. When my brothers were young, they studied by themselves at home, till sleep overcame them in the small hours of the morning. As they grew older, they were permitted to join the men in the house of study. Early in the morning they would return – and sleep most of the day.

I hide my head in shame while admitting that my very first impressions of Shabuoth were that this was a holiday for sleeping for the men, new summer dresses for the girls, and fruit and cheesecake for all.

My childhood's perception of this holiday, the sleeping during the day, was the first to go. As my father and my brothers left home on the fourth day of the war, there were no men in the house to sleep off the night of study. The cheesecake was the next to disappear and the new clothes, but we always managed to adorn the apartment with greenery: a few green branches picked on the way to work out of ghetto. I remember clearly the feeling of elation and festivity that those few holiday-proclaiming twigs brought into our dreary lives in the ghetto and camp. It's like a beam of light among my nightmarish memories of the war.

Rosh Hashanah and Yom Kippur

All during my childhood Rosh Hashanah and Yom Klppur were holidays whose spirited joy intertwined with somber, incomprehensible rituals and customs. To symbolize the renewal of the year, we used to get new outfits. The dresses, the shoes, underwear, even the large taffeta bows that perched on our heads all summer long like large, colorful butterflies, had to be changed into new navy-blue or black ones.

During the weeks preceding the holidays, beggars used to come in droves. Every morning the tray with the change for aims had to be replenished several times. Answering the doorbell before the holidays was a full-time job in our house. The beggars used to come before noon, the afternoon being the time for a virtually uninterrupted procession of "guests" coming to "see Father."

As was always his custom, everybody coming to "see him" was invited into his study for few private moments. It was not easy to keep count of the glasses of tea Father offered his guests every afternoon, but no one, not even Mother, knew the exact amount of money he gave away. Whenever she tactfully implied that he might have been overextending himself, he, with his irresistible smile, used to reassure her that some pending deal was sure to bring a large profit or some transaction in process was going to make us rich. Always a chock-ful of ideas, in addition to giving away the allotted percentage of his earnings, he used to distribute from his projected gains. Sometimes those gains did not materialize or a pending transaction ended with a loss, but this never phased him. Arguing with Father was of no avail. Giving charity was his second nature.

The adults readied themselves for the High Holy Days in a way shrouded in mystery. Nine days before Rosh Hashanah, special predawn services were conducted in all synagogues. Those were the mysterious Slihot. It was still dark outside when my parents used to leave the house. Sextons from various synagogues were passing through the Jewish streets, knocking at the gates and low-placed windows and calling in singsong voices: "Yidaleh, Yidaleh, get up for Slihot!" While the rest of the town was still immersed in deep sleep, Jewish Kaziemierz was getting up and quietly filling the houses of prayer.

They were back from the synagogue at breakfast time. As my brothers grew up, they joined my parents in these morning devotions. According to my brother Moshe, who was my religious mentor, participation in this ritual was instrumental in getting admittance to Heaven. I was most eager to join that chosen group, but by the time I became old enough to take part, it was wartime. All Jewish houses of prayer were burned down or destroyed, and the few left were used as warehouses or detention centers for their former worshippers.

An unwritten but nevertheless ironclad rule of Rosh Hashanah demanded that juniors visit all older family members and wish them a happy new year. As soon as we were old enough to speak, Mother insisted that we take part in this ritual. I still remember the rounds to all our relatives I had to make. First I was accompanied by the governess, later I went by myself, but every time I repeated the well-wishing formula, I found it annoying and embarrassing. Just reciting good wishes was not all there was to it. Every time, before I could finish my lines, I became enclosed in a loving but choking embrace and smothered in wet, teary kisses. It always made me feel embarrassed and a bit scared. I was young and happy. It never occurred to me that the future symbolized by those holidays could be anything but wonderful.

Rosh Hashanah abounds in symbols. The round hallah baked for this holiday, sweet and sprinkled with raisins, symbolizes the infinity of life. Throughout the entire year the hallahs were braided into elongated loaves, slightly salted and without raisins. It was only during the High Holy Days that raisins were added and salt was replaced by honey, the main condiment during the period starting on Rosh Hashanah and ending on Simhath Torah.

Carrots, served with every main meal, are *mehren* (multiply) in Yiddish. These roots, when cooked with honey and dried fruit, became symbols of the abundance of blessings hoped for during the coming new year.

The apple dunked in honey is a reminder of the harvest and the bounty nature offers man. The blessing "Shehehianu" recited over new fruit of the season, celebrates the unending cycle of life. At the same time there is something spiritual and earthy in the yearly renewal of hope and the repetition of age-old rituals and customs that bind all of Jewry together.

On Rosh Hashanah girls were required to attend the services during the blowing of the shofar. In Polish shofar is called a trumpet, and somehow – or maybe because of the association with the common musical instrument – this unique part of the High Holy Days services failed to impress my childish mind. As I was brought up not to question religious matters, I accepted without much ado the fact that on certain holidays trumpets were blown in the synagogues. Only after I learned to read did I find out that the shofar is not a trumpet but a ram's horn, and I became aware of the symbolical meanings of the shofar's different sounds

Yom Kippur was a holiday without joy, always preceded by the rite of Kaparoth performed by Mother. This was scary and incomprehensible. Live fowls were brought into the dining room, with its polished floor covered by a large oriental rug. Each female member of the household, including the Jewish cook, had a hen assigned, each male a rooster. Those were the Kaparoth, the scapegoats to whom Mother was transfering all supposed misfortunes that might have been passed on us during the New Year's judgment. I never imagined that my mother, the prosaic person that she was, possessed such powers, but as she stood there – the prayer book in one hand, the other holding a loudly protesting bird and circling it over my head for three prescribed times while repeating the incantations – I believed that there was not one thing in the world my mother could not have done.

Each bird had its feet tied with a narrow piece of colourful cloth, but the wings were left free. It was obvious that this kindly consideration was not appreciated. Flapping their wings and raising their voices in helpless protest, they often soiled the carpet and the polished floor. To Mother's credit I must add that she navigated them over our heads, with such expertise that the concrete proofs of the birds anguish never landed on our heads. It never phased Mother. This habit of Kaparoth was so deeply ingrained that even during the war, as long as it was possible to buy live fish that could be substituted for fowl, Mother would not give it up – except that one fish had to do for all. The four Landerer cousins stood with bowed heads while Mother circled the slimy fish over our heads, praying and hoping thus to divert the cruel decrees.

Once Kaparoth were completed, the equally, difficult part of the preparation for that important day was begun. We were told that before Yom Kippur one must make peace with every person one had sinned against during the entire year. Even ask forgiveness. If not, we would not be forgiven our sins. Every child's conscience is full of transgressions and guilt, and it was quite a task to remember them and beg pardon for all. To my despair my own list of sins seemed to be endless. My brother Moshe, the religious mentor of my childhood, took this matter very gravely. According to him, it was either sink or swim – Hell and Damnation for the sinners, Heaven and Paradise for the righteous. Not a chance to repent later. Who would want to burn in Heil for all eternity, whatever it meant? Who would want to miss out on Heaven with no school, no getting out of bed on a cold winter morning, and chocolate and candy free for all?

In our family it was not customary to dress up on Yom Kippur. Unadorned attire and felt slippers we all wore, the plain beret Mother donned instead of a hat somehow added to the somber mood of the day.

After I learned the Hebrew Alphabet, Moshe gave me my first instruction in "davening," reciting the prescribed prayers. According to his explicit instructions it was imperative to remain standing during the entire prayer of "musaf." Equally important was to hit one's chest while reciting the confession of sins: those committed intentionally, those committed unintentionally, and even those one might have only thought about. Feeling myself a lowly sinner, I struggled to decipher the long, uncomprehensible lines, while my fist was pounding at my skinny chest with all the strength I could muster. It seemed to me like an eternity had gone by and I hadn't even reached the middle of the prayer. When Mother returned from the synagogue, she found me near exhaustion from the double effort of unintelligible reading and standing. My left hand was clutching the prayer book, while the right was rhythmically striking heavy blows at my chest. Mother absolved me from standing, and after I reluctantly sat down at the edge of my chair, I finally managed to finish the prayer.

For years after, until we were forced to leave our home and most of our possessions behind, I cherished the little prayer book full of penciled instructions in Moshe's childish handwriting: "Sit ... stand ... beat the chest!"

Part Two • Occupation

Have the gates of death been shown you,
*   the gates of the gloom have you seen?*
Can you take in the breath of the earth?
*   Tell if you know it all.*

Job, 28, 17, 18

6 · *The end of childhood*

On September 1, 1939, Nazi Germany invaded Poland, and the most devastating war in history was launched.

I was fourteen then, my sister Lela seventeen. Nothing in our serene childhood could have made us ready for an overnight transformation from affluence to impoverishment, from sheltered girls into young women beset by danger on all sides. One false move, one trespass of the streets not assigned to Jews, one book taken from the lending library, one momentary lapse – forgetting the identification papers, crossing the path of the wrong German – could have meant death.

But even on those first few days, we knew that a bad time lay ahead. The Polish radio urged people to leave their homes and go east, go east – perhaps in hopes of blocking the army's retreat. High treason was rampant at all levels of Polish society, and many radio stations were taken over by turncoats. Nobody knew what or whom to believe. Panic spread like an epidemic.

Frightened people fled their homes, leaving everything behind. Skeptics in the morning joined the stream of refugees in the afternoon. By the end of the first day of the war, it appeared as if the whole nation was on the run. Masses of people clogged the high ways – children in their arms, bundles on their backs, the elderly leaning on walking sticks, farmers leading animals, carts piled high with oddments of household gods. The more fortunate rode on horse-pulled wagons. The few cars that were not confiscated by the army were left by the roadside, out of unobtainable fuel, and many beasts expired beside them.

Many people perished on those roads as well, some from exhaustion, some from strafing by the marauding Luftwaffe, some from the attacks of robbers and anti-Semites taking full advantage of the chaos. And some who survived those nightmare days lived to envy the ones who had died.

The Balkens, my father's sister Ryfka and her husband, were now comfortably settled in Sambor, far to east. Earlier that summer, our beloved Grandmother Landerer had gone back to living with them, and it seemed like the perfect haven in a nighmarish turmoil. Despite the dangers of the road, thirteen members of Mother's family had left Myslenice and joined the throngs of refugees streaming east. Our immediate problem was ourselves: Should the Landerers too take refuge east to Sambor?

There was really very little question about the men of the family. My parents, like others of their generation, could remember World War I, when men and boys had often been conscripted as laborers by the moving armies, so it was settled that Father and my two brothers and Uncle Haskel should leave for Sambor. But what about Mother and Lela and me, Aunt Sala and her two children? How would women and girls fare on those dangerous, panic-choked roads?

It was decided that we should go too. The family must stick together.

September 4, 1939. I will always remember that day as one of the most important of my life. That was the day that the human flood spilled over Krakow, the day that our family broke up forever.

The night before we hardly slept. In the gray morning hours we stood on the balcony that faced the main thoroughfare. Total blackout was in effect, and the mass of people milling about below resembled a parade of phantoms. Inside the apartment final preparations were being made for our departure. Our knapsacks, packed the day before, were repacked over and over, as some new possession, impossible to part with, was brought in by one of the children. In peaceful times the family traveled a lot by car and train, but what was needed to survive wanderings afoot on the roads not one of us knew. The only knapsacks left untouched were those of our parents. Having reduced the contents of their home into a few light bundles, they could not bear looking at them anymore.

At the accustomed time we gathered at the dining room table for our last meal together, served by the red-eyed Jozia, our devoted maid, and Hela, the Jewish cook. We, the youngsters, brought up sheltered and secure, were secretly excited about the impending "adventure." Growing up under the influence of romantic Polish literature, we thought that a refugee was synonymous with a hero. But our parents saw no romance in the situation. No one spoke, no one got up from the table. I counted the crumbs on my plate, and my sister kept stirring her empty teacup. Father and my brothers quietly recited the grace after the meal, then silence fell.

All of a sudden Mother's calm voice broke in: "I have changed my mind. The women will remain at home."

Father was stunned. "How can I go and leave you alone with the children?" (Lela and I were seventeen and fourteen, but in Father's eyes we were still children.)

"The girls are too young, the roads unsafe. I won't trust my young daughters to such ravages."

My parents discussed the matter. My father said that if we women stayed, then the men would too. "No, no, the men must leave." She insisted, and reminded him of experiences from the first war, when hostages were taken in every town occupied by the Germans. Father's prominence in business and communal affairs made him a prime candidate for hostage, should Krakow fall into German hands.

Despite this, it was thought that women would be safe. They trusted to the security of their homes and the supposed German respect for the Geneva Convention.

Today such a viewpoint might seem bizarre, but the innocents of 1939 could not have foreseen the approaching barbarity. People were totally in the dark, not because they lacked political savvy, but because the information they had was vague and incomplete and based on out-of-date experiences. The U.S.S.R., its borders hermetically sealed, remained an enigma; moreover, communist or not, Russia was the land of the Cossacks, traditional pogromists and Jew murderers. On the other hand, Germany, in spite of rumors about Dachau, *Kristillnacht*, and callous mistreatment of Jews, was firmly entrenched in people's minds as the bastion of Western culture and civilization.

To the people of Krakow, German was the language of Goethe, Schiller, Kant, and other humanists, the mother tongue of Mozart, Bach, Beethoven, and Brahms. German-speaking people could not be perceived as a real threat to their lives – certainly not to the security of their women and children.

My mother often recalled to us her memories of the Austrian army unit that occupied her hometown of Myslenice. It was early in the first World War, and the town, today in southern Poland, was then part of the Austro-Hungarian Empire. Mother was in her early twenties, pretty, poised, and fluent in German. Naftali Horowitz, my grandfather, was one of the *parnassim* (men active in public affairs) and often acted as spokesman for their small, self-contained Jewish community. But his German was not as good as my mother's. When the German-speaking Austrians arrived, Grandfather made her his interpreter and liaison between them and the Jewish Orthodox group. Whenever a mission took him to army headquarters, she went with him.

One evening, while all the men of the family were at the synagogue, Syma, a poor widow who had a stall at the market, stormed into the house. "Hacia – Hacia, help me!"

"Why, what's the matter? What's happened?"

Sobbing uncontrollably Syma grabbed my mother's hand and covered it with kisses and tears. Hacia tried to free herself, but Syma clung tightly and managed to blurt out between sobs: "They took my Mojsiele!"

"Your son? Who took him?"

"The *Soldaten*. They need young boys to care for the horses, they said. Early tomorrow they are leaving for the front. My only child! My Mojsiele! Will I ever see him again?"

"But Syma, what can I do? I cannot give orders to the army."

"Go to them! You know their language. I can't even talk to them. I tried to make them understand that he is my only child, my whole life, my 'Kaddish,' my everything. ... But they only laughed at me!" She appeared to be half-delirious. "If only someone could explain it to them, Hacia." Weeping, she sank to her knees and wrapped her arms around Hacia's legs.

Immobilized by the embrace and shaken by the poor woman's despair, the girl did not dare to move. It seemed to Hacia that the loud pounding of her heart filled the room, but it was only the steady ticking of the kitchen clock.

"Hacia!" My grandmother's voice cut briskly into the uneasy silence: "There is no time to be lost. The battalion is leaving soon. You take your coat and run!"

"Without father?"

"It is late. Your sister will fetch Father, and he will follow you as soon as possible."

Hacia reached army headquarters in no time, but to her dismay she found the offices closed. Not one to give up easily, she ran over to the army barracks and was directed to the quarters of the commanding officer. Her shy knock at the door was answered with a sonorous: "Come in!"

She opened the door and remained standing at the entrance.

The officer was stretched out on his bed, dressed only in breeches and a white shirt, while his highly polished boots rested on a chair. Surprised, he sat up. "Come in *schones Fraulein*, what brings you here?"

Her face was familiar to him, since she was often seen at headquarters, but always accompanied by her father. To find one of the Horowitz girls alone, visiting the barracks in the evening was very unusual. He stared at her.

"Her Offizier," she started bravely, "I came to ask a big favor from you."

"My pleasure. What is it you are asking for?"

"Your men, sir, conscripted a young boy from our community. His mother is a widow. They are very poor, and he is her only child. She is desperate. Please, kind sir, have pity and let the boy go."

"How is it, *Fraulein*, that you were not afraid to come alone into my room?

It hit her like lightning. There she was, first time alone with a man in his private quarters – a gentile and a soldier to boot. Her father wouldn't even know where to look for her.

"What is there to be afraid of an Austrian officer?" she answered, smiling.

Taken aback by her quick answer, the man said in mock seriousness, "I have a gun – I could shoot you."

She breathed deeply with relief. "Not likely, right?"

"What is your protege's name. I must know it, because just a while ago my men brought in twenty more young men from your community."

Did she hear right? Twenty more men? So Syma's *kaddish* wasn't the only one.

"I am so happy, sir. I knew that you would be kind. But I am ashamed to confess that I don't know Mojsiele's surname. Everybody just calls him Syma's *kaddish*. Anyway, let me tell you that all those boys would be more trouble to you than the horses themselves."

He burst out laughing and called for his adjutant. They spoke in rapid German that she could not follow. Then the adjutant left, and the officer turned to her.

"*Shones Fraulein*," he said with a humorous salute, "request accepted. And now wish me good luck. Tomorrow we are leaving for the front."

"Sir, I promise that not only I and my family, but our entire community will pray for your safe return." (and they did, too.)

"Thank you, thank you. Permit me to walk you to the gate."

No one in Myslenice ever heard from the gallant young officer again. But in front of the military compound, Hacia was met by a group of twenty-one ex-stable-hands-to-be, waiting to escort her home.

So with memories like that my mother was not afraid to remain behind after the men left. When Father reminded her of German hatred for the Jews, she scoffed. "Such anti-Semitism. It can't be worse than the Polish."

Unspoken was the thought: There has always been anti-Semitism, and yet a most vibrant Jewish community has survived in Poland for many centuries. Sometimes things grow a little worse, sometimes they grow a little better, that was what to expect.

"You must go, Wolf."

I didn't see why Daddy had to leave, but Lela understood the gravity of the situation. Always composed and clear-headed, she nonetheless broke out crying. "You must go, Daddy, 'she kept repeating between sobs.' I swear by God, you must go! You must leave right away!"

That set me weeping, too. "You must leave, Daddy," I echoed, partially blinded by tears. "Daddy, darling Daddy, you must leave!"

Father wept unashamedly himself in front of the whole household and gathered us into his arms, where we clung desperately. Father could not let go of me. "My baby, my baby!" he wept, his tears mingling with mine.

Another hug, and finally we tore away from each other. The door closed with a bang. My father, my two brothers, and our Uncle Haskel had left.

Unfamiliar quiet, interrupted only by stifled sobs, spread over the entire floor. They were gone!

Mother locked herself in the bedroom – she had to be alone. Lela and I ran out to the dining room's balcony and watched them disappear around the corner. They already looked like strangers. In order to be able to blend with the crowds without attracting attention of Polish anti-Semites and hooligans, they had left their Hassidic garb at home.

After they vanished, my sister and I looked at one another. We did not know it then, but we had just said good-bye to family life and happy childhood.

7 · The Occupation begins

Stunned by the sudden breakup of our family, we hardly noticed that war had arrived in Krakow. The feared air raids were few and the damage negligible. We soon grew accustomed to the sounds of sirens and artillery coming from far away, and instead of running to the cellar during raids, we stayed on the main floor in the superintendent's apartment, listening to his battery-powered radio. Broadcasts about the heroic defense of the Westerplatte (September 1–7), the Polish outpost in the port city of Danzig, kept up our hopes in the imminent triumph of the Polish army. But even as we fantasied about Polish victories, that nation was being abandoned by its own leaders. Right at the beginning of the fighting, the highest ranking officials and commanding officers deserted to safe Romania, taking along the national treasury.

Krakow surrendered without one shot being fired. The army retreated in chaos, its soldiers bewildered and helpless. Abandoned and betrayed by their leaders, equipped with World War I arms and virtually no tanks, their tiny air force destroyed on the ground on the opening day of the war, they were expected to halt the endless motorized columns of Hitler's vast war machine. No wonder Germany appeared invincible.

Wednesday, September 6, was bathed in sunshine, a typical day of the proverbial Golden Polish Autumn. But this time, instead of *Babie Lato* (Gossamer Summer) when silk-like threads spun by spiders freely floated in the air, fear hung over the city. Single passerbys were seen hurrying through the deserted streets. The park benches, where maids, nurses, and mothers gathered every morning, and the sand boxes, where the tots played, were desolate. Only the squirrels made good use of the quiet and chased each other on the well-manicured lawns. The gardeners, usually everywhere, were nowhere to be seen. Neither were the children, who stealthily trespassed forbidden areas to collect chestnuts from the ancient trees. (The chestnuts of Krakow were not edible, but nevertheless cherished by children as playthings.) The kiosks selling candles, pretzels, soda, and newspapers were padlocked. Even the majestic swans disappeared from the pond. All that was left were soggy crumbs of bread and rolls floating among the water lillies.

The city, usually bustling with life, was as still as a graveyard. Sparrows, the merry chirpers, were alarmingly quiet. The familiar sounds of tramway wheels screeching at the turns were missing. The newspaper boys, always trying to outrun and outscream each other, disappeared from the streets – the free press in Poland had died. The marketplaces, usually the noisiest and busiest places in town, resembled ghost towns; the stalls were dismantled, and in place of the usual neat rows of booths, pushcarts, and peasants squatting behind baskets full of produce, there were scattered broken boards, wood shavings, and dirty straw blades.

The most oppressive of all was the absence of the familiar sound of the church bells. Krakow had fifty-eight churches, and the sound of their bells accompanied people throughout their entire lives. All bells tolled in harmony: when this grand chorale ceased, it was as if the heart of the city had stopped. This superimposed silence was more frightening than the wailing of air-raid sirens and sounds of artillery combined.

The melancholy mood of the city was increased by its disfiguration. Scarring every patch of green were zigzagged trenches resembling monstrous lips, grinning in mockery. The red flag, embellished with the loathed black Hakenkreuz (Swastika), hung from the tower of Wawel, the castle of the first Polish kings. The inhabitants of this ancient capital became enslaved by the members of the Master Race. Drunk with their easy victory, charged by the enthusiasm of unfought battles, the Germans released their unspent energy upon the helpless population.

First came the looting of the Jewish stores. It was obvious right from the beginning that the occupying army was wholeheartedly committed to the destruction of the Jewish population. The "heroics" of the soldiers were usually assisted and applauded by the Poles, who, when no goods were left, vandalized the fixtures of burglarized Jewish stores. The Polish policemen, taking advantage of the prestige of their uniforms, joined openly in this free-for-all plundering.

Opposite our house, on the corner of Bochenska and Wolnica, was a liquor concession. It had the distinction of being the first Jewish store in our neighborhood to be robbed by the German soldiers in broad daylight. Frightened and disbelieving, we watched from our window as the door was kicked open, and the soldiers rushed in, followed by the mob. What shocked us more than the break-in was the appearance of a well-dressed man holding a briefcase under his arm. At first, seeing him plunge into the lawless mob, we felt like cheering his courage; then he emerged from the store, a bottle of liquor in each hand. After hiding his spoil in the briefcase, this "gentleman" smoothed his slightly disheveled hair and continued on his "distinguished" way.

This fun did not last long. The small stores, once emptied, could neither be restocked nor reopened. Jewish businesses of any substance were taken over by German management.

When no more Jewish stores were left to raid, the beatings began. These were no mere sporadic incidents, but well-orchestrated open-air circuses, attracting crowds of enthusiastic Polish spectators. City streets became traps, and German warriors poachers and trappers of Jews. The Orthodox segment – highly visible because of their traditional garb, beards, and earlocks – was the first to be attacked, but secular Jews were not ignored either.

All Jews caught on the streets were herded by the cursing and obscenity shouting sciders into one of the squares or marketplaces. When enough encouragement-shouting spectators were gathered, the side show began. One of the most popular numbers with the street performers and their audiences was the shaving of the beards. This was usually administered with a knife, flashed below the nose and close to the frightened eyes. This was considered almost as funny as the shaving of the eyebrows, a most comical number. Many soldiers preferred to tear out clusters of beard, handful by handful, or to burn it off with a match. But the loudest applause of all was reserved for the favorite performance: cutting off one earlock. Orthodox Jews allow the hair in front of their ears to grow, leaving two long curling locks. The shaving – or pulling out, or burning, or cutting off – one earlock, while the other was left dangling from the trembling head, never failed to delight the audiences.

Hidden behind the window curtains and watching these macabre spectacles, we held our breath and wept silently. The humillation was painful, but worse than that was the enthusiasm of the spectators, our Polish compatriots.

The town was in disarray, and laborers were needed badly. The problem of manpower was solved by *oblawy* (raids) on the Jews. Jewish men, regardless of their age, status, and physical condition, were picked up from the streets, herded into closed vans, and carried away to different places, where they were forced to perform any labor imaginable. Clergymen cleaned latrines, physicians unloaded crates, scientists painted walls, lawyers scrubbed floors, merchants moved merchandise – often their own. Most of the goods were "confiscated" from the Jews. Usually the men returned at the end of the day abused, beaten, and hungry, but alive. It was not unusual however that men kidnapped from the streets were never heard of again. It was hard to be in Poland in those days – but to be a Polish Jew was the worst imaginable fate.

On September 17, while the German army was scoring one easy victory after another, the Russians attacked Poland from the east, and in a few days the two armies met at the banks of the River San. Many refugees, overtaken by the fast-moving German army, returned to their homes in the west, while those who crossed the San found themselves under Soviet occupation. The deceivingly benevolent attitude of the Soviet administration toward the Jews convinced many that, indeed, they had reached the Promised Land. Others, reasoning that the end of fighting on Polish soil was tantamount to the end of danger to their lives, returned to the territories under German occupation.

In the beginning, the new border was loosely guarded, and the smuggling of people and goods went on almost openly. These repatriates brought along information about life in the eastern provinces and regards and letters from members of separated families. We were one of the few families without any news. In addition to Father, Haskel, and the boys, Mother's family from Mysienice had fled, too, and all together eighteen members of our family were unaccounted for. When the beatings and *oblawy* started, we were relieved by the belief that our men had reached safety. But as days, and then weeks passed without any word from them, a heavy mood invaded our home.

Haskel's wife, Sala and their children, Eva and Bubek, moved with us. We stayed together in our large apartment, believing that home meant security. How wrong we were was proved to us soon enough.

Mother and Aunt Sala tried to hide their worries from us. My uncles Josef and Haim Horowitz began a sleuthing campaign, searching for anyone who might have heard about the departed Landerers. Josef, coming every morning to cheer Mother up, brought bits of information which we tried to verify during the day. Many people had seen them passing on the road; others heard someone talking about seeing the Landerers, but nobody could give us concrete information. Weeks went by, and we didn't know if they were still alive. It was unbearable, and gradually we sank into despair.

Then one day, out of a blue sky, my sister announced that she had decided to go and search for Father.

"To search for Father"?

"Yes. If we haven't heard from them by now, it is obvious that they must have reached the Russian zone."

When my sister Lela made up her mind, it was impossible to dissuade her. Anyhow, in her orderly thinking, she had it all planned out. When she declared her intention, she was ready to go. Jozia, who never married and had no children of her own, adored us and volunteered to accompany her to the border.

Even today it seems like a dream. One moment she was proclaiming, "I am going to search for Father till I find him," the next she and Jozia were gone.

Her courage and determination are difficult to describe. Those were days of lawlessness. Even in normal times in our circles seventeen-years old girls did not travel alone. Mother, taken by surprise, had hardly time to protest. Two days after the pair left, Jozia returned, telling us that their trip was uneventful. My sister had decidedly Aryan features, and the two women traveled on the train undisturbed. They reached the border safely, and Jozia saw Lela leaving for the Russian side with a group of people led by a reliable (we hoped) smuggler. She asked Jozia to tell Mother that soon she would be back with good news.

She returned after ten of the longest days and nights in our lives. After having crossed the border, she came to the Soviet part of Przemysl (about 160 miles from Krakow) and went to David Landerer's house, where she found Father, Haskel, and the boys. To our immense relief the whole Myslenice contingent was alive, well, and together in a neighboring village. For some unexplained reason the numerous messages they sent us never arrived.

After the war Father used to reminisce about this reunion with his older daughter. Everybody in town stopped by to see "the girl who came to search for her father." He begged her to stay, promising even to enroll her at the university in Lvov.

Lela had been the most brilliant student in every school she attended. She graduated from a public high school with a perfect score. Like all public schools in Poland, it was very anti-Semitic, but in spite of that – in spite of being the only student in the school's history exempted from attendance on Shabbat and all Jewish holidays – she was always at the top of her class. Her school's claim to excellence stemmed from the fact that most of the teachers were lecturers at the Jagiellonion University (University of Krakow). At every parent-teachers' conference Mother was the envy of all other parents. My mother was told that her daughter had an outstanding literary talent. The mathematics teacher said that a student like Lela was a rarity and a blessing for a professor. Her art work was sent to schools abroad as examples of superior achievement. She strove to perfection in all she did. Her life's fondest dream was higher education, but she was born into the wrong family. Hassidim in Krakow did not approve of high secular education, especially for girls, and Father had always conformed to the norms of his closely knit community. Nevertheless, he offered Lela a university education if she would remain.

But in vain. Lela had promised Mother to return with good news – and she kept her word. People who were with Father at that time told us later that for days after she left he was inconsolable.

The news that the Landerer girl had returned from the "other side" spread fast, and soon we were besieged by people from desperate, broken-up families, as frantic for news of departed relatives as we had been before Lela's gallant journey. Only then did we realize that our ordeal was not unique. My brave sister had smuggled many letters, out of the Soviet zone, mostly for people she didn't know. Others wanted information about the crossing of the border and the passage to the "good life" on the "other side."

The majority of refugees under Russian occupation survived, each and everyone from our family, including five little children, who were under the Soviet occupation, lived to see 1946. Even the winter they spent in Minora, the farthest outpost in northern Siberia, seemed like merely an unpleasant interlude in comparison to what we went through under the Nazis.

But pulled by some unknown force, or maybe the inescapable destiny of an individual, Lela returned to Krakow.

8 · Midwinter nightmares

Life went on, and people tried to maintain the pretence of normalcy. The changed criteria made it easier. It was perfectly normal not to have coal or potatoes, the main staple of everyone's diet. Families were torn apart. People evicted from their apartments turned into refugees in their own hometown, and active, healthy men hid in dark corners, trying to avoid confrontation with the Germans. In a city teeming with refugees, we could not live alone in our large apartment and voluntarily took in some of the evicted and two homeless girls. One part of the apartment was seized by the Germans, but we were permitted to keep two rooms, Jozia stayed in her little room, and the bathrooms were shared by all.

As we had the use of two rooms only, we doubled up in beds for the night: my mother and I in one, Aunt Sala with Eva, and Bubek on the couch. My sister, claiming that her seniority entitled her to privileges, slept alone in our former nursery. We did not turn the lights on in the large bedroom, because our windows faced the street; lighted windows attracted attention and could bring feared visitors. Also, the coal we had was irreplaceable, so we could not afford to heat the room either.

Aunt Sala was ten years younger than mother and took the forced separation badly. She lost a lot of weight, and in no time, Eva's once beautiful mother resembled a haggard old woman. She had difficulties falling asleep in the cold dark bedroom and used to talk to Mother. Eva and I often pretended to sleep and instead listened to them:

"Hacia?"

"Yes, Sala."

"Hacia, I am scared."

"Don't worry, Sala. Don't be scared."

"Hacia, what is going to be with us and the children?"

"We must trust God. You will see, everything will be good at the end."

The long scary nights, starting with early curfews, were dreaded like an enemy. The terrible fear of the unknown, the longing for fathers, husbands, and children, and the ever-present terror became magnified in the darkness. In the quiet of the night every sound from the street was spine-chilling. Loud voices usually preceded "search," a euphemism for plunder, confiscation of possessions, beating, often arrest. The screeching of car tires often announced sudden deportation of some neighbor to a place of no return. When the mewing of a stray cat broke the night's silence, we heard frightened children crying in the apartment above us.

One of those fearful nights in our neighbourhood occurred when the contents of the warehouse and most of the belongings of the Schenkers, our next-door neighbors, were "confiscated."

The hour was late, We were in our beds. In the deep darkness the night seemed deceitfully quiet. Suddenly, the sounds of approaching cars were heard. I felt my mother's body stiffen beside me. Gradually the noises grew stronger and more distinct. It was evident from their volume that there was more than one truck. We heard them entering our street. The roar grew louder. Beams of light invaded our room through the narrow slits between the shades and the window frames. The cars stopped. We heard voices, footsteps, banging at the gate and angry commands: "*Aufmachen! Aufmachen!*" (Open up! Open up!)

"Pretend you are all asleep!" Mother, as usual was calm, composed, and in control of her emotions. Aunt Sala was trembling. Eva, weeping softly, clung to her mother. My heart was pounding. The stomach felt as if it had a piece of rock in it. I pulled the cover over my head, hoping to disappear in the depth of our bed. We heard the heavy gate being opened and waited for the dreaded banging and kicking at our door. Meanwhile my sister Lela, whose room faced the courtyard and Schenker's warehouse, tiptoed into our room and murmured: "They are at the Schenkers."

Everybody caught a deep breath, but it did not bring relief. Who knew what the night held for us? A minute later Jozia seemed to have floated soundlessly into our room. "They are at the Schenkers," she whispered.

A moment later we heard a slight knock at the door. It was the superintendent's wife, a coat wrapped over her nightgown, her hair – usually fixed in an elaborate arrangement of braids – falling in disarray over her shoulders. Nearing our bed, she bent over in a hardly audible voice said: "They are at the Schenkers. What should I do if they bang at our gate?"

"If they do, you must open immediately," Mother told her resolutely. "We have nothing incriminating in our possession."

Mother pretended to be unperturbed, but she was no fool. In the fall of 1939 being a Jew was the most incriminating thing of all. "Everybody back to beds!" she added in her usual authoritative voice. "Should they decide to come and search our house, they must not find us all awake. They might not like to see so many witnesses to their activities."

Jozia and Nastalkowa, muttering prayers under their breath, left the room. My sister, after lingering a few more minutes, returned to her "privacy."

The darkness of the familiar room felt somewhat menacing. Dreading lest they hear us in the adjoining building, we hardly dared to breath. The hours stretched into infinity. We heard shouting, curses in German. While the trucks were being loaded, we heard the soldiers enter the house and come out again. The night seemed longer than one at the North Pole. Finally the gate closed with a bang. Men's loud voices and footsteps were heard directly below our windows. We froze in fear. The tension was interrupted by Aunt Sala's whisper: "Do you think they are coming to us now?"

"Mommy, I am so afraid!" Eva cried softly.

But then we heard the sound of motors being started. Beams of light galloped wildly over our ceiling and walls. The force of the deafening roar seemed to shutter the windows. Gradually weakening, it finally disappeared. The uneasy quiet of a night in a town under German occupation had returned.

It was a gray November morning. The weather was already cold. As if ashamed to show its face, the sun hardly ever shone over the tragic land. Our apartment was cold, and Bubek, Eva, and I lingered under the warm covers. Our mothers, as usual, were up early. They used to sneak into the kitchen, where they kept themselves busy. Aunt Sala became an expert bread kneader; many of her early mornings were spent kneading the dough. Reluctant to leave our warm beds and face the world that had become so hostile, we were often greeted by the aroma of freshly baked bread that seemed like a promise of a lovely surprise.

This morning, instead of the quiet, lazy sleepiness usually spread over our floor, a strange commotion was taking place. We heard soft knocks at the door, the sounds of the chain being removed, the door opening and being closed softly, and our superintendent's wife agitated voice: "Jesus, Maria, Josef ..." the rest we couldn't make out. Jozia walked in, and the way she entered the room made us sense that something was amiss. Usually she knocked and waited at the door. This time she walked in and stood close to my bed. She was deadly pale, and her trembling lips were moving in silent prayer.

Three frightened voices blended into one: "Jozia, what's happened?"

Jozia did not answer. She was crossing herself, which she ordinarily never did in our presence, and was whispering between sobs: "Holy Mother of God, Holy Mary of Czestochowa, have mercy on us, protect these children!" Before she had time to compose herself, our mothers were back in the room, Aunt Sala white as a sheet, Mother, the captain of the sinking ship our home had become, remaining in control.

"Everybody get dressed immediately! Put on your walking shoes, two pairs of socks, double underwear, sweaters. Have your coats, gloves, hats ready. The entire Jewish neighborhood is surrendered by the German army. We don't know yet what it all means. ..."

We, the youngsters didn't listen anymore but ran to the window. What we saw made us freeze in terror. While we slept, the peaceful neighborhood had become transformed into a motorized army camp. Military vans were parked in the side streets, and Wolnica Square had become headquarters for the operation Plunder and Humiliate the Jews, later to be referred to as the *Grossaktion* (Grand Action).

Streets were empty of civilians. A military sentry was posted in front of every building. Except for the sounds of an occasional military truck or jeep passing, the streets were frighteningly still.

Paff! Paff! Paff! Dry, short sounds interrupted the silence. Strong arms pulled us away from the window.

"They are shooting! Those were gun shots! Merciful God ..."

100

"Quiet!" Mother's steady voice sounded reassuring. "Children away from the window! Everybody into the back room. We are captives in our house, but we must not panic!

As we tiptoed into the back of the house, I could not believe it. Could those short, dry coughs be real gunshots? The sound was familiar, like that of the toy gun we used to shoot caps with. Was this all it took? A tiny bit of lead, and all would be over? All hopes and dreams and even the ever-present fear could be cut off in less than a second? Could life be defeated by a tiny, hardly visible thing? I was not ready to die, not even while life was becoming unendurable. In my dreams I was ready to conquer the sun with my bare hands – but facing the cruel reality, I felt helpless.

Around nine in the morning, the signal was given and the march into the Jewish homes began. The invaders were a regular army unit in full combat gear. With methodical German thoroughness, they searched and plundered every apartment in the district, building after building, floor after floor, flat after flat, room after room. They did not miss anyone.

In a short time the streets, crowded with people's possessions, resembled a warehouse. Amassed on the sidewalks were couches, armchairs, beds, lamps, rugs, assorted pieces of furniture, china, silver, and clothing. The Jews were forced to carry out their own property, accumulations of a lifetime, often of generations.

On the second day, the army unit was nearing our block, and the tension was mounting toward panic. Waiting was a torment. Sitting around the table in our little back room, we knitted furiously, without pattern or design. The steady, mechanical movement of our hands brought a slight release from choking fear.

Finally they came! The sounds of heavy steps climbing our stairs became distinct. Men's loud voices invaded the silence. The door was kicked open. The soldiers spilled over our apartment. How many of the brave warriors were assigned to fight the Landerer women was hard to tell. They were tall, big, powerful, and so loud that it seemed as if a whole battalion had descended upon us.

"*Los! Los! Schnell!*" We were herded into the bathroom, where we remained locked for the duration of the time it took to empty our house of anything that took their fancy.

Listening to radio broadcasts was forbidden right from the beginning. Aunt Sala had a beautiful radio, which she had brought along when she came stay with us. (Uncle Haskel, the musician, had to have the best possible reception and spared no expense.) Not knowing what to do with it, we decided to have it wrapped, sealed, and put away in the dirty-laundry closet. We used up a whole stick of sealing material, and it was obvious that the radio was not in use. While the soldiers were ransacking the house, they found it. We were all in the bathroom when suddenly the door was opened.

"Whose radio is it?" thundered over our heads.

Aunt Sala stepped out. "Cursed Jewess! Out!" The brute pushed her out and forced her to pick up the heavy radio. Bubek, twelve years old at that time, followed his mother. When the soldier pushed her out to the staircase, the boy hurled himself at him, grabbed his arm and begged in a mixture of Polish, Yiddish, and German: *"Lieber Herr. Susser Herr. ich will tragan dus radio!"*

"Weg!"

He was tossed away, and his mother disappeared behind the heavy iron door leading to the cellar.

An hour later she returned. As it turned out they ordered all men from upstairs into the cellar, where they were forced to stand facing the wall, in the classic preexecution position. My gentle Aunt Sala, frail and delicate, was thrown in and forced to stand facing the wall for an hour, all the time holding the heavy radio. When they finished with the looting of the entire building, they let their captives go.

When Sala came back, we were still in the bathroom. Drained of all strength, she could hardly talk. We did not ask any questions. She sat on the floor, her children huddled close to her, covering her red, swollen hands with kisses and tears.

We remained in the bathroom for a long time after we heard the front door slam. We were scared and did not want to look into the rooms. When we finally went back, we could not evaluate the extent of the plunder. All doors, cabinets, and drawers were open and the leftovers spread over the floors. Numb from fear and relieved that Sala had come back unharmed, we did not care.

Our relief was short-lived. Our tormentors were still on the prowl, our door wide open. The soldiers told one another where the wealthiest Jews lived, and hordes of them returned, again and again. It was like being on the street.

For two days and two nights this orgy of German bestiality lasted. All that time we sat in our little back room, afraid to go to sleep, to undress, even to go to the bathroom, because the soldiers were still staggering in and out of the house, still searching, stealing, and destroying.

Next day the loudspeakers blared loud German radio broadcasts: "*Die Deutsche Wehrmacht marschiert siegreich fort!*"

9 · Black Friday

December 4, 1939, will go down in the annals of Krakow's Jewry as Black Friday. The day started like any other Friday. Our mothers were up before dawn, because the meal had to be prepared early and hidden till the evening, lest we get an unexpected raid. When German soldiers raided Jewish homes and found tasty food, they "confiscated" it without any qualms. This, of course, was in addition to pillaging the house thoroughly.

Usually they came in pairs. Keeping watch at the window and warning all tenants when two soldiers were seen approaching became part of everyday life.

No one could foresee what fresh disasters each new day would bring, but no matter what, Shabbat would not be ignored. We spared no efforts to maintain the Friday night tradition. The clinging to our old way of life helped us to retain our self-respect and boosted our courage. The Nazis had the power to rob, torture, imprison, take away all and kill. But we possessed something intangible they could never take from us or destroy. It was our *Yiddishkeit*, the gut feeling that there was reason and order in our lives that transcended human interference.

It was early in the morning. The house was quiet. Under the warm covers, we stretched our limbs. Pungent aromas of fish and soup began to permeate the long hallway as we lazily woke up. But the sensation that something was missing from our daily routine gradually crept into our awareness.

"Eva, did you hear Uncle Josiu coming in?"

"No. Did you?"

"I did not. Wonder what takes him so long today?"

"I hope —" Eva was interrupted in midsentence by a muted sound, as if someone was scratching at the door. Then we heard Mother's familiar step followed by the click of the chain being removed as she opened the door. Someone began to talk fast in a low voice. The superintendent's wife – a bad omen! My heart felt like it had suddenly skipped a beat, and then it started racing without restraint.

The news she brought was very bad indeed. Podgorze was surrounded by the SS.

Podgorze a section of Krakow, was mainly populated by Jews. Nearly all its streets were inhabited by Jews only. We lived in Kazimierz, but most of my family lived in Podgorze: My mother's brother Josef and Wolf Horowitz, the Weinbergers, my father's two married nieces, Ryfcia and Hania. Before she moved to Sambor, my Aunt Ryfka Balken had lived there too.

Now no one was allowed to go near Podgorze, and no one knew what was happening there. All day long our superintendent, Antoni, his wife, and their two sons kept coming with different, often contradicting reports:

"They are rounding up everybody."

"They are rounding up all Jews."

"They are rounding up all men."

"All Jewish men are being rounded up."

"All Jewish men are taken away."

Evening came, and we were still in limbo. Our mothers lighted the candles, but their hearts were not in it. We all moved about the house like wound-up toys. When it was time to sit down at the table, we changed into our Shabbat dresses out of habit. We had to go on. The painstakingly acquired and prepared food was forced down, leaving a bitter aftertaste. The fate of our uncles and cousins was constantly on our minds. All we could do was pray, hope, and wait.

Somehow the night passed. As gray morning light filtered into the room, another day of despair and hope had begun. There was no curfew for Kazimierz Jews, but nobody ventured out. Even the Poles shunned the streets. They did not know what to expect. Rumors circulated all day long, each one more confusing than the other.

Finally, this bleak Shabbat came to an end. As usual we were crowded in the former nursery, the smallest room in the house, the only one we could afford to keep warm. All huddled around the stove, not so much for the touch of its warm tiles as for the feeling of physical closeness, so reassuring in times when hope and courage are waning, and words have lost the power of consolation.

Antoni, his face drawn, came in silently. Switching weight from one foot to the other, he remained standing at the door. His hands were kneading his shapeless hat. The usual merry gleam of his eyes was gone.

"Come in, Antoni." Mother motioned him. "Tell us the news." He remained at the door, as if suddenly afraid to come near, lest our Jewishness became catching like leprosy.

"Madame," he muttered. "Trucks with the Jews from Podgorze are parked alongside the Kahal building on Krakowska Street." The time was thirty minutes before the strictly enforced curfew at eight. Antoni had hardly finished his frightening announcement when we heard urgent banging at the door and loud voices calling, "Landerer! Landerer! Open!" Two young women whom we had never met before burst into the foyer and said: "Horowitz is on one of the trucks. He asked us to tell you that he needs food and bandages."

In the commotion that ensued, they left before we could thank them. In the shortest possible time a package of food, bandages, and iodine was assembled.

In the darkest corner of the highest shelf in Mother's pantry a piece of dry salami was hidden among empty jars. Mother was guarding her sons' favorite tidbit for the great moment of their return. It was promptly taken down, and while Sala and my sister were making sandwiches, Mother and I put on our shoes and coats and ran.

In order to reach Krakowska Street, we had to traverse the whole length of Wolnica Square. Long, dark, and desolated, it resembled a no-man's-land that we had to pass before we reached the enemy lines. We ran to the corner, where military trucks were lined up alongside the street. Separating the trucks from the rest of the world was a contingent of SS men, forming an impenetrable fence. Mindless of the danger, I darted between the guards. Mother followed like another teenager. Our daring took the SS men by surprise. The breaking through an SS cordon by two Jewish women was not foreseen, and apparently they had no instructions in how to deal with such situation. In late 1939 they did not shoot the Jews point-blank on the streets. Not yet. Conforming to discipline, they waited for orders from their commanding officer, while we, taking advantage of the momentary confusion, ran along the vans calling "Horowitz! Horowitz!" There was no response. Those Black Marias seemed to be props in some macabre play. Suddenly the tarpaulin covering the back of one parted, and my uncle appeared. Or was it a ghostly apparition resembling my beloved Uncle Josef? He was deadly pale. Blood, oozing from an open wound on his forehead, was smeared all over his face.

"Uncle, darling uncle, what did they do to you?"

"Nothing, nothing, my child."

Mother seemed to have lost her voice. "Josele, Josele," she whimpered.

"Hacia, Hacia," he sobbed and stretched his hand to her. Before the brother and sister could touch, the SS men surrounded us, shoving and shouting at us with fury: "*Weg! Frauen weg!*" I threw the package at him. He caught it as other captives were pulling him back, and in a moment the tarpaulin had been tied together again.

We turned back. Astonished by our bravura, the somber wardens let us pass. The cordon of the SS closed behind us. We walked home hardly seeing them. The image of Josiu's bloody face blocked out everything.

As it turned out, it was all an innocent fund-raising event. The prisoners were divided into two groups. The younger were sent to Lublin, the older to Arbeitslager Pustkow. A price was set on every Jewish head. Shortly thereafter, they were back. The community was poorer in money but richer in knowledge of the ways of Nazi rule.

An unspoken agreement during the war was that people did not talk about their sufferings and humiliations. Just going through the day was a feat of endurance and courage, taxing human resilience to the utmost. It was only after forty and some years had passed and our emotional wounds had healed enough, that we could talk about what happened on Black Friday.

After being dragged from their homes in the morning, the men spent the rest of the day standing in the police vans. When the entire section of the town was combed through and all Jewish males above the age of thirteen were loaded on the trucks, they were transported to the dreaded Monte Lupich Gestapo prison. Before they were sent off to their respective destinations, all had to pass inspection by Hans

Frank, governor of occupied Polish territories. Tired, hungry, and dumbfounded, they were assembled in a large hall.

What pitiful sight they presented, those POWs from Jewish Podgorze, as they stood at attention waiting for the super-Nazi to enter. All ranks of life were represented in that pathetic formation of defenceless males. Flanked by my two cousins, Aron Horowitz and Iciu Weinberger, stood their beloved teacher and mentor, the Koloszycer Ruv. The rabbi was deeply pious – not an old man, in his early thirties only. His lips moved silently as he stood motionless, oblivious to his surroundings. He was reciting the daily portion of the Psaims by heart. His long, threadbare caftan was open, showing the religious garment he wore over his shirt. Its long, white fringes were hanging down, openly manifesting blatant disregard of German prohibition of religious practices. This unusual apparition caught Frank's attention. His loud voice cut through the silence, making the men shiver.

"Jude!" What are you wearing under your coat?"

Governor Frank stood in front of the rabbi and fixed his stare on his victim. He was absentmindedly twisting his leather whip with one hand; the other rested on his holster. He was an uncommonly handsome man, Governor Frank, outwardly a credit to the Teutonic tribe. Tall, erect, dressed in the full regalia of his power, he towered over the entire assembly – a giant Goliath, the personification of absolute power, gazing down with contempt at his opponent. Facing him stood the Jewish scholar, frail, slouched, dressed in worn-out Hassidic attire. Their eyes met, and the rabbi, poised and calm, replied in a clear voice:

"This garment, Herr Governor, should be worn by every Jewish male."

"Those fringes there, must they be hanging out too?" It was obvious to all but the rabbi that the governor was mocking him.

"Yes, Herr Governor. It is of utmost importance that those fringes always point down."

"If I may ask, what is so important about it?"

"Because no matter how high a man rises in his lifetime, these fringes serve as constant reminder that at the end, everybody must return down, to the earth."

The rabbi's voice, usually soft and a bit hoarse, resounded loud and clear. Holding their breath in panic, the stunned prisoners stood at

108

attention, fearing an outburst of fury. To their disbelief Frank, the terror of occupied Poland, remained silent for a moment, then turned around – and walked out. The sound of his fast steps gradually diminished, until they were heard no more.

The Koloszycer Ruv's oblivion to the world outside of the study of his beloved Talmud, plus his unshakable faith, defeated one of the most vicious Nazis, if for a moment only. As David's little stone penetrated the giant Philistine's armor, so did the rabbi's answer, in its innocence and verity, touch a man, otherwise incapable of emotion.

With grief and sadness, I must report that, in time, the saintly Rabbi Moshe Aron Halberstam, thirty-five years old, the Rebetzin Haya Yetta, and their six children perished at the hands of the Nazis.

10 · Wedrowka

Those uneasy allies, Germany and the U.S.S.R., divided Poland between them. When persecutions of the Jews began in all German-occupied territories, many people packed up whatever they could carry and resumed the refugee march eastward. Poles called this Wedrowka (flight, wandering away). If the refugees managed to cross the River San or the then loosely guarded land border, they found themselves under Soviet rule and were allowed to live a relatively persecution-free life – at first. I suppose the Soviet government simply didn't know what to do with them, and while it was making up its mind, it did nothing.

We had many relatives in the Russian zone: the David and Avroom Landerers in Przemysl, the Balkens and Grandmother Landerer in Sambor, and the refugees from Krakow and Myslenice. My father and my two brothers, Uncle Haskel Landerer, mother's sister Ruchcia, her son Moshe and daughter Dina Reifer with husband Getzel and baby Moshe, Nehame and Josef Rottenstreich with Rachel and Motti, Dina Anisfeld with Moshe, Bracha, and Rachel. The Balkens received all refugees with open arms, and Grandma was quite rejuvenated. Once again she had a house full of small and big children who needed her, and as she had done in her youth, she took care of them all. Her greatest pleasure for her was to have them all seated at the table to wait on.

After Lela's visit to Father and Uncle Haskel, we did not worry about our menfolk so much. Haskel, who had many friends in Lvov, moved there, resumed his old business connections, and soon began to prosper. Semiofficial trade sprang up between the conquerors and their new subjects. Mother Russia was starved for material goods of almost every kind, and the enthusiastic tovariches gobbled up everything they could find.

But after eight months of being left in peace, everything changed. In June of 1940, agents of the NKVD (as the Soviet secret service was then called) began to arrive in all the towns and villages where refugees from German-occupied Poland were concentrated. It had been decided to deport the Polish Jews to Siberia.

The first hint that the Sambor contingent had was the large number of boxcars that suddenly appeared on sidings at the train station. (In Europe, massed shipments of people always employed freight cars, usually cattle cars; even soldiers were transported from place to place by freight, as in the French "40-and-8's" of World War 1). As soon as word reached Haskel in Lvov, he boarded the first train for Sambor and was with Father when the NKVD came for them.

They were awakened in the middle of the night, given an hour to get ready, and then herded down to the train station. There they were separated – men in certain groups, women and children in others – ordered to board the freight cars, and shipped off into exile.

They remained in the freight cars for three weeks, until they reached Irkutsk in southern Siberia. There they boarded large barges for a week's travel, after which they were disembarked, loaded onto trucks, and jounced and jostled for three long days until they reached the banks of the River Lena. Then it was back to the barges again, smaller ones this time, for a three-week "cruise" to Yakutsk. Another series of barges, another three weeks of travel and at last the 2,000 exhausted deportees reached a clearing in the taiga – the swampy subarctic forest that covers most of northeastern Siberia. But that was not the end of their journey, either. They were split into two groups. One, consisting of mainly young, healthy people, was sent up to Yur, the other, consisting of families with elderly members and children (that meant my family) sent to Minora, another three-week trip along the Allahjun River. There they remained for the next fourteen months.

The living quarters assigned to them were old, dilapidated wooden structures, half prison barracks, half peasant huts. Each unit consisted of a single room, to which three or four families were assigned. During the long ten-months-lasting winter, the temperature often reached −40 to −50 degrees centigrade. In the early morning, they used to chop blocks of ice off the walls and melt them on the iron stove for the morning's cup of hot beverage. Often this cup of hot water was all they had for breakfast before leaving to toil at their assigned jobs.

All able bodied – and some of the not very fit, too – were sent to slave away in the gold mines or to cut down trees and saw wood. All "political" prisoners – former teachers, businessmen, shopkeepers, lawyers, rabbis, even, some of the women – were forced to work at hard labor, under the most primitive conditions.

To satisfy the unrealistic expectations of the current Five Year Plan, the ancient land was violated. The virgin forests, the Arctic tundra, the swampy coniferous woodlands called taiga were mindlessly destroyed. Day after day, the men tramped out of their cold and barren huts to ravish land that had lain dormant for thousands of years, in order to fill some bureaucratic quota.

Other bewildered exiles were forced to become gold miners, burrowing through the bowels of the earth to extract the precious metal.

These people had the hardest time of all. They spent their days in darkness, and in summer, when they emerged after a long day of toil, they found that it was still daylight out. Adjusting to the "white nights" of the extreme north was especially difficult for them.

In order to subsist under the brutal rule of the labor-camp guards, the refugees had to use cunning and daring. At first they had been able to alleviate their lot by bartering their possessions with the local people, but then the authorities declared that illegal. A few unfortunates who were caught red-handed were thrown in Minora's jail, where conditions were even more inhuman than at the camp. After that, acquiring and "illegal" loaf of bread or quart of milk for the children became, in Soviet eyes, subversive activity. Nevertheless, such bartering went on clandestinely. In order to survive – and, above all, to see that their children survived – people endangered their lives every day.

It was under these conditions that Uncle Haskel's gift for music came to his rescue. With his weak lungs, lumbering in the bitter cold or mining in the dangerous dark would have spelled an early death. But somehow or other he acquired a fiddle, the only one in the whole settlement, and began to play it nightly in the local tavern. This dreary place, where the guards and their superiors hung out when they were off duty, suddenly became gay and lively. The bosses liked his music so much that they promptly assigned him the most coveted job in the camp – night watchman in the cooperative's warehouse. It was the beginning of a highly privileged existence. Every night, after the tavern closed, Haskel departed for the storehouse, where a warm room was ready for him.

Then on June 22, 1941, a year after the deportation had begun, Germany invaded the U.S.S.R. This, of course, portended a ghastly fate for Russian Jews, including the Balkens in Sambor, as we later learned, but for the refugees, it meant an early release from labor camp. Amnesty was declared for all "political" prisoners, and that included all civilians deported to Siberia, all children, all old people, my whole family. In late summer 1941, Minora's exiles were relocated to Yakutsk, where they spent two years, then to Saratov on the Volga in south-central U.S.S.R., where the climate resembles that of Central Europe.

Father, Uncle Haskel and his fiddle – a favorite with Saratov's local population, too – and the others remained there until the end of the war. Cut off from communication with the outside world (and us), they bided their time, spinning dreams about returning home.

Meanwhile, in German-occupied Poland, persecution of Jews was progressing at a steadily increasing pace – from minor nuisances to blatant abuse, from sporadic executions to mass murder, from resettling large Jewish populations to sending them all to extermination camps.

Although certain streets and sections of towns were assigned specifically to Jews, the term "ghetto" was not yet in use. It was in the beginning of 1940 that rumors began to circulate about an enclosed ghetto being set up in Lodz. But Lodz seemed far away, and with the incurable Jewish optimism, people in Krakow told one another that there must have been good reasons for ghettoing Lodz, but *man meint nicht uns* (they would not think of doing it to us).

Then the formation of Ghetto Warsaw began – over half a million Jews crammed behind the walls that separated them from the rest of the world. To many of them there was something almost reassuring in belonging to such a large community. Some Jews even entered the ghetto voluntarily, believing that the autonomy given to the Judenrat (Jewish Council) would help them escape persecution. After all, Jews always helped one another. Surely the big Warsaw community would survive. As for Krakovian Jews, they commented that Warsaw, as the capital of Poland, was under different status from Krakow. And again, *man meint nicht uns.*

Not one of us suspected that the massing of population in a few centers was the first step in the implementation of Hitler's monstrous plans for the Jewish people.

But soon, even in Krakow, *man meint nicht uns* was no longer heard. As more and more Jews were evicted from their apartments, driven from outlying parts of the city, the idea took hold that we too might end up in a ghetto. And at last, in the winter of 1940-41, the establishment of Ghetto Krakow in part of Podgorze was proclaimed. We were not overly worried. At worst, we told one another, we would move in with our family in Podgorze till "after the war." Then we learned that special permits would be required to move to Podgorze, and we realized that our chance for receiving them were nonexistent.

My sixteenth birthday, celebrated on February 15, 1941, was bittersweet. The one certain thing in my life was that this would be my last birthday in our home. A few days later came the dreaded letters with the *Aussledlung Ausweiss* (population-transfer certificate) for us and Sala with her children. We were given a few days to wind up our affairs and disappear. It was decided to move to Tarnow, fifty miles east of Krakow, where Mother's brother Hirsch Horowitz had settled, after escaping from Myslenice.

How Mother accomplished that move in a few days, I will never know. It had always been my parents' policy to shield the children from difficulties, so she solved her problems by herself. We – the girls and Bubek – packed our clothes, and Mother and Sala tied up the few household goods we were taking along. Mother did not want to be encumbered by possessions – she sensed that this might not be our final move.

Still we expected to return eventually. Some things were left with our superintendent. The furniture that somehow we had managed to retain was turned over to the Poles who lived in our building. Mr. Konicki, who took over the apartment of the Eder family (disappeared at the beginning of the war), admired Mother's bedroom set and offered to safekeep it for us. Mother gave him a fictional bill of sale, so he could prove to the Germans that he was a rightful owner, and he in turn gave Mother the word of honor of a Pole that he would return the set after the war. Later, when Father came back from Russia, he tried to claim it, but Mr. Konicki denied having made any such agreement and threatened to denounce Father to the NKVD. This was how a lot of Jewish property entrusted to "honourable" Poles was lost.

The Wabersichs, who declared themselves Volkdeutches (Poles of German origin) and pledged allegiance to the *Reich*, lived in the part of our apartment requisitioned by the German command; they ultimately disappeared and with them the things left with them. The only people who showed compassion and honesty after my family returned from the U.S.S.R., penniless and broken in spirit, was our superintendent Antoni and his wife Maria Nastalek. Mrs. Nastalek hid a portrait of my sister and me. When my oldest brother married in Krakow in the year 1946, she returned it to him. When I married in Israel in 1949, he passed it on to me as a wedding gift. It is my only memento from my childhood and home.

On a cold afternoon in February of 1941, I closed the doors of our apartment and downcast trudged through familiar yet hostile streets for Aunt Blimcia's apartment. Till arrangements could be made for us to join Uncle Hirsch in Tarnow, my aunt was to keep me hidden in her apartment.

There was no coal to heat the bedroom, so Reeva and I huddled together in the cold bed, surrounded by darkness and insecurity. Our happy past seemed like a fantasy, our future too frightening to imagine.

When our trusted Polish maid Jozia arrived the next day to take me to the railroad station, I said a brief good-bye to the Weinbergers: Aunt Blimcia, Uncle Meir-Haim, Iciu, Moniek and the girls. I thought I'd be seeing them again before long.

11 · Ghetto Tarnow

Tarnow had two claims to greatness: Its train station and the street-car. Otherwise it was not different from other provincial towns scattered along the railway tracks. Its crooked, climbing-over-the-hills streets blended into the picturesque countryside so that it was hard to tell where one ended and the other began.

The city is located at a major crossroad in the south of Poland, and during the war its train station was heavily guarded by the military police, the Gestapo, and the polish milicja, all united in their fervor to arrest Jews. Otherwise it was – and is – a large red brick building, hideous but functional, a tasteless reminder of the elegant Habsburgs.

Tarnow's streetcar was considered a joke even by its most chauvinistic citizens. Its single track stretched from the main artery to the other end of the town. Smack in the middle of its route was the crossing, highly visible because of cars patiently waiting for the right of way. "When in a hurry – walk," went the standing Tarnow jest. "When you have time to kill, take the tramway."

When we arrived in Tarnow, the tramway and even many of the Jewish streets were declared out of bounds for Jews, as absurd as that may appear. You came and went by back doors. Often, in order to reach the back entrance to a house, you had to circle around the block. Still, after the oppressive atmosphere in Krakow, this place seemed ideal, because Jews still had some freedom of movement – limited freedom, but better than nothing.

The entire population of the town and some neighbouring villages were crowded into few city blocks, composed mainly of deteriorating buildings. The density was unbelievable – in each room a family and later a family in every corner. In those surroundings the eternally optimistic race tried to recreate a semblance of normalcy, sustained by hope – the religious people with their expectations of Messiah, the

116

secularists with their scientific theories. All were strengthened by the conviction that this was just a transition period, till "after the war."

During our entire stay in Tarnow we lived on Debowa Street, number 4. It was quite a departure from our previous life. In Krakow we had often been sirgled out because of our opulent apartment. In Tarnow, we lived no better than any poor refugees. The building was old, dilapidated, without modern plumbing, only two stories high. This decrepit edifice had only two concessions to the twentieth century, electricity and gas, and shortly after our arrival, even they were disconnected. A long, dark hall led to our apartment, and we soon learned to grope our way in the darkness. Holding on to the wall, one proceeded along a tunnel-like corridor, until a creaking board, followed by a sinking one to be skipped over, announced the entrance to our apartment. In order to get into our room, we had to pass through the kitchen and bedroom occupied by our landlady, Mrs. Rosenzweig, and her two daughters, Dora and Zina.

Our room had two windows facing the street. It was furnished with three iron beds, one couch, a large table surrounded by assorted chairs, a dresser between the windows, and one piece of furniture transported from Krakow – the battered old white cupboard from our nursery. (How Mother managed to move it to Tarnow, I don't remember anymore. Probably she arranged for an official permit to ship it.) Its poor condition would not betray our prosperous past. It stood leaning against the wall, camouflaging a door that led to another room, which used to be a part of the Rosenzweig's residence. Later on this cupboard was to play a crucial role in the destiny of our family.

One section of the room was set apart by a folding screen. It served as a combination kitchen-bathroom, and was furnished with a cupboard, an iron stove, and two water pails. A small basin standing on a wooden crate performed the function of a sink. In spite of the cramped living conditions, we maintained immaculate personal cleanliness. All we needed was a kettle of hot water, a piece of soap, and a towel. Once a week we scrubbed our clothing and linen on the washboard, and then the floor was scoured with the soapy water.

We were proud of our new home, where we lived in harmony. The ever-present danger formed the strongest imaginable bond among all the people in the apartment. Unfortunately, this experiment in communal living did not last long.

With the optimism of my youth and zest for life, I adjusted to the new surroundings. As everybody above fourteen years of age had to be productively employed, I was assigned a job. It was my good luck to become employed by the Judenrat as a hygienist responsible for sanitary conditions of one ghetto street. In order to qualify for the job, I had to pass an examination in physiology and hygiene given by a medical doctor to whom I had to report subsequently. After first getting acquainted with the people and making detailed health charts, a hygienist had to check the sanitary conditions. The plague of lice had reached Biblical proportions, and a typhus epidemic was on the loose. Most of the buildings had no modern plumbing, which rendered the situation worse.

One of my routine tasks consisted of personal body control. If even one louse or nit was found, the entire family – or rather all families living in the infested apartment – had to be taken to the baths and their clothing fumigated. Being hauled off to *Entlausung* in a police cart was tantamount to the primitive custom of dragging tarred and feathered criminals through the marketplace. And then, too, ir-replaceable clothing was often ruined during this procedure. Not even seventeen years old, I was forced to grapple with the dilemma of whether to perform my official duty or just let it go. Having been brought up in an orthodox Jewish home, I had the concept of human dignity deeply ingrained in me, and I truly believed that shaming a person was one of the gravest sins. But sometimes, the health of the community being at stake, I had no choice but to report people for *Entlausung*.

Two of those cases, were most unusual, even for those abnormal times. I was conducting inspection in an old house on Wekslarska Street one day, and as I felt my way along the wall in the dark staircase, my hand encountered a doorlatch. I pressed it down, and a door opened, leading into a dark cavelike space.

"I am a hygienist from the Judenrat." "Does anybody live here?"
"Yes, come in, come in."

As my eyes adjusted to the darkness, I saw few steps leading down from the staircase into what appeared to be a human dwelling. I inched my way down. It was a long room with a tiny skylight at the far corner, so dusty and covered with cobwebs that hardly any light came in. The place was totally devoid of furniture. At the end of the room an old straw mattress, with no sheet or pillow, was spread on the floor, and from that mattress a pair of large, black eyes was staring at me. As I approached, I saw that they were the eyes of a badly deformed child. A disheveled woman was crouching beside him, and under the window a short man was standing among broken umbrellas.

I stood there speechless. It was the fall of 1942, and at that time I had seen already a lot of human misery, but I have never before seen people subsisting under such conditions.

"Come in! Come in! *Shalom lakh! Shalom!*" Smiling broadly, the man limped toward me. His friendliness was disarming and helped me to appraise the situation.

"Who are you?"

As it turned out, he was an educated man, a Hebrew teacher in a high school in his former life. At present he was fixing broken umbrellas for a living, and the family subsisted on his meagre earnings and one meal a day from the communal kitchen. They had another child, a girl, who was at the day-care center, (located in the Jewish orphanage, which had all the necessary facilities), one of the social services provided by the Judenrat for children from indigent families. I was told that the little boy had an advanced case of rickets. The only part of this poor child that seemed human were those large, sad eyes. This was one family that did not object to taking hot showers.

I tried to help in any possible way. He was such a friendly, nice man, so grateful for every little thing. Sadly, they were beyond help.

The encounter with the *Maggid* (an itinerant preacher) left an unforgettable impression on my memory. While covering a new territory, I checked out a large corner building on Zydowska Street. I verified all the charts except of one that had written on it only one word: "The Maggid." I climbed the steep staircase leading to the mansard attic and reached the top breathless. Disappointed that there were no apartments under the roof, I was about to turn around when I heard a sound. I moved in the direction from where it was coming, and a most unbelievable sight met my eyes. In the corner, partially hidden behind the beams supporting the roof, was a table with a large volume of Talmud open. Other books were piled on the floor. Behind the table sat a Hassid with his *pe'ot* (ear curl) and beard intact, his head covered by a large, velvet hat, religious garment protruding from under his *halat* (Hassidic long coat). When he saw me approach, he got up from his chair and, in the customary way of Hassidim looked away from me.

"I am a hygienist from the Judenrat. Who are you?"

"I am the Maggid from Tarnow."

"How come you stay under the roof? How can you go out looking the way you do?"

"I do not go out. I don't remember when I saw the daylight."

I stared at him astonished.

"How can you live like that? How do you subsist?"

"Occasionally friends bring me food. If the Gestape finds me, that will be God's will, may His name be blessed!"

Needless to say, I destroyed his chart, and as far as my files were concerned, he did not exist. But, as it turned out, most of Ghetto Tarnow knew about him – a well-kept community secret. Deeply impressed by this unique man and the heroic continuity of his way of life, I ran home to tell my landladies about my discovery. Not only did they know about him, but he was a kind of mythical figure. They told me that he had been a very earnest and promising young student, a son-in-law of a renowned rabbi in Tarnow, whose name I do not remember anymore. This rabbi had a daughter who was not quite balanced. When the match was proposed to the young yeshiva student, he was told about her condition. As unbelievable as it appears, he answered that no personal sacrifice was too large for the honour of becoming the son-in-law of such a great scholar and having the privilege of studying under him. Besides, he had faith that the Almighty would help.

I did not go up to the mansard attic again. During the first Action, most of the inhabitants of this house were taken away to "resettling." The Maggid's fate is easy to guess, as is the one of my friend, the Hebrew teacher, and his unfortunate family.

There was more to the work of a hygienist than just checking for cleanliness and lice. People were displaced, uprooted, widowed, and orphaned. Sometimes they just needed someone to talk to, but often problems were tangible: malnutrition, hunger, illnesses, or serious problems for which solutions had to be found. The hygienist, a

120

makeshift social worker, psychologist, analyst, marital and family counselor, had to be able to answer all questions and supply the needed help. At times solutions were simple. Tickets for free meals in the community's kitchen, food supplements for a rickety child purchased by pocket money, admittance into the hospital, clothing collected among friends. My cousin Bubek, who worked in a crates factory, supplied one poor family with wood shavings for cooking, which he brought every day on his back from outside the ghetto. Those little achievements gave us all the first sweet taste of real accomplishment. In retrospect I realize that it was part of our survival as human beings. We, the youngsters in the ghetto, felt instinctively that if we didn't succeed in protecting our humanity, physical survival would have no meaning.

The breathing space allowed to Tarnow's Jews began to shrink rapidly shortly after our arrival. As more and more streets were becoming Judenrein, (Jew-clean), eviction notices effective immediately became the order of the day.

The Judenrat, a distorted outgrowth of prewar autonomous Jewish administration, was under the jurisdiction of the local Gestapo. To Tarnow's tragic fate, it was commanded by four clones of Mephisto: George Grunov, Johan Novak, Klaus Rommelman, and Ludwig von Moltke. In the narrow, crowded ghetto streets, this quartet became a constant, dreaded fixture. Always preceded by their vicious dogs, they used to stroll at a leisurely pace, all the time scanning their surroundings, trying to memorize every miserable Jewish visage. Those eye-to-eye encounters were counted among the most traumatic of ghetto experiences. Any attempt to avoid the foursome was useless. They seemed to possess ten pairs of eyes. Nothing escaped them. Not the slightest sign of panic or fear, not a gesture or movement. Often one was doomed by their whim solely. The finger pointed toward the victim, and then the feared command; "*Jude, komm her und lauf!* In moments, shots would ring out, and that was the end of one more life.

In their never-ending quest for thrills to break the monotony of life in a provincial town, the Nazis invented a spectacular act: marksmanship with life targets, the Jews. Jews were readily available and no trouble to replace. It was easier to kill a Jew than a dog. No trouble disposing of the corpse – Jews always took care of their own, even the dead. A challenge to the supremacy of the Aryan race? Why, one shot them down without pity.

The situation became so horrific that a day in the ghetto when only a few people were killed was considered good.

Often, in order to amuse themselves a bit longer, the Germans took their victims away, but most of the time executions took place right on the spot, in full view of all. After each of their "walks" in the ghetto, new graves were added to the Jewish cemetary.

This was how my uncle, Szymon Anisfeld, found his death. At the beginning of the war, Szymon's wife, Dina was vacationing in Myslenice with their three young children. Three times he set out to bring them home, and every time he was forced back by the retreating Polish armies. Eventually Dina and the children reached Sambor (now in the Soviet Union), where they found safety under the Russian occupation, but the young family never reunited. Szymon lived in a tiny room on the ground floor of a building in Tarnow. Distraught and broken by the forced separation, he sought solace in the study of Talmud, and this was how the Nazi henchmen found him. On that fatal day he was so deeply wrapped up in the dialectic of the ancient text that he did not notice their approach. They spotted him through the window. When the door was suddenly kicked open, it was too late to hide the large volume.

"*Jude. Komm her und lauf!*" The slight man obeyed the order. A brutal kick pushed him out of the room and into the courtyard, where a broom abandoned by the frightened janitor was pushed into his hand. He was ordered to sweep the ground. His head bare, the fringes of the forbidden ritual vestment flipping with his every movement, Szymon obediently followed the command. A shot in the back killed him instantly.

Thirty-one years old, Szymon Anisfeld, an only son, a husband, the father of three young children, the descedent of long line of scholars, businessmen, and community leaders, ceased to exist. He was buried in a common grave with twenty-nine other Jews murdered on the same day.

Then in winter 1942, while we were still mourning the murdered Szymon, we had the rarest of all experiences for those days: some good news.

Early one cold morning, we were awakened by a sudden banging on our door. Everyone sat up, white and shivering. This could mean one thing only: *Gestapo!*

"Landerer! Landerer!" we heard. "Open up! Open the door!"

In the ensuing confusion, somebody opened the door. A tall peasant barged into the room, followed by a shorter one. The first man wore a long jacket with big bulging pockets, heavy boots, and a large woolen hat pulled over his ears, partly covering his face. In one fast move, he pulled off the hat.

Five jaws dropped. Five pairs of eyes popped with disbelief.

"Hacia! Sala! Bubek! Girls! Don't you know me? It's Avroom!"

It was indeed Avroom Landerer, the erstwhile black sheep. We had assumed he and his family were penned up in Ghetto Przemysi – if they hadn't already met a worse fate!

He was all over the room, hugging and kissing us, pushing into our hands bundles of money, and talking incessantly: "Don't worry – don't worry. Don't worry about anything! Everything is going to be all right!"

"Avroom, what are you doing here?" my mother demanded between kisses and hugs. "How did you come? And – and where is your Jewish star?" This last was almost a shriek, because to be caught without one's identifying badge was virtually a death sentence.

"My Jewish star? Here in my pocket!" Laughing happily, Avroom pulled out a crumpled, dirty armband and twirled it around his finger. "You all look well, thank God. We will soon be together again."

"Uncle Avroom, did you hear from my daddy?" Eva asked softly.

"Who? Your daddy? Haskel is fine. Everybody is fine. You will see, we will survive. I will take care of you all. But first you must promise me not to worry. I have a good job. They assigned me to the purchasing department of the army. I am buying hides."

This, he explained, was an important position. "They" needed him. Because of his expertise, he had been promised that his entire family would be allowed to remain in Przemysl.

"I told my boss about you, so he promised to include you too," he went on. "So, as you see, you have nothing to worry about!" As he spoke, he was hastily pushing into our hands packages of tea, salami, a jar of honey, all long-forgotten delicacies.

Mother, the skeptic, was not satisfied. "But still, I don't understand what you are doing here."

"I am on a buying expedition. My train was scheduled to stop in Tarnow, so I decided to pay you a call."

"Always the same Joker. And this Ukrainian with you?" she added in a low voice, glancing at Avroom's shorter companion. "Who is he? I am afraid of him."

"Who, Him? He is my helper. Very devoted. Without him I couldn't have come to you. He helps me pretend to be a Ukrainian, too. I almost forgot. There is money so you won't lack anything that is still available. But now we must leave. Our train is departing soon."

Avroom pulled the hat down over his ears and buttoned the coat, not interrupting his rapid talk for a second. Another round of emotional hugging, then the door closed softly. We were alone.

For a long time after the room remained still, Avroom's happy chatter and laughter echoing in our ears. We were afraid that a spoken word might disturb the long forgotten feeling of well-being that comes from awareness that there is still love and devotion in the world, transcending the artificial bounds imposed by cruelty.

We never heard from Avroom and his family again. When Ghetto Przemysl was liquidated, the Avrooms vanished with it. "Their" promises that Cilla, Gusta, and Lulek would be allowed to remain, that their father's services were needed, were forgotten. Neither his "good" boss nor the Ukrainian "friend" were there to help him. The new life in the New World never came true.

When I think of Uncle Avroom now, I don't remember the griefstricken man who took to gambling. I remember the jovial "peasant," stopping off to visit us, to bring news of our exiled menfolk, to leave gifts of money and food.

To appreciate Avroom's courage and his gallant gesture toward the wives and children of his brothers, one had to live under German occupation. To begin with, any Jew coming from territories once occupied by the Soviets was considered a spy, routinely tortured and put to death. And Avroom – a tall man with a prominent nose and other decidedly Semitic features – ran special risks. And yet he left his assignment on a military train, which carried a supply of hides for which he was responsible, took off his Star of David armband, posed as a Ukrainian, walked in and out of the ghetto without a permit, and, on top of all that, smuggled in food and money.

Avroom Landerer, my uncle the practical joker, the hero.

124

12 · Letters

The following letters parallel the preceding chapters and are self-explanatory.

Father's birthday fell on December 9. We, his children, used to chip in our savings, and buy him a tie. Lela, the writer of the family, composed the accompanying note.

This little scrap of paper traveled with Father everywhere. When he left home on September 4, he took it along. When the NKVD came in the middle of the night to deport him to Siberia, he took the note along. Later on, it traveled with him to the south of Russia, back to Krakow, and finally to Israel. After his death, it was found among the letters from his daughters and wife.

To the Best, Dearest, Sweetest, Most Handsome and Most Beloved, the Noblest of All the Fathers on Earth!

Today, on your birthday, we, your children, would like to prove our affection for you. Oh, don't think that this insignificant gift represents our feelings. This is only a minuscule part of our debt to you.

Today, we promise that we will strive to pay it in fullest and to erase the wrinkles of your brow. Remember, you have children on whose love and devotion you can count every moment of your life.

Today, on this solemn occasion we wish you good health, good luck, loads of success and pockets full of money.

Your children.

P.S. Fathers are individuals who form the foundation of family and society.

Krakow, June 6, 1940

Dear Daddy,

Your letter of May 13 reached us in record time and brought us great joy. Hopefully you are receiving mail from us frequently, because we write every day. In your last letter you ask if the [Weinberger] boys work and how much they earn. They worked only one day. I asked Iciu to write to you, but I can't say when he will. Apparently this sitting home all day long has made him lazy.

The truth of the matter is that we, the girls, don't overwork ourselves either. I just finished a sewing course and am now a qualified dressmaker. The fact that this profession won't make me rich and famous does not affect my perennial good humor at all. I arrived at the conclusion that eating my heart out does not accomplish much. Nothing better and more invigorating than a good and hearty laugh, but it is mainly my faith in the Almighty that helps me in these difficult times.

I agree that the difficult decision whether you should return home or remain there [in Sambor] is not in your hands. We must have faith in God. We would love to see you and Dincia [Anisfeld] with the children. By the way, you are asking if Jozia is still with us. She most certainly is and does not intend ever to leave.

Many kisses. Be well and cheer up, Daddy!

Your Lela

P.S. Special regards for Babcia and the Balkens, many kisses for my brothers.

Krakow, October 10, 1940

Dearest Daddy,

Tonight is the Day of Atonement. We hope that maybe today the postman will bring a letter from you. Tomorrow will be a real Day of Judgment for us. We write often, without knowing if the letters reach you or even if the address is correct. I can't write more because everybody wants to add regards. God willing, we will soon be reunited again.

Regards and kisses for all,
Lela

Krakow, October 11, 1940

To my dearest and most beloved Daddy,

I am writing to you on my eighteenth birthday. The enormity of the distance dividing us [by then Father was in Siberia] makes it a sad celebration. I was deluding myself that at least a note from you would come, but not even this. I only know your address, and that is all. What are you doing, how do you feel, how do you look? Daddy, I want to know how you are, I want to know it so badly that it hurts. The waiting for the mail carrier, watching him pass indifferently by our house is a torment I can't even describe.

Father, my most precious, darling father! I am writing without even knowing if this letter ever reaches you. Maybe it will in a month, maybe two, who knows? When you read those lines (assuming they reach you), I will be my usual self: strong, cheerful, and determined. But today I feel that I must ease the tremendous pressure on my soul.

I imagine being with you and telling you what goes on in my heart today. Today, on my eighteenth birthday, I thank God for having made me your daughter. If only you could know how proud I am of you! I realize that I am not the way I should be, that sometimes I make you upset or irritated, and I know that I am not worthy to be your daughter. But I love you so much! My feelings for you transcend human love. Maybe I am wrong, but it seems to me that no father on the face of earth is loved the way you are loved by me. My love feeds on the respect and admiration for you.

Strangely how this birthday coincides with the new year. This somehow gives me confidence that my prayers will be accepted. Today I have only one request. I am not asking much – nothing for myself. Just begging for your well-being. My mood today cannot even be defined as longing. My whole being is overflowing with the wishes for your happiness. Just to see you smiling would be enough to make me happy. It seems to me that I am not asking for much, even though my wishes might appear selfish. Father, tell me, is it my fault that the realization of your sufferings makes me indifferent to other people's pain?

I often think that if people were less self-centered, the present tragedy would never have happened. And then I realize that even I, the one who works so hard in improving herself, who tries to analyze every action, even I possess a large dose of egoism. And what bothers me even more is the fact that I can't get rid of it.

Daddy, dear Daddy, you are the only person I know to be totally void of selfishness. How do I wish to be at least a little like you! In spite of the realization that it is not right, I just cannot pray to God for all suffering people, and at the end of the prayer just add your name. I must do it the other way. Please, do not ask me to, because I absolutely cannot love other people the way I love you. By the way, Daddy, nobody, but nobody can measure up to you in kindness and nobility. Therefore I do not feel gullty in the least, and I hope that you understand.

Since yesterday I have a ray of hope. Seems like the sun has risen all of a sudden in the middle of the night. We were told that it will be possible to arrange through Kahal to contact the International Red Cross, and through this organization bring you all back to Sambor [that is, from Siberia]. We wrote as well to America, asking them to do all in their might to help you. Do not worry about us! Thank God we are not lacking a thing.

I am waiting for a letter from you with great longing, because we are not even sure that the address we have is correct. How we wish at least to know for sure where all of you are! I am so very anxious to know how you react to the Siberian climate. Do you have underwear and warm clothing fit for the Siberian winter? Write about everything in the minutest detail.

I kiss you Daddy. May God watch over you and bring you to us soon.

Lela

Dear Brothers,

With the coming new year I want to wish you perseverance and strength, so that you do not break under the overload of difficulties. You must believe, you must try to believe that every day gone by is a step bringing us closer together. I make both of you responsible for Daddy's well-being. You must be careful, more than ever, not to annoy him. See to it that his hair does not gray prematurely and that he doesn't change into an old man before his time.

I believe that you miss home, but remember, in order to live through these hard times, we must all reach into the reservoir of the inner strength I know all of us possess. Don't give in to despair, and do not give up hope! Remember, sunny days are waiting for us all. So boys, heads up! Let us challenge our destiny with our unshakable faith that at the end we will be victorious.

Love and kisses
Lela

P.S. Best wishes for the rest of the family. God willing we will soon meet again.

(To Moshe Anlsfeld, six years old at that time son of Szymon, later on murdered in Tarnow)
My darling Pet! Do you still remember me? Please take my place at Uncle Wolf's side and cheer him up. Take care that he is never sad.

Be well, little one,
Lela

Krakow, January 19, 1941

To my father, the dearest of all the people in the world,

Today, after five months of waiting, we finally received the first, so longingly awaited letter from you. At first we rejoiced wildly, and then, as usual, came the doubts. After following your trail on the map, we realized that you are in the coldest part of Siberia where the temperature drops to 40 to 50 below zero, and we don't even know if you are prepared for winter. But I do hope sincerely that the Soviet government sees to it that you all have warm boots and overcoats.

What a tragic comedy life is. When this letter reaches you (if it ever does), the spring will have arrived in Krakow, and most probably in the country you live now, the awakening of the new season will begin. I am really curious how it all looks. Are the barracks built in European or Asian style? Is the salary you are receiving sufficient? While mining gold, don't you lack drinking water? So many questions cross my mind that I can't even list them all.

I am really happy that your letter, written right after your arrival in Minora, is full of hope and faith. Even though I am not terribly observant, I do have great faith that we will not only survive intact, but we will come out of this battle with our destiny as better, more resillent people. As the steel becomes hardened in fire, so does the human character acquire strength by overcoming adversities.

I can easily imagine the nostalgia that is devouring you, and though I cannot feel the same way, I can understand it. My heart is overflowing with strong faith, and on my lips is my heart's prayer that God protects the one I love unconditionally. I know that I am not a worthy person, I have many shortcomings, but in spite of all my faults, Daddy, I love you deeply. There aren't many people who possess my capacity for love.

I don't know if you remember that on the second of October 1940, your daughter friend became eighteen years old. Because I like myself very much, I got me a great birthday present. Would you like to know what? Your last passport photo enlarged and framed. It came out so good that Mommy does not permit me to keep it on the dresser. She claims that you look so alive that she just can't bear it. During the whole day your likeness is hidden at the bottom of my drawer, and only at night, when they all sleep and I stay alone in my little room, I take it out. I sit in front of your picture, and after a while a strange feeling that we are together overcomes me. You look appraisingly into my eyes, and I see a smile hiding in the corners of your mouth. You approve because your daughter was good today. Sometimes I read reproach in your eyes because you don't approve of your daughter's actions and thoughts. But even in your reproaching looks, there is always so much love and forgiveness, so much understanding for human frailities and shortcomings, that I feel relieved. I do not promise you anything, but deep down in me a barrier breaks down, something cries, and at that moment I feel the badness in me receding. Even if momentarily, it can never come back with the same force. It doesn't matter that we are 13,000 km. [about 8,000 miles] apart. I know and understand you so well that it feels like you were close by. How I wish for more details about your living conditions!

You all are probably curious how we live here. I can reassure you that we are not lacking a thing. The only problem we have is the constant worry about you. We girls don't suffer much from the new situation. As members of the "weaker sex" we even enjoy certain privileges. Do not worry that no one else adds a P.S. to this letter. This is because of a new ordinance that only a letter written by one person is allowed to be mailed. At the same time I am writing this letter, they are all mailing postcards and letters. We are all well, and the apartment is very warm. We have enough coal. Mother acquired it still in the spring. Nobody goes to school because there are no schools, but all of us study at home. Every Shabbat we go to Uncle Josiu for *chullent*, I am sure all of you miss Aunt Bala's culinary mastery. At Aunt Blimcia's there is no news. They are all writing to you too. Aunt Haya visits us often. She comes gladly, claiming that our ever-present good humour has a beneficial effect on her nerves. As you see, even Mother and Aunt Sala joke and laugh often.

Szymek [Anlsfeld] will probably write tomorrow; he moved in with his parents. I am not sure that I accounted for everybody, but at the moment I cannot recollect more. Aha, there is still Hesiek, who lives in Tarnow and visits us often. Szaye and family are back in Chrzanow, as is Yankel [Horowitz] and family, and Wolwek [Horowitz] is in Limanowa. In case I forgot to mention somebody, you can interpret it that everything and everybody is absolutely fine!

Don't you think, Daddy, that the proverb "Everything bad has a particle of good in it" Is based on truth? Can you imagine how angry Mother would be (because she did not change, it doesn't take much to get her angry) that I filled the whole letter with my scribblings. I would probably be called selfish and who knows what, but because of the new law no one can say a word against my long letter.

Personally I did not change much. Maybe just gained a bit because of the potato diet and forced idleness. But don't worry, because it really is not too bad. But Lala is really beautiful! From day to day she is prettier and attracts general attention. What a pity you can't see her.

You know I just realized that the length of this letter might land it in the censor's wastebasket. A little too late to change, so I am mailing it anyhow, hoping that it will reach you. Oh, well, good-bye, stay well,

Lela

Krakow, February 2, 1941

To my most beloved father,

It is midnight. I am alone in my little room (the rest of the family is fast asleep), typing this postcard. Writing to you has become my favorite pastime. Your portrait, my eighteenth birthday gift to myself, is standing on the table. I look at you and try to read your eyes. My thoughts are flying to cold, snowy Siberia, to the land of the Yakuts. I see you, Daddy, I see you and your terrible longing for us. Tears are gathering under my lids, but I don't let them go free. I am strong!

Daddy, I understand how deeply you suffer, I feel with you. The vast difference dividing us does not scare me a bit. It really does not matter. What does matter is our devotion to each other. How I wish to be able to send you one sun ray to warm up your aching, lonely heart. Daddy, please, don't be sad. Cheer up, look up. High up, where the sun hides behind the clouds, reigns the One who watches over us all. He is all Justice and Mercy. We believe in Him with all our might. Right, Daddy?

Love and kisses,
Lela

Krakow, February 3, 1941

My dearest all,

I have lost already the count of all letters and postcards we mailed to you. At present the month of February has begun. White, fluffy snow piles high over the city streets. I try to imagine the cold you have to cope with; here the winter is very harsh too. However, when and if you do get to read these lines, here will be spring in the fullest bloom, and by you too the nature will be awakening from the long winter's sleep.

My dearest, does anyone imagine how much I envy this little scrap of paper because it is embarking on a journey to you? That soulless and lifeless object will bring you the news from us, and joy and hope, and I, a human being, have to stay here, totally helpless. This little postcard will provide you with information and reassurance that there is absolutely no reason for you to worry about us. We are not lacking a thing but . . . a tiny scrap of paper with a stamp from a far-away Siberian country. How we wish to be able to get just a glimpse of you all, to see how you are! How terribly unbelievably difficult to fulfill that one wish. We are patient and we wait. Meanwhile, through the vast expanse of land and sea that divides us, I am sending my love, regards, and kisses to all of you.

Yours,
Lela

Krakow, February 4, 1941

Dearest Father,

It is February already. Behind our windows falling snowflakes are blanketing the roofs and streets. White, fluffy snow. My eyes follow the rapid movement of the snowflakes and I think of you, Father. Is it possible that at the same time you are standing at your barracks window and sending your thoughts to us. I imagine seeing them rapidly moving through cold, snowy Siberia, racing the strong wind. Until they reach the border where they stop. Thus your and my thoughts are standing on both sides of the border and exchanging greetings. I know what yours are: "Be strong, my child!" while mine are calling to you with all might, overcoming the whining of the wind and reaching you with reassurance: "I am strong, Daddy. Strong and full of faith!"

Those little flakes covering our town are not regular snow. They are messengers from you. Hopefully, this small postcard will reach you and tell you that I wish you could be as strong and full of hope as your loving

Lela

Krakow, February 4, 1941

Dearest Daddy,

Three weeks went by since we received the first communication from you, your first letter, written three days after your arrival in Minora. After the explosion of joy, which I don't need to describe –

133

surely you all react the same way while receiving letters from us – came disappointment. It was such a superficial letter. You mention work in the gold mine, but not a word about who is working and what kind of work it is.

Tomorrow is Saturday, and since we usually receive mail on Saturdays, I hope that we will get a seven-mile-long letter from ours! And since I did reproach you for not being specific, I will attempt to describe in detail one day of our life.

Morning. White contours of snow-covered buildings are emerging through the gray morning mist. Our disheveled hair is spread on the pillows, and only the noses are visible from under the warm covers. All asleep breathe in unison. The silence is disturbed by the sounds of cars honking and the ring of the tramway's bell.

"Yff, half past eight only. I don't feel like getting up," a voice is heard from under the covers. The mothers stir, wake up, and prompt us to get up. But no one feels like getting out of the warm bed.

"You know, Sala, I had a dream." Mother tells her dream. In order not to be left behind Aunt tells her. She finishes, and it is time to get up! Eva and I, we too have dreams. Sometimes we succeed in prolonging the delightful moments, but eventually the entire family gets up, and then the ceremony of washing up, combing the hair, and getting dressed begins. Someone enters the bathroom and slams the door. Auntie pulls her hair in despair: "My skirt!" In one shoe and one slipper she hobbles to the bathroom and starts banging at the door. "My dearest, my most precious, my golden one, have mercy on me, give me my skirt! It is hanging on the hook." Inside the bathroom the kind-hearted soul commences a frantic search, tripping a chair in the process of throwing down everything off the hooks. "Aunt should stop bothering, there is no skirt here." A very disappointed Auntie returns to the bedroom and what? Miracles, witch craft, magic, the skirt is hanging over the chair. While we dress, familiar scenes are taking place in front of the bathroom door. Eventually everybody is dressed and seated at the breakfast table. Sometimes a cup of coffee is spilled or a glass breaks, but we don't let it upset us. It could have been worse. Considering the serving personnel, it is a miracle that all the dishes are not broken. After breakfast, while waiting for the mail carrier, we get busy around the house, so it won't look like all we do is always wait for letters from "ours." Unfortunately we hardly get any mail from you. The doorbell, however, does ring every morning without fail, announcing our regular visitor, Uncle Josiu [Mother's brother, Josef Horowitz]. Every morning he comes, brings good news, and strengthens our morale. "Children, believe me, everything is going to end well. Very well and soon. Soon, soon, maybe even tomorrow. The Merciful One is watching over us all." We too believe in it, together with Uncle and you, Daddy.

Lunchtime! The nicest part of our main meal of the day is the tea drinking ceremony. We often say that if it were possible to record it and send to you, then you would never stop laughing. Try to imagine for at least ten minutes: "Aaa. Aaa. Aaa," In different keys. Suddenly a delighted voice cuts in: "Look, look everybody! I have a tea leaf!" (at that time we don't remember how a tea leaf looks).

Alas, before we could catch sight of the miracle in the glass, a lonely tea leaf is swimming among the sherds of glass broken all over the floor. Before we stop laughing, your efficient wife puts a new glass of tea in front of Sala, this time without a tea leaf.

After lunch we go to work. Eva teaches some children, I sew, Lela is going to a sewing class, and Mommy leaves on her daily rounds to Uncle Haim, Josiu, and Aunt Blimcla, and Sala visits with her sisters. They come to us, especially Binka (Sala's sister) who is here every day. Bubek is studying, or so we all believe. At least he spends some time with his books. His fiery temperament does not let him sit on one place for more than a short while. He misses his father greatly [Uncle Haskel] and considers himself the man of our group.

After supper Mommy explains the political situation, and we try to listen and understand. Seems like Uncle Haim reads all newspapers available, and then he shares them with her. Every evening Lela writes, Bubek is into his regular mischief, Eva and I get ready for bed where we talk till the Mothers and Bubek come in.

For a while the two of us linger with the family. Don't you find too that there is some mystery about going to bed? It is difficult to get into and say good-bye to a day, and it is even harder to leave its warmth and softness in the morning.

Finally, I am in bed. My head luxuriates in the softness of the pillow and the smoothness of the pillowcase. All is quiet again. A curious moon peeps through the window. A glittering star blinks at me. It seems like she has something to say. What is it? I can read her.

135

"Greetings from your father!" Outside soft snowflakes are falling slowly.

Daddy, I enclose a photo and hope that you get it so you will know how your daughter looks now. By the way, I'm taller than Mommy.

Daddy dearest, hoping that soon we will be able to embrace, I send meanwhile millions of kisses.

Your,
Lala

Tarnow, March 8, 1941

My dear Wolf,

As you see, we are in Tarnow. We have a large room by a religious and fine family. It is very difficult to find here a decent place to live, and many people envy us our good luck. We brought along two beds and one wooden crate with household articles. Other necessities I borrowed from Hirsch's [Mother's younger brother] cousin. It is much easier to manage here than in Krakow, believe me, if I knew that you live under comparable conditions, I would be most happy.

We are well but the lack of any news from you saddens us greatly. We trust that this is the way it must be, and it cannot by any other way, and that you are well.

I embrace you and my dear sons,
Mother

Regards and kisses to the rest of the family.

My most precious, dearest Haskel,

Our life here has been described already by the girls, so I will not repeat it again. We have made peace with our situation and pray to God you should not have any worse. What worries us greatly is lack of communication from all of you. We received here one letter only, dated January 10. I'm sure that more were written. We live with the hope that the war will end soon, and God willing we will be together soon.

Hugs and kisses,
Sala

Regards to Wolf and the rest.

My dearest and most precious Daddy,

You probably wonder that I write to you from Tarnow, but we have been here for the last few weeks. Daddy dearest, we write to you all the time, and from you – nothing. I wish so badly for a letter from you! A letter to let me know how you occupy your days, and everything about you. This is my only worry. How is your health, Daddy? We are in the best of health, you have nothing to worry about us. I work together with Lala; we are sewing children's dresses. Do not worry about us, Daddy.

Your image is in front of my eyes every day, and my thoughts are always with you. I kiss you. Be well! Regards for Uncle Wolf and the rest of the family.

Eva

Dear Daddy,

We have been in Tarnow for two weeks. We all live in one large, sunny room. I work in a crate factory and they will start paying me soon. What is doing by you all? How do you feel? Write about every detail of your life.

Love and kisses
Bubek

Because no space was left for me I limit myself this time to sending regards only. I always think about you, Daddy, and I have deep fate in God.

Love,
Lala

Tarnow, April 4, 1941

Dear brothers,

This is the first time I am writing directly to you. All my previous letters were addressed directly to my dearest friend, our father. I am very curious how you adapted to the new conditions and if you are giving Father all the spiritual support you can muster. As far as Mother is concerned, I don't even have to try because she is great! She is the strongest of the whole bunch, and she supports everybody.

We have adjusted to the new conditions quite well. So well that I can say that we are content in our new situation. Living in one room has a tremendous advantage. Everything is handy, and when something gets misplaced, no energy is wasted in search.

All the time I wonder about your living conditions. Next week are the holidays. Unfortunately, we will not be telling each other the tale of our wanderings. We mustn't lose our hope, we must cling to the belief that our dream about a large "seder" for the whole family will come true sooner than expected.

Chins up, brothers. Right on,

Lela

Tarnow, April 11, 1941

Dear Wolf,

Yesterday we received a postcard from Kolomyja [now Kolomyja, U.S.S.R.] informing us that Szymon Anisfeld's aunt had a cable from Dina. You cannot imagine how happy it made us. We are ready for Passover. Thank God we are not lacking a thing. If only I knew that your situation was no worse than ours, I would be much relieved. The Almighty should only allow us to be together next Passover, and then each one of us would have his own haggada [story, parable] to tell.

Be well, love,

Chaya

[a familiar form of Mother's name]

To my most precious father,

In spite of the great distance dividing us, my thoughts and my heart are always with you. Don't even think about us! Do not worry. We are very pleased here, if only mail from you would come, then we would have a real joyful holiday. I miss you greatly. Maybe we will be again soon

Lala

Regards, kisses and have a good holiday

Sala

Love and kisses

Eva

All the best wishes to all of you.

Bubek

138

My dear father,

Reasons beyond our control forced us to move to Tarnow, and we are quite pleased with this change. We have here one large room that serves as our bed-dining-bathroom and kitchen. We only pray and hope to God your living accommodations are as comfortable as ours. Our only worry is lack of communication with you. But I do hope that with the coming spring thaw our contact will resume, and we will receive mall from you because I am deeply convinced that you write to us.

For the time being I am not very busy, but I am trying to find some occupation, because this lazying around is driving me crazy.

As of present our family left Krakow. Uncle Meir-Haim and family are in Nowy Sacz, Uncle Josiu in Brzesko. Do not worry about us because we are all in a good mood.

Heads up! Love and kisses,
Lela

Tarnow, April 30, 1941

My dear father,

Having little confidence in the efficiency of postal service, I decided to describe our living conditions again. This is the third week since my arrival in Tarnow, the fifth since the coming of the rest of the family. I stayed on the outpost (our home) till the last possible moment. I don't have to spell what leaving Krakow meant to me. Who understands me as well as you do? Right, friend? I don't intend to write that this change of location was happily anticipated by me, but the truth is that I was curious about those unusual changes. Being young and full of curiosity of what life might offer, I feel excited, in a way, by every change. But when the time came that I was forced to part with the little room where I spent my childhood, and where the first page in the book of my life was written, I was heartbroken. Hidden between the four empty walls remained my illusions, dreams, and memories. In spite of everything I am confident that one day the dreams and hopes of long ago will become reality. My faith and my love for you strengthen my spirit.

Father dearest, I guess you must be wondering how we settled here and what our present conditions are. I'll do my best to describe them to you as truthfully as possible, so that you will be able to visualize them. So please, sir, follow me on a guided tour of the Landerer family's new residence.

We enter the house on Debowa Street, number 4, and enter the first apartment on the main floor. We pass through the kitchen and the room inhabited by the Rosenzweig family and stop at the door leading to the Landerers. Let us pause for a moment and have a good look around. At the first sight it looks like one room only, but this first impression is very deceiving. Have another closer look, friend, and see for yourself. The big table at the center of the room is the dining room, and where the beds are lining the walls is the bedroom. And now please, look at the right corner behind the partition. There you will find the kitchen. Feel free to enter and explore. Do you remember our old gas two-burner? Here it is, keeping us company and warming our food. And the coal bin? Hard to recognize, right, because the unforeseen circumstances forced this modest piece of furniture to assume a new identity. It became a working meat table. And the tiny, malformed table covered with a piece of oilcloth? This is our dairy counter. I will divulge to you the secret of its origins. This is a wooden crate which was used for packing. Due to circumstances it became elevated to the status of a table. God's designs are hard to understand! The large kitchen breakfront was lent to us by friends. So, how do you like our kitchen? Wait please, wait one moment! I have more to tell you. This kitchen is not just a kitchen. It is a hiding place of a secret. Not treasures or valuable objects as you might have guessed at first. No, not at all. Every night, after the rest of the family succumbs to deep sleep, there appears on the funny little table my old desk lamp, my little, always locked carryall, and I myself. The family is curious what I do there every night of the week, but they are not going to find out soon. Only you, dearest friend, can share my secret. All I can tell you is that behind the partition something is being created. I am putting in words my thoughts, feeling, and emotions. A day will come, and you will read my book.

Father dearest, I don't know if you received any of the letters I wrote you. If you know that I own a picture of you that is so much lifelike that looking at it I get carried away and forget reality. I look into your eyes, and in the moment my soul transcends the distance between us, and I am with you, bringing you comfort and solace. This photo becomes reality. It is you, my father, my friend, alive, close to me. Hcw well do I know you! As I look into your eyes, I see little sparks flickering, disappearing behind the sadness and longing, and then coming out again. But I do believe, with my whole being I do believe that the moment when your eyes will be sparkling with happiness is near.

Spring is coming. The first warm sun rays are embracing the earth. Even though it seems that now the sun had forgotten us, the moment when it will shine upon us is near. We will return home, to the place where we used to be so happy. A tale will be spun, just like the Passover haggada, only this will be our story.

The holidays are near. We will observe, divided by a distance of 13,000 kilometers, and yet so near. Heads up, Daddy! Hold on!

And now I say: See you soon!

Lela

Tarnow, May 2, 1941

Father dearest,

I worry that you might be angry at me because lately I only add regards to letters [of other family members]. As you well know, I cannot write just for the sake of writing, to fill pages telling about rain, or the mud on our street, or that the crystal vase we salvaged from home broke. There are many things I would like to write to you about, but they are all too personal to be put in a letter that might never reach you, or fall into strange hands. All I can write you at present is that I miss you badly. I can add that every day we wait for the mailman, and when he does not bring us letters from our dearest, we are bitterly disappointed.

We are very satisfied with our room, which is almost as big as our salon. The people we rent it from are very nice, and we became good friends with them.

Today we received a letter from Cousin Avraham Rosenbaum from Japan. He sent for you to Sambor $100, and he will try to get help from your sister, Gela Brandt. He asks for your personal data. I have to finish because everybody has to add regards.

Kisses, kisses, kisses
Lala
Best wishes send from the bottom of my heart to my dear family. I kiss you all.
Hacia
Regards for all. Be well
Lela
Many kisses from
Eva
Greetings from Bubek
Loads of love and kisses Sala

The above are some of the letters Father received from us. It is only by chance that they lasted through the ravages of time, because in those days people hardly thought of preserving any mementos or historical documents. All attention was focused on survival.

After my mother passed away at the age of 89, I found among her papers a few of the letters from Father and my brothers, written during the period of 1945–1946, while they were already at Saratov, and Mother and I in Tel-Aviv. Those few yellowed pages express the magnitude of the Jewish tragedy and despair very poignantly. They are part of the last chapter – unfortunately, there is no happy ending to my tale.

13 · The Weinbergers in Nowy Sacz

Shortly after we were evicted from our apartment in Krakow, the Weinbergers were forcibly relocated to Nowy Sacz, a town in the Carpathian mountains, about fifty miles southeast of Krakow. Luckily for us and all dispersed families and friends, postal service between the ghettos went on for quite a long time. (When exactly was it cut off, I don't remember, because after it stopped the family communicated through trusted Poles.) The regular exchange of letters among families and friends was a lifeline for us – unfortunately a very tenuous one as it turned out.

In Ghetto Tarnow I regularly exchanged letters with seventeen of my friends, displaced like myself. Very few of them and not one of my family, remained in Krakow. My father's oldest sister, Haya Goldwasser, who lived on Starowislna Street with her husband Alter and three unmarried children – Henia, Dorcia, and Benek – returned to her hometown Makow Podhalanski. Mother's brother Wolf, his wife Miriam, and their children, Iciu, Haim, Monius, and Rahela went to Miriam's family in Limanowa, not far from Nowy Sacz. Haim Horowitz – another of mother's brothers who lived in Weglowa Street – his wife Sala and children Hasiu, Monius, and Rehusia went to Sala's mother in Nowy Sacz. At that time a travelling permit was available to Jews – for an exorbitant fee, of course – and my Uncle Josiu who settled in Brzesko, had one and visited us often. The oldest brother and an incorrigible optimist, he regularly made the rounds of the entire family to be sure that no one was lacking essentials.

After the Weinbergers unpacked the few meager possessions they were allowed to take with them, they found themselves a refugee family of eight persons, without means of support. Meir–Halm's business was long gone, and this devout Taimudic scholar was totally unprepared for the only business possible in the ghetto, black market dealings. Morever, he was then in his fifties, an age the Nazis considered unfit for labor and, as such, not deserving to live – so it was dangerous for him even to be seen.

It was clever, brave Recha who came to the family rescue. She started a class in designing and sewing women's dresses. The first course was so successful that she soon had more students than she could handle and was busy teaching from morning till evening. Women and girls came to learn how to redo clothing from whatever scraps of fabric they could find. Many an old coat was made over into a new jacket, a bedspread into a dress, a tablecloth into a blouse.

I suppose remodeling old clothes reinforced people's hope. In those years we accepted all hardships as inevitable parts of the war. With our eternal Jewish optimism, we assumed that bad times would eventually pass, and life would return to what it had been, as it always had before.

It was my darling Uncle Josiu who with pride told us how Blimcla's family managed in Nowy Sacz. They roomed with Meir-Haim's younger brother, whom Blimcia had taken into her house after both his parents died. Soon after Blimcia's wedding, she found herself taking care of a five-year-old boy, and she raised him as one of her own, until he married a girl from Nowy Sacz and settled there. Thus, when the time came for the Weinbergers to leave Krakow, it was natural for all concerned that they would go to Naftall, who was doing well and had a large house.

As Recha's establishment grew, she needed help, and in no time her little sisters became assistant teachers. Blimcia and Reeva cooked, washed, and cleaned, trying to maintain an acceptable standard of living, as much as it was possible under the prevailing conditions. The classroom, which during the night served as the family bedroom, had to be prepared early in the morning. Putting away all the bedding and clothing, serving a hasty breakfast, and to top it all, having to deal with Naftali's four little children, who delighted in the new additions to their family and were constantly under their feet, was quite a task. The boys, whenever left alone by the milicja, stayed at home and hid in the corners, studying. Imitating their father, they tried to make themselves unconspicuous.

144

In spite of all the hardships, hope and faith in the future were kept alive in people's hearts. It must have been this same optimism that caused my aunt and uncle to take seriously a marriage proposal for Iciu – arranged by a third party, as it goes without saying. In spring, just after they had moved to Nowy Sacz, Iciu the scholar, became engaged to Rochma Klagsbald. The Weinbergers were delighted with the future bride. Our family already had a connection to the Klagsbaids of Chrzanow (one of mother's and Blimcia's brothers, Szaye Horowitz, had married a Klagsbald girl). "Our fiancee," they wrote to us in Ghetto Tarnow, "Is beautiful, charming, sweet, absolutely ideal in every sense of the word." And to the Hassidic community as a whole, the engagement was an act of faith in God and the future.

Alas, this charming young girl and her scholarly betrothed never reached the bridal canopy. Shortly after the happy letter announcing the engagement came a somber one, reporting that Iciu and Moniek had been rounded up with some others and shipped off to the concentration camp at Rzeszow. Moniek was seventeen and Iciu twenty-two.

During the winter of 1943 we could still communicate by mail – or perhaps it was through a friendly Pole, I do not remember. One of the communications we received in Bochnia from our relatives, was a gray postcard postmarked Rzeszow. It was from Moniek. It informed us that his beloved brother Iciu, the apple of his parents' eye, had died of consumption.

Mother and Uncle Josef, who adored Iciu, read those lines dry-eyed, but Aunt Bala could not contain herself. "That poor child, that poor child," she sobbed bitterly. It was not clear which one she was crying for – the young life so brutally destroyed, or the orphaned brother left alone with his grief and terror.

Through a friendly Polish woman we tried to arrange help for Moniek. Mother and Uncle Josef wrote him and sent him food and money, but we never heard from him again. How and when his suffering ended, I do not know. In 1943 the concentration camp at Rzesnow was liquidated. Moniek Weinberger was then eighteen years old.

And the rest of them? While we were running for life from Tarnow to Bochnia and again forth and back, the ghetto in Nowy Sacz was liquidated. How and when exactly we did not know. The rumours that reached us were horrifying, but still, we refused to accept them as certainty, hoping that maybe they were really resettled, and somewhere, someplace, were still alive. We had to believe in our hopes and dreams of tomorrow, the tomorrow that became a nightmare.

14 · Action in Tarnow

Totally undisturbed by human sufferings, time went on, and seasons changed. Spring of 1942 arrived and with it more triumphs for the victorious Wehrmacht; but for the Jews in Europe, that spring, the symbol of hope and renewal, brought only despair and tragedy.

Flowers were in full bloom when the first Action took place in Tarnow. It lasted eight days, and when it was over, the community that had counted over thirty thousand members was reduced by close to nine thousand. A few days before this Action had begun, rumours circulated that people without working papers would be deported. All Judenrat employees were busy stamping the *Judenpasses*. The passess of people without valid work papers were stamped with a black letter *K* – as it turned out, shorthand, for *Kugel* (bullet). Red stamp meant exemption from deportation. Mother and Aunt Sala got the dreaded *K*, as did my sister. Eva and I had our papers approved as hygienists, Bubek worked for a crates factory classified as indispensable to the war effort. A day before the Action, my sister, thanks to the intervention of our landlady, Dora Rosenzweig, had her *K* changed to a red stamp. Believing their children to be safe, our mothers resigned themselves to their fate.

The night before the Action very few people in the ghetto slept. Fully clothed, we dozed on and off. The gray morning found us all ready.

The SS men checking the *Judenpasses* were working their way to the center of the ghetto. As long as they did not pass our street, we did not dare to leave home. It was already the second, or maybe even the third day, of the Action when the SS men entered our street and approached the house. Sala was frightened.

"Hacia, let us go to the vestibule. Let us not stay in the room. They may take the children with us."

"Calm down, Sala. We don't have to run to meet them. They will come for us soon enough."

As they were whispering, we heard heavy footsteps outside the door and men's loud voices speaking German. Suddenly Mother, acting like a woman possessed, grabbed Sala by the shoulder and pushed her behind the white cupboard, then followed herself.

"No, Hacia! no! If they find us they will take the children too."

Mother put her hand over Sala's mouth.

The door opened, and a young SS man, not much older than ourselves, entered the room. The four of us holding our *Judenpasses*, with the precious red stamp on it, surrounded him. He checked carefully. We all had the same family surname, and he assumed that we were siblings. Seeing Lela's crossed-off K and the proper red seal affixed in the right place, he remarked: "*Du hast Gluck gehabt* (you were lucky)."

"*Eltern* (parents)?" he asked next.

"*Ausgesiedelt* (Deported)," we answered. He had no reason to doubt it. Very few Jewish families were left intact.

Meanwhile other SS men were going through the cellar, the attic, every nook of the old house, till they rounded up all "illegals" and "undesirables." The elderly, the children, and the unfortunates stigmatized with the letter K were taken away. For a long time after, our mothers remained in their improvised hiding, afraid to come out lest the SS men return and take us all away.

Long after the commotion in the street died, Mother and Aunt Sala emerged from behind the white cupboard. The whole house was quiet. We did not rejoice. The Action was still going on. Wagons – usually used to transport hay from the fields, but this time loaded high with human corpses – passed through the ghetto streets. The programmed destruction of the Jews had begun in Tarnow.

Hirsch Horowitz, my mother's brother, was a man of faith. In his person was found the ideal of Hassidic piety combined with virtue. Hirsch loved people and in turn was loved by all who knew him. His father's favourite among fourteen children, he became an adoring husband and father, a devoted son and brother, a doting uncle and a faithful friend. In spite of his young age, he was elected by the community as the head of Kahal (local governing body) in Myslenice.

He was a capable businessman, a yeshiva boy with knowledge and understanding of secular world.

Religious faith was a domineering power in Hirsch's life. His was the purest, most sublime emotion a human is capable of. Like the biblical heroes whose faith never faltered, so did Hirsch's belief in the justice of God's ways remain unshaken till the tragic end of his life.

My recollections of Hirsch go back to my early childhood: tall, young Hassid, dressed all in black. A flaming, red beard and earlocks framed his face and emphasized his fine features and white even teeth gleaming in a broad smile. He was an optimist, who even during the war, when life often became unbearable, believed that everything that happened was an expression of God's will.

While in his early twenties, Hirsch married Lieba Landau, whose father, Bernard Landau, was the head of the Kahal in Auschwitz. (In prewar days, before the notorious concentration camp was built there, this city boasted a large Jewish community.) Just as Hirsch was tall, broad, and exuberant, Lieba was small, petite, and quiet. They had two daughters, Rachela, lovingly nicknamed Lalusia (Dolly), and Fela.

This is how I remember the girls from Tarnow when Fela was six and Lalusia ten years old. The two looked alike, with their reddish blond hair always neatly braided, apple cheeks, little upturned noses. The older inherited her father's temperament; she was quick, sharp, exuberant and courageous. Little charming Fela, dimpled and round faced, always shyly turned down her stare and followed her big sister adoringly.

There was a German store in Tarnow that catered to German civilians and allowed the Poles to buy some of the nonrationed products. As children below the age of twelve were not required to wear the Star of David armband, Lalusia used to buy there items that did not have to be redeemed by coupons. Once a large transport of lemons arrived, and Fela begged to be taken along. She was permitted to go because those were the days when people still believed that little children would not be harmed. How could anyone think otherwise?

The older sister agreed to take Fela under the condition that once inside the store they must behave as if they had never seen each other before. Dressed alike and looking like carbon copies of each other, the two sisters pretended to be strangers. While leaving the store Fela dropped one lemon, but she didn't notice it until Lalusia's familiar voice called: "Little girl, little girl! You dropped a lemon!" Her sister, ten years old at that time, manifested presence of mind fit for a seasoned actor in a well rehearsed play.

This minor incident illustrates how fast the children matured during the war. What a promise of human potential those children carried, and how senselessly it was destroyed!

Before the war Hirsch was a successful businessman. As was the custom, he studied in a yeshiva until his marriage. Then he became a producer and bottler of soft drinks – a lucrative business because *krachel* was as popular in Poland as Coca-Cola in the United States. His house was built at a walking distance from his father's, and every day of their lives they saw each other. At the ground floor of Hirsch's house was the bottling plant, on the second floor his apartment. Myslenice had no public water supply, but Hirsch's house had running water, a modern bathroom, and flush toilets. Every few days water from a well was delivered, and the large tank supplying the plant and the apartment was filled. The house bordered a large orchard. During spring, summer, and fall the fragrance of flowers blooming, fruit ripening, and cut grass filled the air.

In Ghetto Tarnow, Hirsch did not work. He absolutely refused to have anything to do with the German war effort, Judenrat, or any kind of black-market dealings. Legal business was nonexistent, and he could not function in the stealth and secrecy the situation demanded. He paid his dues to the Judenrat, and his family supported itself by selling what valuables they had managed to carry away from Mys-lenice. (The plant and the apartment were looted by his neighbors, the Poles, even before the German army entered.) Not having a binding schedule, he became a steady visitor in our house, mostly at dinner-time. Pretending to be passing by and just stopping in to say hello, he used to linger till we started to eat.

"I don't understand my brother," Mother used to complain. "Doesn't he know that one does not 'drop in' on people at meal time." We were annoyed until we found out the reason why his visits always coincided with the main meal of the day. No one realized that he wanted to assure himself that we ate properly every day.

One noon day, we were seated at the table, and Hirsch was standing at his usual "post." Leaning against the white armoire, he slouched a bit forward, like one afraid to miss a detail. Mother got up from her chair and suddenly found herself enveloped in her kid brother's embrace. His eyes were full of tears, and he was choking with emotions.

"Hacia, dear Hacia! I was afraid to ask you, but Lieba and I worried so much about you. But I see that, thank God, you are able to manage quite well."

We had made up our minds that, one room or no one room, our standard of living must be upheld as high as the situation would permit. We never ate on the oilcloth, clean tablecloth was as important as the rationed slice of bread. Every day we set the table with double china plates, remnants of the household we lived in once upon a time.

"Don't worry, Hirsch. I have enough to last us till 'after the war.' If only they let us live, we won't starve."

"Hacia, God is our father, and you know that a father never forgets his children."

"From your mouth to God's ears" was mother's reply.

Other times I remember Hirsch, standing in the middle of the room and spinning dreams and tales about the great future awaiting us all. There was not the slightest doubt in his mind that our sufferings were not in vain. He believed that this generation had a special mission and that the arrival of Messiah was imminent. His belief that the Heavenly Father is all goodness and mercy came from the core of his being. For him everything was clear and simple. The meaning of life equaled submission to God's will.

In his last, dark hours his unshakable faith stood him in good stead. Hirsch Horowitz, the notorious noncontributor to the war effort, became a nonperson; before the first Action his papers were stamped with the dreaded letter K.

A day before the Action Hirsch came to his sister with desperate plea. He was told that, for a large bribe, his name could be put on the list of Judenrat employees, but he did not have the necessary funds.

"How much do you need?"

Hirsch named a sum that would hardly have been covered by all of Mother's possessions. She did not hesitate a second.

"Hirsch, I still have my big diamond, I have some dollars, the children have their jewelry. Everything is yours."

"Hacia, how can I take your last?"

"Don't worry. We will manage. We could eat in the soup kitchen. We will not starve. After all it will only be till 'after the war.'"

Hirsch hurried out to find his contact. Few hours later he returned, his eyes blurry from fatigue, the face drained of color. It was too late. All lists had already been taken over by the Gestapo, and nothing could be done. Brother and sister embraced silently. That was the last we saw him.

Hirsch Horowitz and his family were among the first to be taken away. His neighbors who survived this Action told us that when the SS men entered the house and ordered them out, Hirsch asked for a few minutes, delay – just enough to let him say farewell to his friends. Such was the kind of spiritual strength emanating from this young man that the barbarians relented. Breathless, he ran from one apartment to another, shaking people's hands and embracing his close friends. His last words were: "Do not be sorry for me. I am going to sanctify God's name. Good-bye, good-bye! Don't forget to tell my sister that I went happy because such was God's will, blessed be his name for ever and ever!"

Our friends, who lived on a street leading to the train station, watched from behind closed shutters. They recognized Hirsch running with Fela in his arms. His wife and older daughter were not with him. Prodded by rifles, kicked, pushed, and falling over, they were forced to race for the train that was taking them to their doom

This is the last we heard of Hirsch Horowitz, thirty-one years old, and his young family.

15 · Escape and return

How difficult is to single out a most important moment in life. As one looks back over the years, many events that seemed of utmost importance when they happened now appear void of meaning. Years go by and are forgotten, but certain moments remain in the memory forever: first day in school, first book read, first love, first kiss, first disappointment, first tragedy, and so on. Childhood and youth memories are mostly happy; it is in remembering the mature years that a person encounters disillusion and sorrows. Often strangers, even my own children, ask me how I could have survived the Holocaust, how it was possible never to break down. Answers are hard to find.

But memory brings back one incident, seemingly unimportant, something that happened during my stay in Ghetto Tarnow. I recall it because it was characteristic of my attitude to life at that time and that of other young people.

It was summer of 1942. I was a teenager, and in spite of my being in the eye of a hurricane of cruelty, I believed in life and the future. We had only the barest necessities and lived in one room with three other families, ten people together. Anything unexpected – a loud sound, a knock at the door, commotion in the street – could mean death, sudden and unexpected. But our will to live was so overwhelming that we separated ourselves from the ever-present danger. Death seemed inevitable, but we forced ourselves to believe that we must survive. It was against logic and reality, without any hope except the one in our dreams, but it enabled us to keep going.

We were a group of friends, in our teens and early twenties, to whom it seemed absolutely impossible that a life could be stopped by a tiny lead bullet. Maybe it was the result of our isolation from the world outside the ghetto, but we considered ourselves an important part of the universe. Paying as little attention as possible to our surroundings, we created an unreal world, full of emotions, love, friendship, together building castles in our dreams and hoping against hope. While being marched out of the ghetto to work, we recited poetry to the rhythm of our steps. During work we hummed songs, finding in the sad lyrics reflections to our situation. Books were forbidden, but we always managed to get some reading material, savoring every word. We used to learn by heart passages that had relevance to us. *The Flames*, a book about young revolutionaries by a Russian writer named Brzozowsky, had a very special meaning for us all. We had ties with the Underground, and we identified with the heroes of the story. To retain sanity we had to reject the idea of senseless death, death merely because one was a Jew. The heroes of this book died fighting for their ideals, and we too had ideals we were ready to give our lives for.

I distinctly remember the chapter "Breneisen's Testament." Breneisen, one of the main characters of the book, was ambushed and killed by the *milicja*. He left a will in which he wrote: "What could be better than a sudden death? It closes the door behind you and absolves you of all responsibilities. You are not responsible anymore for the evil and injustice around you... ." This was what we all secretly wished for: if death must come, let it be sudden, taking us unawares. Our helplessness made us feel guilty. Strange choice for young people, but our lives were unbelievably cruel. Death was the only logical outcome of the situation.

Brzozowsky's language was magnificently rich, and in the sea of poverty that the ghetto had become, every page of his book was a treasure. Everything and everybody was drab, poor, and gray. Even the few remaining trees and bushes seemed to have changed color from green to gray, as if they too were ashamed to look unaffected. People's language reflected their predicament; the vocabulary shrank to essentials. Therefore we savored Brzozowsky's description of the Russian countryside, so much like the Polish, because we loved the country we were born in, and it was refreshing to be reminded of its beauty.

One day my cousin Bubek smuggled a flower into the ghetto. I remember it distinctly! A sweetpea in different shades of purple. It was exquisite! We put it into our best glass and placed it on the dresser

154

so everybody could enjoy it. The same day that we got the flower, a new ukase was proclaimed: One part of the ghetto was annexed, and all Jews within it must vacate their homes immediately. This came as a complete surprise, even to the Jewish *milicja*. No arrangements could be made for the new refugees on such short notice. Luckily, the evening was warm, and the majority could camp outside. The next day they became absorbed by the small community. Unbelievable how many people fit into one room.

In our courtyard, a few of the displaced families were preparing for the night. The most amazing part was the total silence. Afraid to attract the attention of the Gestapo, still roaming the streets and checking for curfew violators, they moved about like mute, gray shadows. I was standing on the balcony with my two friends; after what was pompously called supper, we used to meet there for a little "privacy." That evening we couldn't talk. Standing together we tried not to look at or to see the people in the yard, and they too moved around without looking up and seeing us. All tried to behave casually. We were leaning on the railing looking at each other, ashamed of the people's plight and our own helplessness, afraid to mention tomorrow's insecurity. Suddenly I had an idea. "Wait for me," I whispered and ran back into our room, took the little flower, and brought it out to my friends on the balcony.

Speechless, they caressed the little flower, smelled it, kissed it, held it close to their faces; it was a revelation – a sign from the outside, a message from the world of beauty, nature, life. The little flower was a living proof that ghetto was not the only universe.

The darkness of the night covered the world. The courtyard with its sad inhabitants seemed like a bad dream. We talked again about the future, about life and the happiness we wished for. Suddenly my friend Mina Nattel said: "You know, girls, if we are still able to rejoice because of the beauty of one little flower, then Hitler will never win the war against us!"

I don't remember the other girl's name anymore. She lived upstairs in one corner of a kitchen allotted to her parents and their two daughters. They all perished during the second Action.

Mina Nattel left Ghetto Tarnow after the second Action, which took away her sister Luna. Mina was a member of the Shomer Hatzair movement, and they provided Aryan documents for her. She went to

Warsaw, where her friend Regina Reinhold had succeeded in establishing herself as an office manager. Mina found a job as a governess with a Polish family living on the land. The few months spent there were a perfect bliss for her. Unfortunately, someone suspected her identity, and she had to flee. The last communication I had from her was on a card postmarked Lublin. It read: "Dear Irene [my Aryan name], Don't write until I notify you of my new address."

The notice never came.

Ghetto Tarnow became a metaphor for hell on earth. At the same time that more people were being brought in daily from surrounding communities, less space was allotted to each person. We were lucky because our house was in the area originally designated for the ghetto. Every time the Jewish quarter shrank, we took in somebody to live with us. By the time the ghetto was sealed, our single room housed ten people belonging to four different families.

How could we stand it? We were happy just not having to beg for a space to spend a night. Our one room contained everything we needed to live at that time. The problem was how to remain alive.

Right across Debowa Street was the ghetto wall. From our windows we could see the gate with its sentry booth. The wall was only a wooden fence, but the sole fact of its existence reminded us constantly of the frightening reality. For me the gate became a symbol, the gate to life.

Unable to reconcile myself to the reality, I became obsessed with the idea of escape. Most of my free time was spent in front of the mirror, trying to figure out a disguise that would make me look Aryan. I parted my hair in the middle, pinned it up, pinned it down, to no avail. I was always known as the girl with the black eyes, but during the war my best feature became my curse. What I wouldn't have given for wishy-washy myopic eyes and stringy blond hair. New criteria for beauty were Aryan features. Dark, semitic faces with eyes like mine were a bane.

Language was another problem. Yiddishisms, injected into Polish conversations, were a giveaway and could be more treacherous than my black eyes and wavy, dark hair. In preparation for escape, I started to practice a new way of speech, a new personality. My mother's ring was exchanged for forged documents. I became the proud owner of a Kennkarte (identity card), a Polish passport required by law to be on

156

one's person at all times. It christened me Irene Zahorska, and with all my imagination I tried to become her. The name "Zahorski" indicates noble roots. The making out of a jewish nonperson a member of Polish aristocracy was the forger's benign joke.

My seventeenth birthday passed unnoticed. What was there to celebrate? We lived from day to day, surrounded by instant and constant suffering and death. Like every young person in time and history, I tried to define the meaning of life. Passivity was worse than death. So was the submission to fate and the loss of pride. Maintaining self-respect under those circumstances was quite a feat.

At night I doubled up in bed with my cousin Eva, in a room shared with eight other people. One outhouse on the entire floor was used by twenty people. We were deprived of space to move around freely; there was hardly enough air to breath. Privacy was an archaic word whose meaning was long forgotten.

In spite of the hardships I did not want to look into reality's face. I would not accept it.

"Mother, Mother I want to live! Mother, do you understand, *I WANT TO LIVE!*"

For the first time in my life Mother did not respond to my demand.

"Mother, do something. Mother, talk to me, say something!" Finally it dawned on me. Mother could not answer. She had ceased to be my comfort. The mothers in ghetto had to be pitied more than anyone else. Forced to witness the destruction of their children, theirs was the most tragic fate. Motherhood had become a curse!

And the rest of us? We became people stripped of everything. All we had was taken away. Even the Star of David, the symbol of our pride, became transformed into a badge of shame and inferiority. But Polish Jews never gave up hope. They clung to their lives with a tenacity difficult to describe.

Were there any questions asked? No. Were there any solutions to those unasked questions? None. Did I think that my unspent youth entitled me to anything? Oh, yes. If death was to be the destiny of my short life, then I wanted it to come while I was fighting for life. I would run! I would not wait for "them." Let "them" catch me running. Let "them" shoot me in the back! That was how I wanted to die!

In the summer of 1942 I escaped for the first of many times. My last hour in ghetto was spent in a little makeshift beauty parlor, where the tattletale hair was straightened and lightened, and my thick, black eyebrows plucked thinner. Thus beautified, I felt very Aryan. Projecting the air of genuine, nonghettoish self-assurance, I approached the ghetto gate.

"I am leaving," I blurted to the astonished Jewish *milicja* man. He looked away, and before the Polish policeman could stop me, I was already on the other side of the street. Hardly believing my luck and quietly praying, I walked briskly. In order not to break out in a wild gallop, I had to exercise the utmost of my self-control. In a moment I was out of their sight. My good luck held out. Not one Gestapo man – or plainclothes policeman, not even a single one of the Polish anti-Semites constantly watching out for escaping Jews – accosted me.

I felt like jumping, laughing, and crying, or yelling at the top of my voice: "World, I am coming! Life, wait for me! I will live, live, *LIVE*! Daddy, do not despair, we will meet again!" The doomed girl, Lala Landerer, who missed her father and dreamed of life and future, was left behind the ghetto wall. A young Polish woman by the name of Irene Zahorska took her place among the living free.

As arranged before hand, a friendly Polish woman was waiting for me. There were Poles who helped the Jews, usually for a fee. Our Mrs. Smajda from Bochnia was trusted and her fees were affordable to our quickly decreasing reserves. We didn't talk. She nodded her head, turned around, and walked while I followed her from a safe distance. When we reached the train station, she bought the ticket to Bochnia for me. Train stations were most dangerous traps. Because of their strategic importance, they were heavily guarded.

Everything proceeded as planned. There was no delay in schedule, and after an hour's ride the overcrowded train reached Bochnia. Once there I felt safe. The manager of the station was a trusted man by the name of Smajda, the husband of my guide.

What a relief it was to leave the tightly packed compartment and inhale Bochnia's fresh air. The train station resembled a beehive. People were hurrying out. I almost lost my guide in this human wave fast rolling toward the exit. In Bochnia she was known as the wife of the station manager and could not be seen in the company of an escaping Jewess. I followed her from an uncompromising distance, and when she entered a door with a large sign "The Station Manager,"

I went in after her. There I was safe, if for a few moments only. I still had to steal into the ghetto.

I was tired. The tension of the last hours was taking its toll. Through the bolted windows and shut door of the manager's office muted noises were heard. First the heavy puffing of the steam locomotive, then the shrieks of the screeching wheels, long walling whistle of the locomotive, and the train departed. A lonely voice called, "Good-bye! Good-bye!" and then all was quiet. We heard the watchman closing the gate. "We are the only people in this part of the station, and it would be safe for you to leave now," said Mr. Smajda.

The major part of my trip was over. All I had to do was to smuggle myself into the ghetto, where my uncle was waiting for me. With the naivete and recklessness of youth I wasn't worried at all. The frightened Jewish girl was left behind in Ghetto Tarnow; the person who emerged from Bochnia's station manager's office was sure of herself and confident.

I followed Mrs. Smajda to the spot where one board of the ghetto fence was loose. I cashed under while she continued walking without looking back.

I found myself in a meadow, bordering the backyards of ghetto houses. After a short walk, I reached a street teeming with people. This was the ghetto's thoroughfare, Kowalska Street. The faces were familiar, the white armbands with the Star of David made me feel at home. Suddenly I felt that I did not want to be Irene Zahorska anymore. Anyhow, who was she? As I was walking and musing, I felt a gentle tap on the shoulder.

"Lala, when did you come?" It was Maryla Lichtblau, another escapee from Tarnow.

"Maryla! When did you come?"

It was good to be among Jews again!

My mother and my sister, whose looks were decidedly Aryan, followed me to Bochnia, where we joined my Uncle Josef. His family had just escaped deportation from the ghetto in Brzesko, and they arrived in Bochnia a few days before we did. My uncle's family of six people was allotted one room only, and every night each one of us Landerers slept at different people's homes. Sometimes it was a shared bed, and often a blanket on the floor. We did not have a thing we could call our own. Afraid to resemble Jews escaping from ghettos, we left with pocketbooks under the arm only. We had our lives, all right, but at the same time we learned that without even one change of underwear, life was difficult to enjoy. The meager remnants of our valuables, which could be hidden in our clothing, was all we had. After a short time we decided to return to Tarnow.

Ironically, reentering the ghetto was more difficult than leaving. One could not walk up to the gate and tell the guard that, after all, life "outside" was not so great. We made it by joining a group of workers returning in the afternoon. The groups employed outside the ghetto were escorted by the Jewish *milicja*, who just pretended not see the "illegals." People covered up for each other. A person returning to the ghetto usually stepped into the moving formation of laborers.

While the marching went on undisturbed, an armband with the Jewish Star was passed on and pulled over the right arm of a former fugitive. The greatest danger was at the ghetto gate, where the list of returning workers was often checked by the Gestapo. The three of us went in undetected.

We were back in Tarnow. Sala and her children were overjoyed to see us, and we too were happy to be together. But the feeling of home was gone. During our short absence Tarnow had become a different place. The small ghetto was a cross between a wasteland and a cemetery. No one knew the exact number of missing, but most of the people I had known weren't there anymore. From our small apartment building alone, ten people were taken away. The total missing from the entire ghetto was too scary to acknowledge.

I do not remember anymore the exact date of the second Action, but it is safe to assume that it took place during, or just before Rosh Hashanah, 1942. I was in Bochnia when my friend Maryla received a letter from her boyfriend in Tarnow, telling about the Action. That was on Yom Kippur, and the Germans usually conducted Actions against the Jews during Jewish holidays. So it was fortunate that we celebrated New Year's in Bochnia.

The Action that we had escaped, emptied the community of old people and children. The ideal age to be was between fourteen and thirty-five years – the most suitable for slave labor, the equivalent of the right to live.

People disguised themselves to appear the right age, and were a pitiful sight. Gray hair was bleached or colored, pale cheeks revived by specks of rouge. Young girls dressed up, their hair combed into grownup styles, chests padded into a semblance of bosoms, precariously balancing on old, worn, out-of-shape shoes. A few small children, miraculously saved from the last carnage, were hidden indoors. This precaution was not needed anymore because the Gestapo's daily tours stopped after the second Action. Nobody rejoiced. Any change of the usual routine was an omen of worse to come.

As the German army continued its victorious *Drang nach Osten*, workshops supplying the needs of the army were organized closer to the front. No new workposts were created in Tarnow for the Jews, and there was a large group of unemployed in the ghetto. No reorganization took place after the second massive deportation, and the feeling of suspended danger pervaded the atmosphere. The department of hygiene was disbanded. There was no more sense in pretending that fighting lice was possible at all under the present conditions.

The summer of 1942 was nearing the end. With every passing day the feeling that a noose was being tightened around our necks was growing stronger, acquiring the dimensions of physical pain. Fear and hopelessness began to take their toll. Some people became resigned to their fate, others reacted violently. Exchanging their last possessions for food and booze, they went on eating and drinking sprees. Abandoning all restraints, they tried to get at least a taste of what life could have offered them if they had been allowed to live. Rejecting all accepted social mores and restraints, they lived by the motto: "What the hell! Either the grave or the ditch!" But the majority of young people wanted desperately to live and refused to abandon hope.

Shortly after our return from Bochnia and the second Action, the Jewish *milicja* received orders to bring all former hygienists to the Judenrat. There in the courtyard they arranged us into columns of three abreast, handed cleaning equipment, and thus, armed with brooms, pails, brushes, and rags, we were ordered to go. Not knowing where we were going, or why, but well aware that our macabre procession was being watched from every window, we marched resolutely. It was a warm summer evening. The eight o'clock curfew was strictly enforced. In the quiet of the abandoned streets, our steps and the loud orders of the *milicja* men reverberated in all corners of the ghetto. From windows opened into dark rooms, frightened eyes followed our advance. The invisible grapevine was fast, and the news that all hygienists had been brought into the Judenrat and then taken away spread fast. People were petrified. This had no precedence, and it was hard to figure out what it could mean.

We had already passed the ghetto boundary and could not guess where we were being led. Somebody started to hum a marching song, another mockingly directing the rhythm of our steps: right, left, right, left. Anything to keep the spirits from sinking. An uneasy feeling of helplessness and resignation crept over the marchers as we finally reached our destination. It was a former housing project that few of us were familiar with. It had, among other amenities, a large basement where steam and shower stalls were located.

We were ordered to clean the entire basement. It looked as if a band of savages had bivouacked there recently. Different objects scattered on the cement floor indicated that, whoever those people were, they were a very mixed group. A doll's arm, a man's sock, a bloody handkerchief, a soiled diaper were strewn over the floor.

Scrubbing and cleaning diligently we tried to guess what might have gone on in that place. It was only later on that we found out that we were the first of Tarnow's citizens forced to clean a steam bath where people had been steamed to death. What happened was that some of the SS men got bored with the repetitious routine of the second Action, and directed a cattle carload of people to the steam bath. There the unfortunates were exposed to a continuous flow of hot steam. People gasped for air, choked, fainted. Some did not survive. Those who did were conveniently shipped off to "resettling," from which they were never heard of again.

One family who lived through this ordeal eventually returned to the ghetto. These were the Cytronenbaums, one of Tarnow's old families. The head of the family was a member of the Judenrat and as such not included in the deportation list. Their oldest daughter, Tosia, was my friend, and she told me their story. Confident that their father's position as a councilman of the Judenrat made them immune to deportatior, they stayed at home during the second Action. Two SS men gone berserk broke into their house and dragged them out. Their protests that they were not on the list were quickly and efficiently quieted. The Cytronenbaums had forgotten that their Jewishness qualified them for unconditional humiliation.

Tosia was reluctant to talk about their ordeal, but as hard as she tried to block it from her memory, this nightmare kept coming back. She told me how her whole family, the parents and four children, were forced into the crowded steam room, where she passed out. She remembered hearing her father's voice, calling to her as if from another time and space: "Tosia, Tosia, wake up, wake up! Come back to me, my child, my life, come back! Please, oh God, help me, Tosia, come back!"

She felt hot drops falling on her face, and as if someone were ungluing her lids and opening her eyes. She looked up, and it was her father bending over her, weeping unrestrainedly. His face was close to her as if he was trying to breathe life into her. Both Tosia and her father were convinced that when he found her, she was dead. At the beginning I was skeptical.

"Tosia," I said, "how can you say that you were dead?"

"My father told me later that, when he found me, I was stiff, cold, my lips were blue, my eyes without any sign of life."

"My father's tears and cries brought me back to life."

I understood and fully accepted this explanation. I too had a father who possessed a great gift for love, and I was convinced that parental love could even reclaim a child from the clutches of death. Sometimes.

Cytronenbaums' good luck did not last long. During the liquidation of the ghetto, this whole family was loaded into the death train that took them to Auschwitz, where they all perished.

Shortly after the hygienists cleaned this infamous basement, the entire complex, comprising a number of buildings, became converted into a large warehouse labeled *Judische Vermogens* (Jewish estates). The booty from Jewish homes was stored there. Workers were needed to sort out the wares, and the four Landerer women were drafted. Every building was marked according to the "merchandise" it contained. One housed Torah scrolls, prayer books and shawls, phylacteries; heavy volumes of Talmud, musty manuscripts, and new Hebrew books – torn, dirty, desecrated – were scattered over the floors. Another building was full of clothing; one floor had only coats, another dresses, another one suits, lingerie, blankets, and beddings. A whole building was filled with furniture, rugs, drapes, and curtains.

The saddest of all was the floor filled with shoes. Small shoes, large shoes, heavy boots, working shoes mingled with dancing slippers, evening shoes, tennis shoes, winter shoes, and summer sandals.

Thrown in disarray over the entire floor, they resembled a collection of different footprints. If only they could talk ... Limp, untied laces seemed to be ashamed of their uselessness. Open buckles appeared to beg for someone to fasten them. Single shoes, dispersed and forlorn, were like lost lovers looking for their partners. Most of the children's shoes stored there were worn out, patched up, torn, and the more wear and tear they showed, the sadder they appeared. No one needed them. No more little feet waiting to slip them on.

As a former hygienist I was assigned to disinfection. Everything had to be disinfected and sent to the appropriate department. Physically the work was light, but emotionally it was murder. Hardly a day passed without one of our crew finding some of their family's belongings.

"Oh God! This is my sister's dress!"

It was hard to go on working after each discovery, but nobody drove us. Our foreman, who had been forced to witness the execution of his wife and children, was beyond caring. Someone sitting in a corner, weeping and clutching a garment, was an everyday sight in our work unit. Each one had a private day of sorrow. Eventually my day came. While sorting a pile of clothing still warm from the oven, I found two dresses belonging to my little Horowitz cousins, Lalusia and Fela.

Two little girls' peasant outfits, reminders of carefree summers in Rabka. But in that dark basement those two dresses seemed to poke fun at me, my suffering and longing after my family. The soft fabric mercifully accepted and soaked up my tears. I was supposed to fold garments neatly, so that not even one crease would mar their perfection, as befits garments for a child of "superior race". – for all things from *Judische Vermogens* were being sent to Germany. I could easily imagine a plump, well-fed, blond *Hausfrau* dressing her plump, well-fed, blond daughters in the dresses my Aunt Lieba used to put on her daughters every Shabbat. Closing my eyes I buried my face in the soft fabric. Not a trace of the sweet, familiar smell of their bodies. Only the repulsive odor of carbolic and the sterile warmth of the oven. Reddish-blond braids, two lovely faces shining in disarming smiles appeared in front of me, and the sound of their giggles rang in my ears.

To let those dresses be sent to Germany, where they might be worn by the murderers' children, was like letting my little cousins be killed for the second time. I could not let this happen. I sneaked those two dresses under my clothing and brought them back to the ghetto. For a while we cherished them like a precious treasure, the only thing left of the family of my uncle, Hirsch Horowitz. But when the time came for our next and final escape, we destroyed them. The only mementos we could take along were those in our hearts.

16 • "Dus Pintale Yid"

After the first deportation a new face appeared in Ghetto Tarnow. A young German, dressed in full regalia of a Hitlerjugend organization, the read armband with a large, black swastika in the middle flashing with his every movement, was courting a Jewish girl. Fela was one of the most capable nurses in the Jewish hospital. The two made a striking couple: the tall, blond, blue-eyed Aryan and the slight, dark, black-eyed Jewess. Every day he waited for her at the hospital, located outside of the ghetto boundaries. He became a permanent fixture during the evening hours, when most of the people escaping their crowded apartments were taking to the streets. Soon people ceased paying attention to this anomaly. In time he became friendly with Fela's crowd and seemed to have found a niche in ghetto society.

When I returned to Tarnow after my first flight, the young Aryan god seemed to have vanished. This time nurse Fela was being escorted by a ghetto inmate proper, wearing a white armband with a blue Star of David, like the rest of us. The former boyfriend was forgotten. Every time I saw the lovers, they were holding hands or walking with their arms entwined. Having eyes for each other only, they seemed oblivious to the world around them. Who was the new man in town?

This magnificent Teuton and the new Jew were the same person, by name Horst Werner. His parents' only child, Horst was born in Berlin, where he grew up under the regime that equaled love of the Fatherland with adherence to the Nazi party. Thus young Horst joined the Hitlerjugend corps as a natural outcome of his upbringing.

This little family went on with its happy existence, totally oblivious to the suffering inflicted on Jews by Germany's revered Fuhrer. It appeared as if the Graces had bestowed all their gifts upon the youngster: beauty, loving family, privileged position, and promise of a good life.

166

Then one day, fate chose to play a most cruel joke on the Werner family. German Bureaucracy, relentlessly searching for anything that might undermine the purity of the Aryan race, discovered that Werner, the father, was of Jewish ancestry. And, worse, his Jewish ancestors came from Poland. The newly discovered trace of Jewish parentage disqualified the senior Werner from citizenship in the Third Reich. The bewildered new Jew was automatically stripped of all honors and privileges and promptly deported to Poland. How he landed in Ghetto Tarnow I do not know, because Fela was not one of my personal friends. Apparently, after his father was sent to Tarnow, Horst arranged to be transferred there, too, and his mother, middle-aged civilian, simply packed up and followed.

At the beginning the Werners lived in the section of town set apart for German citizens, and they visited every day in the ghetto. When the ghetto fence went up and it became obvious that it would be closed in a matter of days, both the mother and son renounced their German citizenship, registered with the Judenrat, received *Judenpasses*, and moved in with father and husband. (It happened while we were in Bochnia.) At the end they shared his fate. Tarnow's "great transport," the last one, went straight to Auschwitz and its crematoria.

What was the force that made those two people reject their privileged position, renounce all they had believed in and lived for until the shattering discovery, then voluntarily take up poverty, degradation, and certain death? Nazi Germany was at the top of its glory. The army was advancing on all fronts. The mast of the German flag was raised above most European capitals. If a woman only were involved, it could be passed on as another moving story of love and sacrifice. But young Horst?

Why would a man at the peak of his youth give up freedom and life? Was it because of the girl only? Not likely. The land was full of attractive women ready to offer themselves for a good meal or a pair of stockings. Was his devotion to father stronger than a young man's will to live? Not likely either. At the same time that Horst denied his allegiance to the Nazi party and all it represented, there were countless youngsters in the ghetto willing to give their right arms for a chance to breathe freely and walk unafraid, if for one day only.

Horst's choosing death with his father's people, rather than life without conscience, came from the spiritual strength hidden in every

Jewish soul. Folk wisdom identified it as *"dus pintale yid,"* a tiny speck of Jewishness. This minuscule particle concealed in the depth of the Jewish heart, or whatever it is that generates emotions and conscience, prevailed over the evil might of the Nazis. Horst Werner, the former *Hitlerjugend* member, chose to die as a Jew when rejecting Judaism would have given him life.

The mother and wife is more easily understood. Cut off from her world, she had no place to go back, certainly not as long as Germany was under the Nazi regime, which then appeared to be forever. Once her husband and only child were doomed, she did not want to live anymore. This lady was to be considered one of the Righteous Gentiles. Were there more like her, things might have been different.

17 · Faithful friend

I hardly remember the year Jozia came to us. She seemed to be always there. Other maids before her passed through the house like insignificant shadows, but the memory of Jozia is attached to every important moment of our lives. I was a little girl then, maybe four or five years old, when one dark, wintry evening Mother introduced to us a slim, tall woman. She was wearing a long, dark brown coat with a large fur collar. A small hat was perched on top of her head.

"This is Jozia, and she will be staying with us," Mother said. Jozia seemed very shy, and we, eager to go back to our game, did not pay much attention to her.

Next morning we heard a gentle knock at the door, and Jozia came into our room to start a fire in the big heating stove. This is how I remember her best: crouching in front of the stove and poking its insides with a long iron, to rake out the ashes from the grate. Once it was done, she put in old newspapers and few kindling sticks, lit them with a match, closing the stove door and waiting for the fire to catch. Tucked under the warm comforters in our beds, we watched the slim tongues of flame climbing over the wood, mirrored in the polished floor. The sound of crackling wood broke the silence, signaling time for the coal to be added. This was carried out by an established procedure: first small pieces, then big ones, always followed by the same proclamation: "This large chunk of coal will keep the room warm till you go to sleep again." Like a priestess performing an ancient rite, she remained crouching until all the coals were a glow. Then she left the room quietly.

I remember the long Saturday afternoons, when all the children of the family gathered around Jozia and listened to stories about her childhood in the village. Hers had been a drab and uneventful life, but somehow Jozia seemed to possess an inexhaustable well of emotions

169

and feelings that enriched her memories. An orphan, she hardly remembered her parents. Her stories were about the changing seasons, the passing of the armies through their village in the first World War, and the manor. There was a manor near the village whose young mistress took an interest in the quiet little orphan girl and used to invite her over. One story I remember particularly well. Jozia, then eight or nine years old, was invited into the kitchen, where she was served a mug of chocolate and a large chunk of cake, which she hid in her lap to save for later. The dog smelled the cake, sneaked under the table, and devoured it. The little girl sat at the table afraid to move, shamed lest they discover her deceit, and heartbroken by the loss of the cake. A lot of time has gone by since I first heard this story and many things have happened, but somehow, I remember the story of that little girl and her lost cake.

Jozia's splendid poise and tact stayed with her throughout her entire life. She never lost her temper, never raised her voice. Her dignified ways gained her the respect and love of the entire family. Her interests were not those of a maid but of a cultivated young woman. She loved books and poetry; reading stealthily during work hours was her only vice. I used to bring books from the lending library for both of us, and instead of meeting with cousins or friends for play, I walked with Jozia to the park, where on a remote bench we could read undisturbed for hours. On our way home we discussed what we had read. Her remarks were always to the point, as were her observations about my habits, ways, and friends. She had definite preferences and conveyed her disapproval without offending. If she disliked somebody, she never used the person's name. It always was "this girl." Referring to somebody by his name was an unmistakable sign of her approval. I had triple trouble in finding playmates and friends: First I had to like them, then my mother had to be pleased by the company I kept, but the hardest to get was Jozia's approval.

Then came September, 1939, and our lives were brutally interrupted by the war. Jozia's love for her country was deep and genuine, but what crushed her spirit was the Jewish tragedy, obvious and visible to her from the very beginning. She felt embarrassed and personally responsible for her compatriots' shameful participation in the persecution of Jews. She identified with our sufferings; when part of our family fled to escape the approaching Nazis and were later

170

deported to Siberia, she suffered the same agony of separation and lack of information about their whereabouts that we did.

I will never forget the day we received the first proof that they were alive. It was on a cold Saturday morning in January, 1941, six months after the Soviets had shipped them off to Siberia. The house was cold, and we stayed in bed late. All of sudden Jozia walked into the room, her face pale, tears streaming down her cheeks. In her shaking hands she held a grey envelope and whispered: "A letter from ours ... a letter from ours."

This was the first communication from Minora, northern Siberia, where my father, my brothers, Uncle Haskel, and the family from Myslenice were deported to. Even in their perils they did not forget Jozia. There were special regards for her in that first letter, as there were in every letter, as long as she was with us.

Jozia remained with us as long as we were permitted to live in our house in Krakow. Mother let her stay in her little room, and Jozia found day work outside, because we could not afford to pay her. She helped us with what she could. Being an Aryan, she had freedom of movement while we, branded by the Star of David, were restricted.

In winter 1941, forced to leave Krakow, we had to part from her. The last I remember of Jozia was a few weeks after our arrival in Tarnow. One afternoon she arrived unexpectedly with two large suitcases full of our belongings, which she had reclaimed from our Polish friends. "I was afraid they wouldn't see you for a long time, and they might forget that those things belong to you," she said. And time, of course, proved her right. As she took off her coat, we saw that underneath she was wearing ten men's shirts, the first being my father's kittel, a traditional garment worn during the High Holy Days. Her peasant mind grasped the gravity of our situation: "You won't wear them, but you will be able to exchange them for food." Trembling, she added tearfully: "The master will come back and he will need the kittel for the seder."

When my mother offered her reimbursement for the train fare, the generous woman declined. "The lady may need it to buy bread for the children," she said simply, and she was right about that, too.

She left for her home village, and the last we heard of her was one year later, when we received a letter from her sister, informing us that they had buried Jozia the previous week.

Jozia, the master did come back from Siberia, but he never found the kittel you smuggled into Ghetto Tarnow. Nor many of those to whom you gave it. But I promise you, dear friend, that as long as there are Landerers alive, you will be remembered.

18 · Disappearances

It was end of summer, 1942. The only thing on our side was the weather, hot and dry, it made us forget the approaching winter. The fertile land responded to the caresses of sun and abundance of dew with an unexpected bounty. The fields were golden with maturing wheat; in the orchards trees pregnant with ripe fruit bent over, like women about to give birth. Ghetto, the few city blocks enclosing the Jews, appeared like a faded, moth eaten spot on a colorful carpet. A few anemic looking trees, unpruned, neglected, their branches naked and barren, stuck out of the ground. Grass and weeds grew over gardens and backyards. When it rained, rivers of mud drowned the unpaved streets and paths. Our block, composed of solid brick houses, was surrounded by sidewalk, and we were among the few luckies who did not have to navigate through the slush.

It was a time of intense living. Most of my friends had been deported during the first and second Actions. Hala Blitz with her dreams of kibbutz, Irka Goldberg, the skating champion, Lusia Beldengrun, the long-legged beauty, Iziek Flashen, my first boyfriend, David Meltzer, the singing voice of our group, Edek Poller, the quiet philosopher, Cyla Wilk, the brilliant redhead, and many others whose names I don't remember anymore.

My Uncle Joseph Horowitz kept writing and begging us to join him in Bochnia. In spite of his deep faith and incorrigible optimism, he could not deny anymore that the situation was extremely grave. The destruction of the Jews was progressing, according to detailed plan. Most of the Jewish communities in eastern Galicia were already wiped out. Meager remains of what had been the largest Jewish community of the world were concentrated in few large cities.

In the midst of that desolation and death, Bochnia was considered an oasis. The local Gestapo head, Schomberg, was a master of deception.

A most corrupt individual, he masterfully projected the image of a benevolent tyrant. This masquerade created a belief that the chief, as he was called, would eventually save the community. In those days of darkness, even an illusion of hope was better than nothing.

German newspapers were easily available and widely read in the ghetto. All armchair strategists and military experts were busy trying to figure out the truth behind the lies and propaganda. For the first time in our lives we heard names like "Tobruk" and "Sidi El-Barani," read about valiant victories and battles of the Wehrmacht, and could not imagine that our destiny depended in great measure on what was happening in far off North Africa.

Never, not even once, was the Jewish tragedy mentioned in the German press. Only when letters, our sole means of communication with our dispersed family, began to return, did we realize what was really happening. First to come back was the letter from Uncle Wolf Horowitz, who together with his wife and four children had settled in Limanowa, southeast of Krakow. Across the envelope, like mourners' crepe, were large black letters: *ZURUCK. AUSGESIEDELT* (Returned, Resettled). It was self-explanatory. Then the mail from Nowy Sacz was returned. Blimcia and Meir-Haim Weinberger with their four daughters, plus Haim and Sala Horowitz and their three children, who had made their home there after being refused a permit for Ghetto Krakow, were among the condemned.

The day the mail came from Nowy Sacz, I was home alone. Knowing what it meant I had to be by myself with my grief and fury. Why? Why? Our darling Blimcia and her family! Our beloved Uncle Haim, the most brilliant and kindest of men, and his young family! How many of our most beloved would have to be sacrificed? Whose turn next? How do we go on, how do we face another day knowing that our flesh and blood were no more among the living. Our innermost selves depended upon the boundless love and devotion that had always held our family together, and now its members were being snuffed out, one by one.

Next it was Szaye and Rozia Horowitz with their children who fell into the silence. They lived in Chrzanow; right at the beginning this town was annexed as part of the Third Reich. When their letters stopped coming, we forced ourselves to believe that, as German citizens, their lives would be spared. (It may appear insane today, but it was the time when the whole world seemed to have gone berserk.) Leibele Horowitz, his wife, and three sons lived in Sanok, southeastern Poland. They owned and lived on an estate, and we hoped that the good earth would shield them. Instead it seemed to have swallowed the entire family. We didn't even know when they were taken away.

My father's oldest sister, Haya Goldwasser, settled in her hometown, Makow Podhalanski. With her were her five children, including her two married daughters, their husbands, and four grandchildren. In the winter of 1941 my Uncle Alter Goldwasser was taken hostage, together with eleven other people. When a real or imaginary transgression of the imposed restrictions took place, the local Gestapo sent the entire group to the prison in Tarnow. There most of them succumbed to the ravages of cold, hunger, and savage beatings. Whenever the capacity of the prison became strained, those that had not died of ill treatment were shipped off to Auschwitz. Eventually my Uncle Alter Goldwasser was one of them.

But before that happened, we tried to ease his misery. His own family, unable to leave Makow Podhalanski, could do nothing for him, but we were in Tarnow at the time. Uncle Alter's daughter, my cousin Dorcia (who had made the pink flannel bedjacket for Grandmother Landerer when she was sick) bombarded us with letters, begging us to do what we could.

I vividly remember standing near the prison block in a long line of girls and women. Men did not dare come near the prison out of fear of being taken in. Each of the standing women was holding a regulation food package. It was bitter cold. The line had begun to form in the early morning hours, because the wardens accepted only as many packages as they pleased. We stood there, stiff from cold but afraid to move from the line, lest we lose our coveted spot. Often the wardens did not open till noon, and then the Gestapo would come and chase us all away.

Thursday I believe was the day the *walowki* (slang for prison packages) were permitted. How many Thursdays did we come back home, frozen to the bone, our could fingers still carrying the packages. My cold toes were frostbitten, but the despair and disappointment that my uncle and all the other uncles, fathers, husbands, sons, and brothers remained hungry, without sign of life and caring from their families, was harder to bear than the physical pain.

Mother and Josef missed each other badly. The two were all that were left out of a family of fourteen brothers and sisters. Until the beginning of deportation, Jews could purchase traveling permits, and brothers used to visit each other and the sisters. But after the beginning of the deportation, no Jew dared to venture outside the ghetto walls.

As hard as I try to re-create this period, my memory refuses to cooperate. I can't recollect when the decision was made, what arguments persuaded us to part with Sala Landerer and her children and move to Bochnia. Those frightening days lie buried in my consciousness. It was in Tarnow that for the first time in my young life, I looked into death's face. I will try to leave those particular ghosts of my past alone. They are too scary, even forty and some years later. The year spent in Bochnia seemed like a pleasant interlude after Krakow and Tarnow. Alas! Death's voracious appetite was not satisfied yet. Even the smallest child could not be spared. But meanwhile we were gaining time.

All I remember is that when September 1942 came, we were already in Bochnia. Darling Uncle Josiu was pacing the room when I arrived. On the table were prayer books and an open Book of Psalms, a Jew's timeless comfort. During the whole day, while waiting for my arrival, he prayed, fasted, and recited Psalms. His faith, courage, and piety remained with him during the hardest of times.

For the second time, I was the first to arrive in Bochnia, followed by mother and then my sister. Lela fretted Bochnia. She was in love with a young man in Ghetto Tarnow, and she felt that by staying in somewhat safer Bochnia, she was betraying him and her own self-respect. So, she returned to Tarnow after a while.

Lela, the logical, realistic one, the clever independent one, could have survived "on the outside" better than any of us. With her good looks and a set of forged Aryan documents, she could have lived in relative comfort as a non-Jewish Polish civilian and seen the end of the war. But illogically, unrealistically, she threw away her chance – out of love and self-respect.

Final liquidation of Ghetto Tarnow took place during the High Holy Days in 1943. On Yom Kippur, her birthday, we observe the Yahrzeit (anniversary) of Lela's death. She was twenty-one years old when she perished.

19 · Ghetto Bochnia

At the beginning life in Ghetto Bochnia seemed like an idyll. The ghetto was still spread over a large area, and the housing department assigned us a little wooden hut on the outskirts. It was located at the end of a narrow dirt path pompously named the Street Under the Little Linden Tree. There were two or three other little houses, all surrounded by old linden trees. Experts in adapting, we immediately settled in our new abode. It reminded us of a summer home, except that the houses our families used to rent for a season were much roomier.

Our new house consisted of one room and a kitchen; the well and the outhouse were in the backyard. There was a stove in the kitchen, a little table, a chair and an iron bed. The patriarch Szmerl Balken, Aunt Bala's father, slept there alone.

The only room in the house was furnished with another bed, table, and a few assorted chairs. Bala shared the bed with her daughter, mother and I slept on a folding cot, and Josef and his two sons occupied mattresses spread on the floor every night.

We stayed for short time only in this little house, because the Jewish population was soon divided into two parts, Ghetto A and Ghetto B, and segregated according to age. All people of working age went into Ghetto A, those few elderly who were still left plus women with young children to Ghetto B.

The weeks we lived among the greenery of the linden trees, far from the hubbub of the ghetto's center, seemed like a vacation. Our backyard stretched over the steep bank of a stream, which formed a natural border between the ghetto and the rest of the world. For some unexplained reason the small wooden bridge connecting both worlds was left unguarded, for a while giving us the illusion of freedom. Mother and Aunt Bala used to cross this little bridge and barter our meager possessions with peasant women. Our second escape from Tarnow had been well planned ahead of time, and we arrived with "great wealth." Mrs. Smajda was entrusted with two suitcases full of our household goods, and she brought them over from Tarnow. With these goods, we were able to "buy" a few necessities of life. The money printed by the occupying forces had no buying power, and barter became the accepted way of doing business. After every successful transaction, we joked about having for dinner a towel, a pillowcase, a sheet. . . .

When I first came to Bochnia, I noticed that the ghetto's population consisted of much older or much younger people than myself. Why it was so I found out only after we settled there for good. Before the first Action in Bochnia, rumors were spread that all young people would be "resettled" in special working camps, where their lives would be spared. What a diabolic trick! Parents overjoyed at this "chance for life," forced their children out of hiding and into the transports. Many young people, refusing to be saved without their families, begged to be left, but desperate parents, resigned to their own fate as long as their children were safe, literally dragged them out and pushed them toward "salvation."

Anyone familiar with Nazism will have no trouble in guessing the outcome. Not one of the young people taken away was ever heard of again. All those youngsters were driven straight to execution. But we did not know that until much, much later.

Meanwhile the absence of other age peers made the handful of people my age very visible, and in no time I became a part of a group of teens. Most of them were from Krakow, and we had known each other before the war. My closest friend in Bochnia was Lusia Steinfeld. One of many afternoons we spent together is as fresh in my memory as if it happened yesterday.

It was one of the legendary Golden Polish autumn days. We were sitting at the water's edge, throwing pebbles into the brook and reciting verses. Poetry was very important to us. It helped us to put our own emotions into words and, for a few precious moments, to escape reality. Julian Tuwim, a Polish Jew, was the indisputable idol of our youth, and our affections were divided between him and the romantic Polish poets, whose longings for freedom and home mirrored our own. I was reciting a famous poem by J. Slowacki, "Oh,

God, how sad I am," and when I reached the stanza ending with a line "If even the prayer of a small child is rejected . . ." Lusia's angry voice cut in:

"Don't you feel like it was written with us in mind? All this beauty around, the serene nature, the devoted prayer on our lips, and the supplications of our hearts are totally ignored. I feel like a caged animal! Just look at this!"

Out of her pocket she pulled a crumpled postcard. Startled, I took it from her.

"What is it?"

"Just read it!"

She seemed very upset. I knew it could not have been caused by my recitation, because she too knew this poem by heart. I looked at the postcard she handed me. The postmark was Belzec. The handwriting was unfamiliar. It read as follows:

"Dear Miss Lusia,

All I can tell you is that every day we see freight trains full of Jews coming to Belzec, and all day long black smoke comes up the long chimney in the camp. The trains and the camp are guarded all the time by a special *Judenvernichtungs* (Extermination) *Batallion*, and nobody knows what goes on there because nobody ever came out of that camp alive. I only hope that your father was not on one of those trains. We did not hear from him.

Sincerely,
Zosia

"How would you explain this?" Lusia asked. It was from their gentile friend. The Steinfelds had agreed among themselves that, in case the family became separated, they would maintain contact through this friend. Lusia's father had been taken away during the first Action, and since Bochnia Jews believed that deportation meant relocation and survival, the Steinfeld family had been eagerly awaiting news from him. None had come.

Tired of waiting and worrying, Lusia wrote to Zosia, and this was the reply. She had hidden it from her mother and brother, but the secret weighed upon her heavily, and she had had to share it with me.

179

I could not and would not analyze it. And yet it was self-explanatory. *Vernichtung*! It could only mean that humans were being cremated on the premises. People coming in through the gate would leave through the chimney, transformed into smoke. . . .

In spite of living under German occupation for three long years – in spite of our losses, the disappearances, the sudden silences, the voids where there had been beloved family members – we had desperately clung to the conviction that whatever bestialities we witnessed were sporadic. The fact that a state engaged in a major war would divert much-needed resources, employ a whole army of men, and create an entire industry – for the sole purpose of destroying a segment of civilian population – was beyond the comprehension of a normal human being.

But Lusia and I saw no point in adding to the heavy mood that prevailed in Ghetto Bochnia. We decided not to talk about it anymore. Lusia tore the card into shreds and threw them into the water. For a while we remained seated, watching the tiny pieces of paper being swallowed by a whirlpool and carried away by rushing waters.

20 · The little action in Bochnia

Gruesome reality was staring us in our faces. We were all on death row – even the valuable laborers from Ghetto A. Our way of thinking became that of people condemned to death. And we, the youngsters of Ghetto A, could only attempt to block the despair by looking up to an imaginary rainbow. At its end was life and a future to dream about, while we, we were just marking time.

It was not easy. Everything but our innermost thoughts was regulated by the ghetto's routine and influenced by the ever-present fear.

First there was the little Action. Rumours about reinforcement of local police and Gestapo began to circulate. Then somebody heard from an important source that additional Gestapo dignitaries had arrived in town. Uncle Josef was spending whole days at the Judenrat, trying to buttonhole well-informed people.

The more information he got, the more confusing it was. One evening he came home later than usual, bringing good news. Somebody talked to "our" Gestapo chief and was told that it was a false alarm. Thank God, there would be no Action. We spread our bedding, undressed for the first time in over a week, relaxed, and slept soundly. Next morning my uncle went out to get water from the well in the backyard and a moment later he was back with an empty bucket dangling from his shaking hands. His face was gray. "We are surrounded," he whispered. "An armed policeman is standing on the bridge."

I rubbed my half-closed eyes. Mother, completely awake, handed me my Aryan clothing and prompted me: "Hurry, hurry, dress quick!"

You have no working papers. They may be taking the young people again. You must get out fast!"

She went outside and pretended to be getting water from the well while she scanned the surroundings. Few moments later, she was back, reassuringly calm and composed.

"There is only one man on the bridge. Plead with him. If he doesn't let you go, give him money."

She tied a white kerchief in a babushka style over my tousled hair and put money into my pocket. To mother's credit it must be said that, no matter how difficult our situation was, she always stuck to the principle that one must have cash ready for emergencies. With a steady hand she propelled me out of the house, and I ran down the steep bank.

"Halt! Where are you going?"

We faced one another. He was young, not much older than myself. The uniform did not match his boyish looks. The hand pointing a gun at me seemed a bit unsteady.

"Let me go!"

"I can't. No Jews allowed out."

"Please! I am only seventeen years old. I want to live!"

"I can't. My orders are not to let a single one out. If I let you go, they would shoot me."

"No, no! Don't shoot! Please, please, maybe you have a sister my age, maybe a sweetheart. Wouldn't you have pity on her? Look away for one second only!" I pushed the money into his hand. He pocketed it and said, "Run!"

And run I did. Over the bridge and onto the main road. Things were happening faster than I could think. In a few seconds, I found myself in unfamiliar territory, where I could not behave like a panicky, running-away Jewess. I had to find the Smajda's house without asking directions.

It was still early in the day, and the streets were deserted. That day no Jews were led out of the ghetto to work. A hurried passersby were hiding in the shadows of the buildings. The Poles knew that it was not wise to attract attention of the police while an Action was in progress in the ghetto. But war had taught me ingenuity, and in short time I was knocking at the Smajdas' door. They took me in and hid me in their house for the duration of the Action. For three days and three nights I shared their meals and slept in one bed with Elzbietka, their daughter. They even prepared a hiding place for me above the chicken coop, in case the search for escaping Jews should spread to other parts of the town. During the time I was there, I forced myself to believe that I was a part of that group, a friend of Elzbietka, high school student like her. I could not let my thoughts run free, to think what might have been happening to my family, and what would happen to me if there were no one left in the ghetto by tomorrow or my family had been taken away.

When the Action was over, I could hardly wait for nightfall, so I could go back. After dark I ran all the way home, exploding with tension. Who was left? Did I have a mother still? Uncle, aunt, cousins, friends? Miracle of miracles, I found the whole family, and they were worried about *me*. We were together again. For how long nobody dared to ask.

Soon after the "little" Action, Grandfather Balken's health began to deteriorate. His mind became blurred, and he had to be hospitalized. He died some weeks later and was buried in the Jewish cemetery. His death from natural causes at the age of eighty and some years brought relief to us all. Soon after his demise the ghetto became reorganized, an we had to move "uptown."

21 · The Baudienst

The beginning of winter, 1943, found us in an apartment in a two-story building on Bracka Street. We were lucky to be accepted as one family with Uncle Josef and Aunt Bala. Our dwelling had one room and a kitchen. In spite of being solidly built out of brick, the house had no modern plumbing, and again, we had to share one outhouse with all tenants of the second floor. By that time we were so used to primitive conditions that it didn't matter at all. The apartment was furnished with beds, enough for us to double up. No more sleeping on the floor. This was real luxury!

In Ghetto A everybody had to have a job. My uncle and his two sons worked as basket weavers; we, the women, in a stocking factory that supplied the Wehrmacht. Everyone worked ten-hour shifts, alternate day and night. Led by police, a long column of workers, consisting of half the ghetto population, was marched to the outposts. Ours was called the Baudienst, and it was situated in an old, two-story building. On each story was a large hall that had been turned into a workshop. The knitting machines, operated by men, were close to the window; the women knitters were seated along long tables. Returning from the night shifts, we passed through the empty streets like a caravan of shadows, and jokers christened it "the march macabre."

Black humor flourished. The graver the situation, the more sinister the jokes. I still remember one:

"Two Jews left in Poland are being led to the gallows. As the hangman is tightening the rope around their necks, one whispers to the other:

"Take heart. The news is very good."

"What is the very good news?"

"Churchill gave a major speech in the Parliament, and he mentioned the Polish Jews."

184

The bottom of our suitcases was beginning to show. Their contents had been bartered for food, and we began to take our hot meals in the soup kitchen. Once a week, though, on Friday nights, we tried to be together and share a semblance of a Friday night dinner. We kept one white tablecloth, and those of us who did not have to work the night shift sat together at the table. My uncle, who was respected and well liked by all, always managed to get relieved on Friday nights, so he could pray and observe Shabbat at home. As long as it was possible to prepare some food at home, we maintained the tradition of having an *oyrech*, a poor guest. There was no lack of lonely people, who hungered after food and companionship.

Bochnia's Gestapo chief, Schomberg, often pretended to be a friend of certain Jews. He was called Shefale, a pun on the Yiddish nickname "Shafale" (little lamb), but he was a sly fox. He adored money, especially Jewish money, but he was not picky. Not at all. Jewelry, precious stones, silver, any kind of valuable was equally acceptable to him. A few people in the ghetto had free access to Shefale. Some worked for him on a daily basis, others were former prisoners of the Gestapo who found out how to buy favors and their freedom from them, and maintained the connection. They reassured people that "our *chief*" was a friend, a kind soul hidden under the Gestapo uniform. Thus, based on those fairy tales and hope against reality, a myth was born that "our *chief*" would not permit his friends in Bochnia to perish. It was understood that this would have a price, but what price life? Meanwhile people bought small favors and big ones, all the time hoping that eventually life would be on sale too.

No one would have believed that when orders to liquidate the ghetto would finally come, this purported friend of Jews would prove himself to be a "most obedient soldier." While Bochnia went through its final Action, I was already far away. But my friend Lusia, who later on escaped from Auschwitz, told me how, during the Action, our good chief himself "took care of" all the people who came in daily contact with him, including Freddy, his personal chauffeur, and his fiancee, the beautiful Nusia Rose. He forced them all to kneel in a row and with his own hand shot each one of them through the back of the head. So much for a friendly, sympathetic Nazi!

We had just made our home in the apartment on Bracka Street when it was requisitioned for the Jewish *milicja*. We moved again and again, until we were separated from the men and lived in a section assigned to the women, only. The four of us, Aunt Bala Horowitz with her daughter Rachela, mother and I, bonded together with the Schiffs from Brzesko, two women and three children. In the men's part of the ghetto the five men from the Schiff family and the three Horowitzes lived together in one room. We had a little iron stove in our room, where the food was prepared for the children and old mister Schiff and his brother. A bunker for hiding the children had to be built in every new lodging we moved to, and that was the men's task.

I hated that crowded little room. Whenever I worked the day shift, I spent the evenings with my friends. We behaved the way a group of teenagers would anytime, anyplace. Once we were out of the grim Baudienst workshops and crowded apartments, we discussed books, philosophy, religion, injustice, poetry, sometimes gossip, but never our immediate prospects. I had two groups of friends, one at work, another after work. Two of the most popular themes were: how things were before and how it would be "after the war." At Baudienst we used to sit at long tables, and when the foreman was not within earshot, we talked. While our empty stomachs were turning, we never tired of discussing our favorite dishes, especially the sweets. The chocolate bark, the rum bombes, the little chocolate cubes by Domanski, Piaseckl's candies, the ultra bitter Rival by Wedel. Salivating hopelessly, we could not stop talking. Or we would reminisce about school, vacations, trips, movies, all the things that we used to take for granted. We fantasized about what life would be like "after the war," when everything would be even better than before. The whole world would reward us for our sufferings.

Were we that foolish or insane? Who was the whole world? But we had to believe that someplace, somewhere, somebody cared what was happening to us. Otherwise it would not have been possible to get through the day.

We had lost contact with the reality outside the ghetto walls, and the world we so badly missed appeared highly idealized. Forced to march on the dirt road while led to work, we resembled yoked oxen. Heads bent low to avoid hostile looks and the smirking smiles of passing Poles, we hardly saw our surroundings. As we sat in the Baudienst's large hall, noisy from the whirr of the knitting machines and full of choking dust, we were modern day slaves. With a daily

186

quota to be filled and the supervisor hovering over us with his favorite slogan, "Production, production," we could relax only during rare moments when he was away from the floor.

It was during one of those rare moments of his absence that Fela Stern, a lively girl working next to me, pulled my elbow.

"Fast, fast, hurry! He went out. Follow me!" and she sprinted out. I tailed her as she reached the staircase, ran up to the next floor, and started to climb a ladder. Mystified I asked,

"Where are you going?"

"To the attic. Don't talk. Just follow."

The attic, full of dust, cobwebs, and bats hanging upside down from the beams, resembled an abandoned cave.

"Watch out! Try not to break a leg!" Fela's giggling voice came from above. I looked up and there she was, climbing a shaft like a cat.

"Wait a minute. Just let me open the trap door," and she slid down. "Now you go up and push your upper body out. Just don't fly out because then I would be in trouble."

I climbed the shaft, raised myself over the opening, and, supported by my arms, looked out. The view made me dizzy. I could not catch my breath. I closed my eyes, and then I opened them again, and still I could not believe what I saw. All around me was the hilly countryside in the first bloom of spring. The entire town looked like one large orchard full of flowers in different hues of pink. Their smell was blown into my face by a gentle breeze. Could this be the same Bochnia I lived in? Impossible! This was an enchanted country where birds nestled happily and swarms of insects buzzed around freely. As I stood there, a small ladybug settled on my arm. As little children we used to catch ladybugs and sing, "Ladybug, ladybug, go up to the sky and tell me what the weather will be tomorrow." When she flew high up, it meant that the day would be sunny, when down, rainy.

"Ladybug, ladybug," I murmured softly – as she suddenly took off and flew away.

"You mean bug!" I cried out, tears welling in my eyes. "You too are turning away from me. I should have squashed you!" "Sh, sh, quiet! Do you want to be found out. Come down. I want to have a look too." Fela, holding my legs, pulled me down.

"That disgusting worm! Even the ladybugs are not the same."

"Don't talk to my legs, just hold on tight!" A giggling voice came from above. But this time her cheerfulness was not infectious. I shuddered. If felt as if an icy wind had swept over the empty attic. How I envied this little bug that could take off and fly to freedom, while I was the one to be squashed anytime, soon.

All it took was five minutes, and we were back. To be away from the table longer would have been conspicuous, and we returned before any of the supervisors could have noticed our absence. The rest of the afternoon was spent dreaming. I could not concentrate on my work. This one short glimpse at the world from which I was banned awakened my old restlessness.

22 • The people from Wisnicz: A Bochnia memory

Our father was unique. Too young to appreciate his character, understand his brilliant mind, and evaluate his modesty, the four of us nevertheless agreed that he was the best, the wisest, the funniest, most intelligent, and kindest of all the people on the face of earth. One of my best Bochnia memories was an encounter with a stranger who reinforced that belief.

One day, as I was walking toward the soup kitchen, I heard rapid footsteps behind me. I turned my head and saw two young men who while overtaking me, stared at me for a moment.

"Yes. That's the Landerer girl," I heard one of them saying.

That unexpected identification left me annoyed. Why did they follow and gaze at me as if I were an apparition? From that day on, whenever I met one of these men, he stared at me, it was irritating, made me uneasy and it bewildered me. What had I done?

One day the puzzle was solved. That week I worked the midnight shift and was free during the day. As I walked alone one morning, I met and cornered him.

"Excuse me, but why do you follow and stare at me always? I find it embarrassing."

"Oh, no. No! Miss Landerer, I never intended to embarrass you. It is only that every time I see you, I remember you are the daughter of Wolf Landerer, and it makes me feel good."

My father's daughter! That made better sense. I felt flattered and relaxed.

189

"You must tell me who you are and from where do you know my father?"

"This is quite a long story."

"Doesn't matter. It is early, and I am not due at the gathering point for many hours. Even the kitchen is still closed. We have lots of time."

"This is a long, long story, dating still from before the war," the man began. And this is the story he told me:

He was from Wisnicz, a village near Bochnia. His father was a confidant of their rabbi, a man as poor as he was pious and learned, and one day the rabbi told the father something and swore him to secrecy. The young man thought no more about the incident until early in the war when, fleeing from their home, he and his father came under heavy bombardment. Then the father, fearful that he would be killed, confided the rabbi's secret.

He had found a wonderful husband for his daughter, a great treasure, a most promising scholar. He had had to promise a large dowry for the girl, and being a poor man, he did not have it. He had to hide his pride and go out into the world to ask merciful Jews to help him raise the money he needed. When he arrived in Krakow, the nearest big city, he was told to go first to Wolf Landerer.

"This was the first time our rabbi had had to beg for money from strangers," said the man from Wisnicz, "but it was not for himself. He had to think of his child and her future."

The rabbi found himself in front of a corner building, its gate wide open. (How well I knew that corner building and that familiar gate!) He entered the lobby and climbed to the first landing, where there was only one door. A copper plate on it was engraved "Landerer." With a heavy heart, he closed his eyes and pushed the button.

A tall gentle woman, wearing a white apron, answered the door and motioned to him to enter. (In my mind's eye I saw just what the rabbi saw when he stood in our hallway: a soft colorful carpet, a paneled wall painted white and interrupted by doors and mirrors, brass coat hangers on the wall. Jozia led him to Father's study, knocked softly, and then opened the door for him.)

Father was sitting at his big desk, his back to the window. He pulled up an armchair for the rabbi and urged him to be seated, and, sensing his uneasiness, asked, "From where comes the Jew?"

"From Wisnicz. I am the rabbi there."

"*Sholem aleichem!* What brings the rabbi to me?"

The rabbi started to stammer, and my father, to ease the situation, called for some tea. After a few refreshing sips, the poor man began to unwind and slowly poured out his story. When it was finished, my father said thoughtfully, "And how big a dowry do you need for this fabulous match?"

Now that the crux had been reached, the rabbi hesitated again. "A lot. An awful lot."

"Well, how much of what you need have you raised already?"

"Nothing," the rabbi admitted.

"How much do you need?"

"An enormous sum. May the Almighty have pity on me."

"How much is a lot"? my father persisted. (How patient he was, always! As the man from Wisnicz talked, it was Father's voice I heard instead.)

The rabbi closed his eyes. "Three hundred American dollars," he whispered. There was a long, long moment of silence; then, forcing himself, he opened his eyes.

Father was smiling at him. "I will give you the dowry money, on –"

"What!" cried the started rabbi, "All of it?"

"All of it," Father said, "on one condition."

"And – and what would this condition be?" the rabbi faltered.

"You must promise," my father said, smiling broadly, "you must give me your word that you will not tell about this to anyone."

"Not even my wife?"

"Not even your wife. This is my condition."

Overjoyed and overwhelmed, the rabbi gave his word and returned to Wisnicz with the money in his pocket. And he broke his promise only once: He told his confidant, who, thinking himself about to die, told his son.

"The rabbi told my father," continued the man from Wisnicz, "that there were people with more wealth than Wolf Landerer, more knowledge, more learning, but nowhere in the whole of Europe was there a man with a heart like his."

I nodded, but I couldn't say anything. There was a lump in my throat the size of a fist.

"But that's not the whole story, Miss Landerer. Listen to the sequel."

The man's father, the rabbi's confidant, nursed a secret longing to meet Wolf Landerer, but he didn't know how. The thought of journeying to the big city and boldly entering a rich man's home – that sent a shiver down his spine. But perhaps fate would intervane in some way known only to the Almighty.

And so it turned out. In 1939, as father and son fled with their horse and wagon from the advancing Germans, they reached a certain village, and as they were about to stop for the night, they overheard someone mention the name "Landerer." Excitedly, the man approached the gossipers and asked if they spoke of the Landerers from Krakow. Why, yes, they said. Wolf Landerer, his brother Haskel, and his two sons were in a neighboring village. The father's fatigue vanished, and he prodded the son to reharness the tired horse, so they could resume their journey before nightfall.

They reached the neighboring village in record time, but the dusk had arrived before them, the blackout was in effect, and the streets were empty of people. But the man was undeterred; he had come to meet the hero of his dreams, and he wasn't going to be put off by mere darkness. The two knocked at a farmhouse and asked where the refugees were staying. A peasant woman directed them to the Jewish street, and a little boy led them to where "the people who came two days ago" were staying.

It was a shabby, dilapidated house. The child knocked at the door and, without waiting for an answer, pushed it open. Father and son entered, almost tripping over the high threshold, and it was a few moments before their eyes became accustomed to the dimness. The room was almost bare of furniture. In the large brick oven, a fire was slowly dying. Along the wall was a bed, and in the bed, covered by a coat, a man was lying. "This is a refugee," said the child guide and then vanished.

The older man approached the bed. "Excuse me, sir, are you from Krakow?"

"Yes, why?"

"Because I am looking for somebody from Krakow. Very important man."

"For whom are you looking? Perhaps I could help."

192

"The man I am looking for is very prominent and wealthy. Did you ever hear the name 'Wolf Landerer'?"

"I did hear," replied the man on the bed. "I even know the man."

The two from Wisnicz looked at one another skeptically. How could this pauper have anything in common with the princely benefactor rabbi had described? "I don't think we talk about the same man," the older man said politely.

"There is only one Wolf Landerer in Krakow, and I know him well. Tell me why you need him."

The father was deeply downcast. Obviously the man he sought was not here after all. "I cannot tell you," he said woefully. "This is a highly personal matter. I have run my poor horse without pity in order to catch up with this Wolf Landerer, only to find out that he has left already. Just tell me where he went. I wouldn't mind riding the whole night." He turned to his son. "Feed and water the horse. We will travel to the next village."

"No!" cried the man on the bed. "Don't go out into the night. It is very dangerous for Jews. Besides – I am Wolf Landerer."

"Father's happiness is hard to describe," said the man from Wisnicz. "The man his rabbi had proclaimed the best of all was stretching out his hand to him, smilling and saying, *Sholem aleichem. Reb Yid.*"

Father and son spent that night in the little hut with Father. In the morning, Father bought another horse, and they harnessed the two of them to the wagon, and they stayed together until the end of their wanderings. The two fathers and Uncle Haskel rode in the wagon, the three sons walked.

"I did not mind giving up my place in the wagon," the narrator concluded his tale. "During that journey, I got to know your father well, and I can tell you – our rabbi was right: In the whole of Europe, there was no man with a heart like his."

After the war, I mentioned this story to Father and asked him about it. He brushed off his share in it lightly, the way he always did when someone wanted to talk about him. "Yes, yes, I remember those people from Wisnicz. Very fine people indeed. They were of great help to us on the road."

"Well, Daddy," I reminded him, "weren't you of help to them and their rabbi?"

Father became very serious. "Remember, my child," he said, "to be able to respond to people in distress and help those who come for help is the greatest privilege, a special grace from the Creator. And remember, too: Never talk about it."

That is the kind of man my father was. We don't see his like very often.

23 · Arbeitslager

The situation was deteriorating rapidly. Ghetto A disappeared from the map. In its place an *Arbeitslager* (work camp) was established in Bochnia. With the new name, came new restrictions and new authority – Commandant Miller, a member of the SS. Right from the beginning, he made clear that his powers over the Jews would be utilized to the fullest extent.

The large field behind the Judenrat was turned into an Appellplatz (area of military assembly), and it became his favorite playground. There, at a moment's notice, regardless of the time of day or night, we had to gather for "inspection." Those endless hours of mortification and helpless rage are impossible to forget and hurtful to remember.

People rushing from all over. Running, pushing, afraid to be late, scared to come early. Not knowing whether to head for the beginning of the line or the end of it. *Milicja* men everywhere. Shouting directions and orders. Bewildered people arranged according to their working units. Older people being shuffled down the lines to be camouflaged among the young and healthy-looking. All bound and united by their fear and hatred of the oppressor.

Thus we stood there, pathetic shadows of our former selves: housewives, mothers, husbands, fathers, doctors, tailors, students, scholars, and those who hardly could write their own names. All found guilty and sentenced to die for the crime of being born Jewish.

The illegals of the *Arbeitslager* the children and some old and infirm who somehow had managed to survive till then, but were not fit to be presented as working potential – were hidden in bunkers. Every building had a hiding place known only to the few who had to use it. Precious lives depended on total secrecy.

The first occasion is imprinted on my memory. The moment the *milicia* men stood at attention, a hush fell over the entire assembly. We knew that our new master, our absolute ruler was approaching, surrounded by his usual retinue: the commandant of the Jewish *milicia*, some lesser functionaries, and few of his assistants. Headed by Miller, the group proceeded leisurely till they reached a large clearing in front of the assembly. Then a loud voice barked, *"Lagerfuhrer! Achtung!"* [camp leader, attention!] and the whole frightened world stood at attention. He faced us, tallest of all, in an immaculate uniform, his boots polished to a high gloss, his collar adorned by the dreaded concentration camp emblem, the skull and crossbones that identified a Death's Head Unit man. With his tall neck, supporting a small, well-proportioned head, Miller was an example of a pure Aryan specimen. His right hand held a whip, the left rested in his pocket. From under the visor of his cap, piercing eyes scanned the scene. One foot resting on a large stone, he leaned forward, trying to get a closer look at the people assembled. Well-fed, tall, strong, handsome in a satanic way, he was a real Prince of Darkness.

Cowed by this display of brutal power, we were kept standing there for hours. A list of names was read aloud by one of the assistants, and everybody, as his name was called, had to step forward and pass in front of Miller for inspection. My name was called, and I went by without incident, as did Mother, but not everyone was that lucky. Miller liked to amuse himself by checking to see if some of the women did wear wigs under their head kerchiefs, or if a man was wearing a religious vestment under his shirt (a crime). He never dirtied his hands by touching one of us, the untouchables. He used his whip to poke and pry.

After that initial acquaintance, Miller went on to make our lives as miserable as possible. His actions were unpredictable. He used to enter our compound at all hours, take leisurely walks and inspect houses and apartments. The few remaining children were trained to run into hiding at the sound of the word *"Lagerfuhrer!"* Lusia had a little sister, Marysia, whom we trained to crawl under the bed at the sound of this feared word and remain there till her mother or sister pulled her out. Fear made Jewish children old before they could be weaned.

We were made to stand attention at the *Appellplatz* many times. Miller walked between the rows, his dreaded whip dancing over our heads, propping up the chin of a head bowed low or lowering one held high. I remember the silent prayer on my lips: Please God, make the earth open and swallow me! After being dismissed, it was back to the Baudienst, to the crowded room, again and again, for how long? Nobody dared to guess.

Even the biggest optimists among us had to face reality. Miller's arrival was a harbinger of worse to come. Rumors begun to circulate, each one bringing more dread to our hearts. Through the underground grapevine we heard about a miracle ghetto in Theresienstadt, Czeckoslovakia. The rumor had it that it was under the auspices of the International Red Cross. Supposedly the school, the symphony orchestra, the theatre were all organized and run by camp inmates. The general consensus in Bochnia was that the luckies in Theresienstadt were sure to survive. For a few intoxicating days things seemed quite simple. We had only to reach this miracle place and the rest would take care of itself! But no one in Bochnia had ever heard of that town, and when we tried to find it on the map, all we saw was the unpassable Carpathian massif dividing Poland from Czechoslovakia. Sadly, we gave up hope of reaching the miracle place.

After the war, we learned the truth. Theresienstadt (now called Terezin) was, indeed, the showplace of concentration camps, the only camp that representatives of the IRC were allowed to see. But it was reserved for "privileged" Jews: the extremely wealthy, German Jews with distinguished war records, prominent functionaries. And even these special categories were not immune to "thinning out" when the facility became overcrowded – shipped off to Auschwitz like ordinary, garden-variety Jews. When I visited Theresienstadt in 1977 and saw the impenetrable fortress that was the concentration camp, I realized what foolish dreamers we Bochnians had been.

The summer of 1943 was almost over when our depleted emotional resources received a severe blow, that shook up the entire ghetto like an explosion. The family of Leser Landau, the most influential go-between of the Jewish community with the Gestapo, had escaped to Hungary, at that time a relatively safe place for Jews to take refuge. (Hungary was an ally of Germany and had not yet been invaded and occupied; its government confiscated Jewish property and imposed harsh working restrictions on Jews, but it still permitted them to live.) The news that they reached Budapest shattered all hopes. Landau had connections with the highest echelons at Gestapo headquarters in Krakow and was always the first to be informed about upcoming Actions; now who would warn us? A few days after the Landau family escape, the Grand Rabbi from Belz (now a town in the U.S.S.R.), together with his brother, the Bilgorajer Rabbi, were quietly whisked out of the compound, and next it was heard that they, too, were safe in Hungary. The two brothers had large followings in eastern Europe, and their disciples in Hungary had arranged and financed their escape. But the Grand Rabbi from Czhow, whom his Hassidim wanted to save, refused to leave, saying that he considered himself a shepherd whose place was with his sheep.

Outside the *Arbeitslager*, a few Jewish families with foreign passports were permitted to live and enjoy some privileges. Some of them used to sneak into our work place and bring the latest news. As time went by, fewer and fewer came. They were "going to Hungary." Again people began to whisper about "contacts," addresses of smugglers, but everything cost money and our funds were almost dried up. A few weeks before when serious rumors about an impending Action were being spread, Mother, according to her credo that one should always have cash ready for emergencies, sold her last diamond. This was a real gem, one carat blue-white, flawless stone, last remnant of a necklace her proud husband had bought her after their first child was born. It brought two hundred dollars, which she divided evenly between Uncle Josef and herself. So, when the time finally came that we might have a chance of escape, all Mother and I had between us was one hundred dollars, and a few towels and pillowcases in the bottom of the suitcase. Budapest shimmered in our dreams like a Fata Morgana that could be materialized only with money.

And then salvation appeared from a totally unexpected source!

How does it feel to be on the high seas during a violent storm and see panicky rats running from one deck to another? Whoever was in Bochnia during the summer of 1943 knows that feeling too well.

While being lined up in front of the compound gate to be marched out to work, I often noticed that one or two of my coworkers did not come. Somehow, every few days one person or another left the compound unnoticed. Jewish officials, although responsible for us, the prisoners, who were supposed to work and be productive till the moment when we were not needed anymore, closed their eyes to these disappearances. I was envious of everyone who left – and at the same time very frightened.

Every imaginable route of escape was being tried, but the number of inmates remained about the same. Many people returned. Discouraged by the hardships of living under false identities among a hostile population or the difficulty of remaining in hiding for a prolonged stay, they stole back into the compound. Having lost hope of "making it" among the Poles, they cast their lot once more with the rest of the Jews.

And then someone living beyond the wall received a letter from a family that had quietly slipped out of the ghetto two weeks before. While sitting in an open-air coffeehouse in Budapest and waiting for their daughters to return from a movie – a coffeehouse! a movie! – they write this letter. Miracles were still possible!

Lusia and I could not stop talking about it. We had known the Selinger sisters well. Through their miraculous escape, our dream acquired the dimensions of reality.

"Could you imagine? People sitting in coffeehouses? Girls going to movies? We must, Lala, we must!"

"What is it we must? Lusia, don't be foolish!"

"Come on! Do you want me to believe that you are the only person in Bochnia immune to 'Hungarian Fever'?"

"No, Lusia. Not at all. I think and dream of nothing but escape. But we are too poor to afford it. Why should I fool myself?"

"I'm sorry. I did not realize that the Landerer treasury was so badly depleted."

"Practically nonexistent."

"Not even for this one trip?"

"Not even for one bribe of one ghetto guard."

One of the people with foreign passports living outside the compound was a woman from Myslenice, hometown of my mother's family. Her name was Ilona Goldman. During the war she married a refugee from Austria. Emboldened by the authenticity of her documents and driven by an inner need to help people, Ilona traveled between different towns, bringing news and helping in any way she could.

She was an unusual woman. Those were bitter days. Even close relatives and friends hid information from each other, fearing that

199

someone else might get there first and steal the chance for escape. In Ghetto Bochnia it was dog-eat-dog and every-man-for-himself.

One day Ilona approached my uncle and told him that she was operating a rescue mission and our family was her priority.

"What do you think about it, Hacia?" Josef asked Mother.

"She probably is convinced that we have the necessary funds."

"Probably," Josef said. "But I will try to talk to her."

The Schiffs were planning their escape with Ilona. As we lived in the same room, they could not hide it from us. But they had a major obstacle. Their old, infirm father could not be considered a candidate for this strenuous, dangerous trip. In addition to his bad health, he, like many of the Hassidim, did not speak correct Polish and thus could not be dressed up as a peasant and put on a train for the border. The question what to do with Father was constantly on their minds.

My mother was always at her best in a crisis. This time she found one solution to two problems. She offered to take care of the old gentleman and remain with him till the end if the Schiffs would take me without payment. Overjoyed, they agreed to the deal.

Mother was ready to put into practice the principle: Give those who are most saveable the best chance. I was the youngest of four children and always Father's favorite. Somehow, she felt that, if I could be saved, this would ease the pain of his other losses. To her brother she said: "Only one of us can go. Lala is young, therefore she has priority. At least there will be somebody to tell Wolf that we did not suffer hunger."

The following day, Ilona came to the Baudienst, where Schiff and Josef worked. When told about Mother's deal, she simply said, "Lala will go on 'my road' without payment."

Astonished and grateful, Josef said eagerly, "You know my brother-in-law." "He will come back after the war, and he will compensate you a hundred times over for what you do for his daughter."

Ilona literally jumped up. "Compensate me? You are insulting me, Mr. Horowitz! It is I who must compensate – for the friendship and support your family has always given me. Please, don't you ever, ever talk to me about payment. On 'my road' Lala will go, and your sister, your wife, your daughter, you, and the boys as well."

To be able to appreciate and understand fully the selflessness of this great lady and the grandeur of such a gesture, you would have had to live in Poland during those tragic days. There were still people in Bochnia who would have showered her with money and jewels for that chance to escape. But Ilona would not think of it. She considered herself a friend of the Horowitz and Landerer families. Her action raised the concept of friendship to heights very few people would ever be able to understand, even less to attain.

Ilona Goldman restored our hope and faith in people. What a pity that the liquidation of Arbeitslager Bochnia cut her plans short. After Mother left, Aunt Bala and her daughter were getting ready to leave next, but they never made it, not even to Ilona's house. The day before they were supposed to leave, the ghetto was surrounded by the SS. The Horowitzes, together with other able-bodied workers, were rounded up and shipped to Czebno. Mr. Schiff, the old father whom the children could not leave behind, was killed on the first day of the Action.

But to my mother and me Ilona gave the gift of life.

24 • Joseph and Szaye Horowitz

Before I tell you about our escape, I have to tell you a little about some of those who did not get to go on Ilona's road.

There was Uncle Josef and Aunt Bala and their family, to begin with. The major force in the life of my mother's oldest brother was love combined with religious faith. Boundless devotion to his family, affinity for people, and a gift for friendship endeared Uncle Josef to everyone.

His love and faith in the Creator knew no bounds. The sheer force of his simple way of thinking, deeply rooted in religion and tradition left an enduring impress on all who knew this unique man. His reaction to the tragic events during the war and the many conversations we had helped me to understand the guiding principles of his faith. He believed that the infinity of God and justification of His ways are beyond understanding of the finite human mind. Only through an absolute affirmation of God as the Supreme Being, Goodness, Justice, and Love, and in gratitude for Creation, is a human being capable of loving God. This is religious faith in its purest, moral height at its tallest, and a lifelong discipline.

The harder and more unbearable life became, the more he clung to his faith. His only response to the brutal anti-Jewish laws was "Praised be the Lord." Neither horrors nor hardships could defeat his gentle yet indomitable soul. All that happened was for him a part of an eternal, logical, impenetrable but undoubtedly just plan. The steadfastness of his belief could be compared to those of Biblical heroes: the patriarch Abraham, who did not flinch when told to sacrifice his only son, Isaak, and his namesake Joseph, whose religious principles remained unshaken, whether at the bottom of the snake pit or at the pinnacle of power as the viceroy of Egypt.

After the liquidation of Arbeitslager Bochnia, as I've said, all able-bodied inmates were deported to Camp Czebno, where they had a foretaste of things to come. Inmates were permitted to meet once a day after work for ten minutes only. Ironically, this was called the rendezvous.

My friend Lusia and her mother were in the women's camp. During the liquidation of Bochnia, she witnessed the cold-blooded execution of all children, among them her little sister Esther-Marysia, who had been so carefully trained to hide under the bed. Lusia, knowing that her mother's age would automatically disqualify her during the next selection, became despondent. The only thing that helped her to get through every day was the "rendezvous" with Uncle Josef. Every day he took off a few precious moments from the time he was allowed with his wife and daughter.

"Miss Lusia, you must not give up hope! You must not despair! God is merciful. We cannot understand His ways, but we must trust Him and love Him because we are his children. We may not abandon our faith because salvation is sure to come. We may not doubt God!"

The daily dose of moral support restored the girl's faltering spirit. While in the cattle train being transported to Auschwitz, Lusia escaped, reached safety, and survived, thus bearing witness to the invincibility of human spirit and faith.

I can visualize my uncle at the barbed wire. Dressed in a prisoner's stripped garb, deprived of human dignity, stripped of everything, hungry and cold, he acquires legendary dimensions. Well aware that every moment of the short reunion with his wife and daughter could be their last time together, he shares his faith with a desperate girl.

In the pit of despair and injustice, in the wasteland of depravity and brutality, this man was capable of embodying the ideal of the Man of Faith as portrayed in the Bible. Josef, the son of Naftali Ish Horowitz, has proved that unconditional faith and the seemingly unattainable steadfastness of the Patriarch Abraham and Joseph Hatzadik is not a parable, but an ideal to be strived for at any time and any place.

From Czebno, the inmates were shipped to Auschwitz, where they remained until January 1945. Even there Josef did not miss one

Shabbat or holiday's prayers and rituals, camouflaging them so that he could not be found out by the Capos. Not once during the entire period of his incarceration, which lasted from the fall of 1943 till June 1945, did Josef fail to recite the Kabalath Shabbat liturgy from memory. No matter how skimpy the daily bread ration and how violent the hunger that tore at his innards, a part of the daily bread ration was always set aside for a Sabbath meal so he would be able to pronounce the benediction over bread and, after swallowing his few crumbs of stale bread, to say grace after the meal.

During the holiday of Sukkoth, a corner of the barrack was declared sukkah proper. Some of the meager leftovers were exchanged for a few raisins provided by a corrupt guard. (Yes, there was black market in every concentration camp.) The raisins were soaked in a jar of water, and thus kosher "wine" was obtained, and the prisoners could fulfill the obligation of saying the blessing over wine in the sukkah, just under the noses of the most cruel SS guards in Auschwitz.

One of my most moving memories from the time of the war was something told to me by my cousin Aron, Josef's son.

It was January 1945. The end of the war was near. The Russians were approaching Auschwitz. The retreating Germans were emptying the concentration camps of people, thus hoping to remove traces of their atrocities. The remains of the emaciated slave workers were forced on the infamous death marches. Pushed and kicked by their bestial captors, they shuffled along on their swollen feet with the remains of their strength.

It was on a Friday night that the prisoners of Auschwitz were gathered on the *Appellplatz* and ordered to march. Arrayed in formations of six abreast, the men set out in the dark, bitterly cold night. Josef tried to keep pace with his sons so they would not become separated. Walking with difficulty, he softly hummed the part of Friday night's liturgy, *Shalom Alelchem Malachei Shalom.*

"I could not believe my ears," Aron said, "but my steps adjusted to the rhythm, and my lips automatically mouthed the words. I felt angry. I could not understand how my father could think about Friday night's *zmirot* while we were in the death march. I was young and bitter. We hoped for a different ending, and Father's holding on to the religious ritual seemed ridiculous. Only now, after I have passed Father's age at that time, am I able to appreciate the depth of his faith and moral strength. My father," Aron concluded, "attained the *medrega* [level] of spirituality possible only to a chosen few."

From Auschwitz they were marched to Gleiwitz (Gliwice). It was a brutally cold evening when the decimated column entered the grounds of this latest concentration camp. During the tedious march Josef's younger son, Moshe, was pushed into another column and disappeared into the night. Josef and his oldest son, Aron, were directed into a crowded barrack. Josef, an old man before his time, sat on an empty cot, his back hunched, lips cracked from cold, the unshaven bristle of his beard underlining his hollow cheekbones, frostbitten hands propping the weary head. Numb from hunger and fatigue, he stared into space.

The barrack was dark and crowded, and it was hard to recognize people. Many of the inmates, too weak to sit, were lying on their bunks, while most of the newcomers, exhausted from the gruelling twenty-four-hour-long march from Auschwitz, sat on the floor. No one spoke. The only sounds heard were those of feet shuffling on the floor, a sigh or an occasional sob. The air in the unheated barrack was heavy with the smell of unwashed bodies and breath from hungry mouths. Aron, wanting to comfort his father, put his hand on his shoulder, but the stiff body did not respond to the gentle caress. The son withdrew his hand. A little speech had already been prepared: "As long as we're together . . ." But the reality was more than the young man could face. All he felt was rage and despair, and he stepped outside.

The wartime blackout was being strictly observed, and in the prevailing darkness the camp appeared deserted. After a while his eyes got used to it, and he recognized human forms moving slowly. At the far corner of the barrack a man was leaning against the wall. Prison clothes hung loosely over a bony body, and he was swaying slowly, as if in prayer. There was a certain familiarity in the quivering skeleton, and as Aron moved closer, he begun to shiver. Blinding tears welling up in his eyes, he cried out in joy and disbelief: "Szaye! Uncle Szaye!"

Szaye Horowtiz, the youngest of my mother's eight brothers, had always led a charmed existence. Life seemed to smile at him always. I knew him well, because once he spent a whole summer with us in Rabka. He had a great facility with words and used to entertain his little nieces with funny improvisations, brought us little gifts from the bazaar, and treated us as persons. A nicer uncle would be hard to imagine.

As kind Providence willed it, that very summer one of the wealthiest families in the county rented a villa close to ours: the Klagsbalds from Chrzanow. They had a daughter, Rozia, who, besides being a great beauty, was one of the sweetest creatures imaginable. In spite of their strict upbringing and the watchful eyes of Rozia's mother and Szaye's sisters and all his nephews and nieces, the youngsters managed to communicate, and a deep affection developed between them. Rozia's father was a disciple of the Koloszycer Grand Rabbi, as was Szaye's father and all his brothers, so it was a desirable match all around, but despite that, it would have been unthought of to permit the youngsters to meet and decide their own fate. A renowned matchmaker was called in, and the match was arranged to the delight of both families and with the blessing of the revered rabbi. Tradition and decorum were preserved and respected.

Szaye Horowitz and Rozia Klagsbald were married in 1934. The radiant bride wore a wedding gown from Vienna, and with the handsome groom at her side, they appeared to be the luckiest couple in the world. They had youth, health, beauty, love, wealth, success, and when a year after their wedding Rozia gave birth to a boy, their happiness was boundless.

Little Avigdor, named after Rozia's grandfather, was called Vigdus. The little boy was exquisite. He resembled his mother in looks and charm. Not only the family, but the entire Jewish community in Chrzanow adored him. A few months before the war, Rozia gave birth to another boy, Naftall, named after Szaye's father.

Everything seemed to be going their way. The in-laws established Szaye in a factory of chemical products, which prospered greatly. Their summers were spent in spas winter vacations in Zakopane, in the Polish Tatra Mountains. Rozia's beauty and elegance attracted attention even in the famed resort Marienbad (now Marianske-Lazne near the German-Czech border). Theirs was a fairy tale marriage.

Aron was stunned. Could this be his handsome, elegant uncle?

"Who are you?" asked the living skeleton.

"Uncle Szaye, I am Aron."

"Aron? Aron who?"

206

"Arek, Josele's Arek!"

"Arek!" It sounded like a wail. "Arek, I bought *shihaloch* [little shoes] for my Vigdus – a day before they took him away."

"Uncle Szaye, wait. I will get my father."

Disfigured by their sufferings and deprivations, broken in body and spirit, the two brothers met. They clung to each other with despair that could not be put into words.

"Szayele 'my breederl' [my little brother] Szayele."

"Yosele, I bought new *shishihaloch* for my Vigdus. One day before they took him."

Next morning the body of a prisoner, formerly Szaye Horowitz from Chrzanow, was removed from the barrack. He was thirty five years old.

Josef, the oldest, the last of the Horowitz brothers, was sent from Gleiwitz to Theresienstadt, where he was liberated by the Russians. A few days later he fell ill with typhus. His emaciated body could not fight the infection.

In the middle of June 1945, Josef's pure soul returned to his Creator. He was buried in a mass grave in the cemetary of Theresienstadt martyrs. At the time of his death he was fifty three years old.

25 · On Ilona's road

On Ilona's "road to Hungary" people were smuggled over the border in small groups of three or four. Next on her agenda was a group of three: Syma Schiff, her brother Tuvia, and I. Full of excitement and hope mixed with fear, I had to act as if nothing unusual was going on.

My mother and uncle tried to spend with me as much time as possible. My forthcoming trip was not to be a pampered, sheltered daughter's journey to one of the most glamorous capitals in Europe but a dangerous foray into a savagely hostile world. Today, a mother myself, I can appreciate the extent of the despair and anguish they hid from me. Even now, living in the free United States, I worry when someone from my household does not come home on time. During the war Jewish parents in Europe could not indulge in the luxury of acting out the most basic feelings. They had to encourage their children to engage in the most risky undertakings, hoping against all odds that they would survive. No statistics are availlable on the percentage of successful escapes. From our small group of three, I was the only one to reach safety at the end.

Only eighteen years old I had already learned that the only irreplaceable things in life were people and their love. Material possessions had no meaning, except for what food and clothing they could buy. In Bochnia, where a few changes of clothing made up the sum total of my estate, this philosophy was easy to practice. The one object I could not part with was a book of poems. One well-worn volume of the collected poems by Julian Tuwim, circulating among my friends, was lent to me for one afternoon. I memorized all my favorite verses. Poetry was the antidote against depression, hopelessness, and fear, and a safe luggage to carry over the border. I still remember the first stanza from my favorite poem "The Dancing Sokrates."

It was end of August 1943. The great day arrived. The three of us worked the day shift, came back with our groups, ate in the soup kitchen, and lingered outside with our friends. Once inside we waited for the children to be put to sleep – an unnecessary precaution, since the little ones understood not to talk about what went on in their homes. We had just changed into our "outside" clothing when a trusted *milicja* man came and led us, the two girls, out through a secret opening in the fence. There, hidden in the shadow, a guide was waiting for us. We followed him to Ilona's house.

This indomitable woman received us as if we were guests coming to a party. Tuvia, who had come from the men's part of the ghetto, was there already and overjoyed to see us. The first step of our flight had been accomplished. The fence was left behind but not the risks and dangers. Ilona's delighted welcome had a balming influence on our mood. For harbouring us she was risking confiscation of her documents, imprisonment, or execution on the spot. But her courage and good mood were contagious.

We all sat around the table set for supper. We three escapees did not feel like eating, but the smugglers devoured the tasty food Ilona's mother had prepared for us. As they gobbled they gave us instructions: Our goal was to reach Piwniczna, a village on the Czechoslovak-Polish border. We would be going to Piwniczna by train and would have to change trains in Tarnow. The most frightening part of it was that there would be a two-hour wait in Tarnow. I forced myself not to think about that. My courage and determination were fed by the exhilaration that I was "going to Hungary." It meant that I was going to live!

Our smugglers, Jasiek and Kasia, were two young natives of Piwniczna. It was the first time in their lives that they had ventured out of the backwoods as far as the "metropolis" of Bochnia. Supposedly they were to be trusted. Anyhow, what were the other odds? Either a bullet or transport to a place of no return.

They handed us our train tickets, and we rehearsed the instructions. Under no circumstances were we to come near them – at any time. Each one of us was to go separately and board a different car. When the train reached Tarnow we would get off and follow our guides into the waiting room. In case we lost them, we would have to find the waiting room by ourselves. Once there, each one would sit alone. We must watch our guides inconspicuously, because when time came to board the train to Piwniczna, they would leave the waiting room without even one look at us. In order that we should not appear to be a group, we would have to follow one by one – but not too close together. It should be understood that under no circumstances would they approach any of us or give signals or look for us. Should anyone find himself lost, he would have to be responsible for himself. Should the plan go awry at any point, they would deny ever having seen any of us before.

It was time to go. Jasiek was the first to leave, followed by Tuvia, then Kasia, then Syma, with me closing up the rear. The train depot was not far from Ilona's house. Bochnia is a small town, and everything is close by. It was dark when we handed our tickets to the attendant, who checked them by a flashlight. The station was crowded, and it took a lot of cunning not to lose sight of the smugglers without following them closely. People resembled shadows. When the train arrived, silent shadows descended while others pushed into the crowded train.

Anxious not to be left behind and at the same time wishing to be invisible, I squeezed my frame into the gray mass and was propelled by other bodies into the crowded car. There was standing room only, hardly any room to move. Once the heavy door closed, a strange kind of conviviality developed, possible only among strangers. People talked, joked, exchanged risky information about war news and the availability of black market items. Outside they were voiceless shadows; in the train they became shadowless voices.

The train glided into motion. Someone started to play a little mouth organ, and several voices picked up the melody; soon half the car's occupants were humming patriotic Polish songs – spiritual contraband. The sounds of the moving train and the soft singing of the familiar tunes of my youth took my mind off my precarious situation. A sudden stop shook the train, and we almost fell over one another. It was an insignificant station. A peasant woman with a large basket on her back boarded the train and crowded us even more.

Gradually uneasiness was taking hold of me. The man on my right lighted a cigarette, and for a split second the treacherous match light slid over my face. Instinctively I tried to cover my eyes, but my arm was imprisoned among pressing bodies. By the time I freed it, the train was rolling at full speed. The harmonica player left and with him the comradely spirit that for a few magic moments had enveloped us all. Suddenly the tall shadow with the matches leaned close to my ear and softly hummed the first measures of Hatikvah, the Jewish national anthem.

It took all of my self-control to remain calm. He was already standing erect and looked away. Who could it have been? An informer, a Jew hunter not very sure of his prey in the dark? Another fugitive trying to communicate? All I saw was a shadow among shadows. Was I dreaming or hallucinating? I tried to swallow, but my mouth was dry and throat tight. Only the stale air passed through with a whizz. An unexpected stop shook the train, and I fell. By the time I was back on my feet, more people squeezed into the tight space. The train begun to move again, now at a slower pace than before. People trying to find their belongings were stirring and groping in the dark. Act One of our escape drama was coming to an end.

"Tarnow! Tarnow! Tarnow!" The shouts of the stationmaster brought back old horrors. I was back in the one place on earth that I never wanted to see again. I had to find my guide without looking for her. To my relief it turned out that we had all traveled in the same car but in different compartments. Pushing to get out, I collided with Kasia, and this surprise made me drop my pocketbook. She picked it up and with a straight face said: "Panienka [miss], this is yours." The instructions we received at Ilona's forbade any encounters, so, suspecting that she might have been testing me, I nodded my head politely. The awareness that Kasia had kept close to me was reassuring, and I followed her. Syma trotted after Jasiek into the waiting room, filled wall-to-wall with sleepy people. All benches along the walls were occupied. In the middle of the large room. oblivious to the noise, dirt, and smoke, a group of weary travelers was bivouacking.

Our two-hour wait for the train to Piwniczna had begun. As we entered, a few people left, freeing some spaces on the crowded benches. I saw Kasia sit down, and I turned to a bench on the opposite side of the waiting room. In the middle sat a lonely nun, holding a rosary in her hand. I approached her and asked if I could sit with her. She just gathered the folds of her habit and made room for me.

I had hardly sat down when I saw Jasiek, who had left the room after his companion had settled down, returning, going over to Kasia, bending over, and whispering into her ear. When he finished, she got up, crossed over the hall to me, bent over, and whispered to my ear: "They took him." "Him" was Tuvia. Then she turned on her heel and returned to Jasiek, huddled close to him, leaned her head on his shoulder, and fell asleep.

Panic and despair blinded me for a moment. Anyone who had lived in Tarnow for a year and a half knew too well who "they" were and what to expect next for poor Tuvia. I wanted to run, to cry, to cuddle up to my mother, my father, to pray to my God – but in that room full of strangers, I was all alone with my fear and despair. There was no one and no place to turn for help. I could not look for Syma. Did she know what had happened? I did not think they had informed her. For some reason Kasia thought it necessary to break the self-imposed rules and inform me of the disaster. Gradually my survival instinct and self-control began to take over. I was well-disciplined. Three years under German occupation had taught me how to behave in moments of danger. The slightest sign of fear might have given me out. At that moment my life depended solely upon myself. Poor, poor Tuvia flashed through my mind, but I forced it out. Sorrow and pity would have to wait.

Tuvia Schiff had gambled his life and lost it. How happy he had been to see me walking into Ilona's house! How he had hoped that together the three of us would walk to freedom and life. And now his life has already ended. Had it? Was he killed on the spot or was he now in "their" hands? If "they" torture him, would he be able to stick to his story that he was alone? Wouldn't he tell about the escape route? Did he tell "them" about us?

My heart was pounding so hard that I feared that those seated close to me might hear it. Trying to evaluate the situation while pretending to be just another passenger waiting for the train, I turned around and looked at the nun. She was a motherly-looking middle-aged woman, and we started talking. She offered me some of her food which I politely declined. "My God," I prayed without words, "let me just hold down what I ate before." I felt nauseated. A bitter taste was in my mouth and a dull pain in my stomach, but the woman's kindness had a calming effect on me. Her plain face had a honest look; it inspired confidence and gave focus to my eyes. I did not dare to look around and didn't dare check to see if Syma or even the smugglers were still there. Huddled up to the nun, I talked to her as to an old acquaintance, when suddenly I begun to sense an almost tangible tension. The room had become disquietingly still. As I looked up, fear – fear like I never knew existed – gripped me. A group of Gestapo men had entered the waiting room and was slowly approaching the people on the benches.

My first reflex was to run out, under an approaching train, into the dark night, anything rather than fall into their clutches. But fear immobilized me, if for a moment only my toes and fingers seemed to have turned into icicles. But my brain was in hot pursuit of clear thought. The Gestapo men had begun from the other side. Walking slowly, they examined every face as if they were searching for some particular person. From my seat I recognized a couple of them. If they spotted me, too, this would be the end of my trip. Before I could clarify my thoughts, instinct made me turn and ask, "Sister, I am sleepy. Could I lean on you and doze off till my train comes?"

"Certainly, child."

I bent toward her and put my head on her lap, and she raised part of her long habit and pulled it over my head. I closed my eyes and waited, praying: "God, please, don't let them see me. If they do, this might be the end of the escape route. They would figure out Jews are escaping from Bochnia and trying to get to the border. And then there will be no one to tell Father that we did not suffer hunger."

On my back I felt the nun's hands fingering the rosary in slow motion. I wanted badly to stuff my fingers into my ears in order not to hear the approaching steps, but was afraid to move. The sounds were getting louder, and I knew that they were coming toward us. Then they abruptly stopped.

"*Legitimation* [identification papers]" thundered above my head.

The nun remained motionless, except for the rosary slipping through her steady fingers. I realized that the person next to us was being checked out. Oh my God, they're checking the documents! Mine were good only as long as no one attempted to verify them. Please God, please ...

Loud footsteps passed me by. The man next to me was the last to undergo the control of his documents. As slowly and leisurely as they entered before, they left.

For a while I was afraid to raise my head, but my guardian angel –

because this was who she must have been — took the cover off my head. Smiling a serene, happy smile, she said, "You slept soundly. They checked some papers, but, God be blessed, nobody was taken away."

At the same moment Kasia got up and started to walk to the exit. I scrambled hastily to my feet. "My train has arrived. I must run. God bless you, sister!"

"God bless you, child!"

The fast moving crowd made following Kasia easy. When I saw her climbing into one car, I boarded the next. I didn't dare to look for Syma. It was only Kasia and I, against the alienated world.

The train left the station fully packed. As it neared the border, people began getting off. A few single passengers got on, and soon I found a vacant place. Seated among strangers, I felt a strange kinship with the whole human race — but the bliss did not last long. At every stop of the dragging train, travelers left, until only I and a man remained in deserted compartment. All the time he sat quietly, apparently dozing, but as soon as we remained alone he became fully awake and started conversation.

"And to where is Panienka going?"

"To Piwniczna."

The words hardly left my mouth when, realizing my blunder, I almost burst out crying. I had given myself out to this stranger! He might have been a secret policeman or a Jew hunter, one of many swarming over every possible route of escape.

"And why is a beautiful young miss traveling alone at night?"

There was no way out, and I had to improvise: "My mother got sick, and I am going to take care of her."

"Mother is vacationing in Piwniczna?"

"Yes. Have you ever been there?"

"Many times. I know Piwniczna very well."

"Nice place."

"Beautiful. I would go with you, but I have some very important business to attend."

"What a pity," I said, while thanking my lucky star for whatever it was that made him busy.

That a young girl traveling alone at night might have been vulnerable was a risk that had to be undertaken. There was no other way of reaching Piwniczna, unless by car, and even so the highways, especially those leading to strategic points, were heavily patrolled by the military police.

I was tired of the man's company already, who turned out to be homicidally talkative.

"You know what?" he went on. "You should get off with me. I live close to the Slovak border. Jews are running away to Slovakia all the time."

"Are they?" was all I could manage.

"All the time smugglers take them out and bring back silk stockings. If you get off with me, I will get you beautiful stockings . . ." and on and on he went with this ridiculous talk and amorous advances.

I didn't know what to do. Afraid to call the conductor lest I attract attention, or to leave the compartment in case he might follow me, I was getting desperate. As it turned out, he did not recognize the hated Jew in me; he was just trying to impress a girl. As the train approached his town, he began to collect his belongings, all the time talking nonstop. Realizing that he would be leaving, I regained my nerve.

You know, you really are a very nice gentleman," I said boldly. "If you would give me your address, I could visit you on my way back."

This propelled him out faster than he intended – and I had hoped for. I locked the door of the empty compartment, stretched my legs, and took a deep breath. My lids were closing, but this night was not meant for sleeping. The town was insignificant, but the railway crossing was an important one and the train was stopping there for thirty minutes.

I was getting apprehensive. What if my CAVALIER went to the police to denounce me? Maybe he could even get a price for my head? In many towns, in order to encourage and reinforce patriotism – strongly tied in many Polish minds to Jew hatred – rewards were being offered for every Jew found outside ghetto or camp. If he alerted police that an escaping Jewess was on this train, then all exits from the station would be blocked off. I couldn't even get off this train unnoticed.

If only I had the invisible hat of my childhood's fairy tales! In those tales Death was always portrayed as a tall skeleton in flowing black robes, holding a long scythe. Alone in the train, somewhere in the

215

south of Poland, I fully believed that this stocky man in a nondescript suit, carrying a small ordinary suitcase, would be my Death.

Dejected and discouraged I sat in the lonely compartment, for the first time resigned to my fate. There was no way out for me. I heard heavy footsteps and loud commands in German, but those were only my strained nerves and imagination. Nothing unusual was disturbing the slow, muted sounds of a deserted provincial train depot. A slight knock at the window shook me out of my stupor. I raised my head and looked out, and there, in front of my compartment window, stood my Lothario, comically stretching his short neck.

"Irenka, Miss Irenka! Have a nice trip! I hope your mother feels well."

"I hope so too. Thank you!"

The train started to move. I remained standing at the window till the lonely figure of a man disappeared completely.

The train was gaining speed. The night's shadows were dissolving in the light of the approaching dawn. I was getting ready for the next hurdle and could not permit myself to think about Tuvia or whether Syma was on the train or how trustworthy Kasia was. I had to remain calm, composed, not ask questions, and hope that nobody asked any of me.

Nestled at the feet of the imposing Carpathian Mountains lies Piwniczna, the first in a chain of mountain spas. During the summers, when the mineral waters and mud attracted guests from all over, the village came to life. Summer guests were the mainstay of its economy. Otherwise the farmers eked out a modest living from the meager mountain soil. The most important employer was the sawmill, owned by Ablosers, one of the few Jewish families in the village. Because of the sawmill, the train made two stops at Piwniczna. As I remembered from summers I had spent there, the train halted at the spa station for exactly three minutes. Just enough for the vacationers to disembark and the wheels to get rolling again. The major stop was a few miles further on, where freight cars loaded with tree logs waited to be attached to the train.

Reluctant to face memories of my idyilic summers of not long ago, I turned my back to the window, at the same time reflecting how cruelly ironic the destiny of my generation was. A welcome summer guest returning four years later as a most wanted fugitive!

216

Before emotions and fatigue took over, the train halted. The door was opened. I was the only one to get off my car. Going toward the exit, I noticed the rails leading from the sawmill to the station overgrown with grass and weeds. At the door, a sleepy controller took my ticket without one glance at me.

I stepped out into the dirt road, the village's main street. Facing me was the once imposing structure of the sawmill, now idle and desolate. Only large letters spelling the owners' name stood out on the white-washed wall. I looked up. Ahead of me Kasia was marching briskly, followed by Syma. I breathed with relief. Thank God! We were in Piwniczna!

26 · Over the border

It was five in the morning as we walked through the village, which had just begun to stir from its sleep. A familiar landscape met my eyes: Piwniczna, where we had spent two wonderful summers. Clouds of morning mist hung over the bright green meadows. On the river bank gracefully bent weeping willows touched the water with the tips of their narrow, pointed leaves. I used to play hide-and-seek among the tall reeds and bushy grasses and make garlands and bouquets of field flowers. Did I really? Was there ever life without that gnawing fear, was there ever time for carefree play?

Kasia turned into a path leading uphill. A little distance from the road, a hut was hidden in a large garden. The gate was not bolted, and we slid between the flower beds and entered the house. Syma, who had preceded me by a few minutes, threw her arms around me, and we embraced withcut words or tears. The time to cry and mourn had not come yet for us.

Jasiek was jubilant. His luck had held. As far as he was concerned, all danger was left behind. The minor fact that just a few hours ago there had been five of us and now there were only four did not trouble him at all. Holding a bottle of Vodka in one hand, a little glass in the other, he was celebrating. Anxious to prove what a good sport I was, I swallowed a few sips, which burned my throat like fire. My empty stomach, used to different breakfast fare, protested violently. I munched on a slice of bread that Kasia mercifully gave me, and it made me feel better. The fatigue and tension of the last hours were taking their toll. I was getting drowsy. When told that we would have to remain in hiding till nightfall, we were glad to leave the celebration and be left alone.

The worry about Tuvia's fate weighed heavily on our minds, but we knew his name could not be mentioned. We had to put the incident in the station behind us and concentrate on the danger that still lay ahead. We had to think of ourselves and maintain our spirits. There we were, two young girls, alone and at the mercy of uncouth peasants. Ahead of us lay an illegal crossing of closely guarded borders. Just to keep calm took a great deal of courage and self-control.

We were led to a barn full of fresh hay. Its scent was soothing, and we slept most of the day. When they let us come back into the house, it was dark already. Famished, we ate ravenously, while Kasia and Jasiek packed a basket with fare to take along. We climbed out through the back window and soon were on the path leading to the forest.

Our climb had begun. It was like stepping into a world of eternal calm. Merrily blinking stars were sprinkled over dark, velvety skies. A narrow crescent moon was floating in their midst. In the dark of the night the mountains, covered with dense pine forests, resembled giant porcupines in repose. Glimmers of scattered fires were visible from the mountain tops.

"What are those lights?"

"Forest men and partisans."

"Don't 'they' know it?"

"Yes, but nobody dares to come into our forests."

"Are we going there?"

"No. We are going to the south."

After a few hours of exhausting climb, we reached a clearing in the woods and were allowed a short rest. When we resumed our march, Syma and I hardly spoke. The primeval forest was mysteriously still; the four of us seemed to be the only creatures moving. There were no trodden paths, and often our feet became entangled in the thicket. Thorns and sharp twigs tore at our stockings and legs. I lost my sense of orientation, but our guides were moving with the assurance of passersbys on a well-lighted street. They had known these trails since they were children and were as familiar with the forest as with their own backyard, and they seemed to glide through the prickly under-brush as though it weren't there. My weariness made me believe that I had reached the end of the continent already, but a few more hours later, I found out that fatigue was not a good indicator of covered distance. The arrival of dawn signalled only the first step of our journey.

Deep in the mountain forest lived the family of a poor woodsman.

The attic of his barn, which housed one emaciated cow and swarms of ferocious wasps, became our shelter for the day. We were left alone. The wasps defended their territory with a wrath worthy a batallion of SS men encountering two Jewish girls. While the wasps were regrouping, we dozed off. Uneasy, each one tried to hide her misgivings from the other.

At the end of the day, the smugglers came back and with them the sorely missed basket of provisions. They rationed us some of the food. After a meager meal, we reentered the forest.

Every summer of my prewar life was spent in the Carpathian Mountains, and I used to climb the hills like a mountain goat. But now that my life depended upon crossing them, I could hardly walk. Every step, every breath became a major effort. My throat hurt, my tongue felt like cardboard, my lips were parched and swollen. There was a bottle of Vodka in Kasia'a basket but no water. I grew thirstier and thirstier until I could scarcely swallow. Every new hill seemed to me steeper than the previous one. As I was reaching the limit of my endurance, Jasiek announced that at the bottom of the next ravine was water. Mustering the remnants of my energy, I started to run blindly downhill. Branches scratched my face, I tripped on a rock, but nothing could have stopped me. When finally my feet splashed the shallow water, I knelt at the edge of the stream and dunked my face in it. Totally unaware that my hair, neck, and collar were getting wet. I drank and drank and drank, till I could take no more. Then, feeling completely spent, I lay at the edge of the water and let the cool water run through my fingers.

My memory brought back to me a passage from a book read long ago. It was about life in a forest during drought. The scene where the animals find a source of water, after a long and torturous search, moved me deeply, even if I could not imagine the extent of suffering caused by thirst. There and then, in the mountain forest, I understood how a thirsty animal feels. It was easy. The last few days I had lived like an animal – by instinct only. Eating, drinking, sleeping, running, and being on constant alert of mortal danger.

Refreshed, I was on my feet again, but the good feeling did not last long. Every step taken made my breathing more laborious. The walking became more and more difficult. Last in line, I followed in a daze. Having lost the concept of time and place, I did not know where I was going anymore. With the greatest effort, I followed the silhouette moving in front of me. As we began the final descent, the going became a bit easier. We reached a clearing in the woods and were told to rest. I dropped on the grass like a collapsed marionette.

"*Panienka*, why don't you take off those heavy shoes? Your feet must be sore," Kasia said.

It sounded like a good idea. I was wearing my hiking boots. They were heavy, and the moment I took them off, I felt tons lighter.

"You stay here with Jasiek and the other *Panienka*, and I will go to fetch the Slovak guide."

"Are we already past the border?"

"We passed the border long ago. We are on the outskirts of the town Nowe Miasto."

"Oh, how wonderful! The people are going to take us in. The first thing I will ask for will be a cup of tea. Delicious, hot tea," I said dreamily.

"You know, if you let me borrow your shoes, I would be able to run fast, and you will have your tea before you know."

Even though I was feverish, I knew that it wasn't wise to antagonize our guides. Their wish was our command. Poland or Slovakia, it made no differece. We were still at their absolute mercy.

"Sure, gladly. Take the shoes and just come back fast."

Kasia disappeared among the woods, and this was the last we saw of her and my shoes. After a long while, Jasiek turned to me and said, "Why don't you put on the other shoes you wore on the train?"

"I can't wear them here. The heels are too high. Where is Kasia?"

"I don't know, and I don't care! All I know is that we must hurry because the other guides are waiting for you."

Like a zombie I put on my high-heeled shoes and began to limp along. At the edge of the forest, parked on a narrow dirt road, a small black car was waiting for us. Before he let us enter, Jaseik made us write notes to our families that we had reached Slovakia safely. He would be paid only after bringing proof of safe delivery of his cargo.

I scribbled a short note to my mother, as did Syma. Jasiek grabbed them and disappeared into the forest.

Was it delusion or reality? Syma and I relaxed comfortably on the worn-out seat of a creaky Lancia, which to me appeared to be a most luxurious vehicle on the face of earth. I could hardly believe our luck.

We had crossed the border, we were in Slovakia! The screeching, groaning old jalopy was crawling over a winding, narrow dirt road. Even though our driver, a short, rough, like a peasant looking man, who failed to respond to our enthusiastic greetings, was the biggest imaginary contrast to a coachman in livery, both Syma and I felt like two princesses riding in a gilded coach. Our weariness was gone. We babbled excitedly – like two kids left out of school, not at all like escapees from a hangman's rope. (In many camps hanging in full view of the entire population became the punishment for attempted escape.) We had made it! Good-bye, Schomberg! Adieu, Miller! We hope you roast in hell!

"This is what I call service. A private car just for the two of us with a private chauffeur. Soon he will take us to the rescue committee. Could you imagine how they are going to receive us? What would you ask for first?"

"Syma, Syma, I am so happy. All I wish for now is a cup of hot tea. Dark, fragrant, real tea. Not the terrible *Erzatz* we drank at home. In a tall glass with a silver holder. I hope they will offer me sugar. Cubes. I will ask for two. Maybe even three. They will say to me; '*Fraulein*, you have not had sugar for a long time. Take more.' I am sure they will have lemon. I will take two slices. Syma, Syma, I can smell the tea already. I see the steam raising from my cup. I will stir it with a little silver spoon, then lift the cup to my mouth, taste the heavenly –"

Screech! The car came to a sudden stop, brutally interrupting our reverie. Aghast, I looked through the smudgy windshield and rubbed my eyes. The car was blocked by men in dark uniforms. I blinked, looked around. They were real. We were surrounded by the border *milicja*. Totally unperturbed, our driver chatted with them amiably.

Syma and I looked at one another. We understood without words. They had betrayed us. Jasiek had delivered us straight into the monster's jaw. Not only that, but unwittingly we had helped those bandits to fool the rest. Letters heralding our triumphant arrival in Slovakia were on their way to Bochnia, to lure others into the same trap. The perfidy of those people! Their false promises had made us follow them through the agony of Tarnow station, the murderous climb over the mountains, all in order to be delivered into the clutches of Slovak henchmen. A prison in Slovakia was worse than a concentration camp in Poland. Here nobody knew us, and we couldn't even talk with our captors. Slovak and Polish are two different languages.

As it turned out, communication was the least of our problems. Our interrogators spoke fluent Polish. I stood firmly by my identity, for hours claiming that I was not a Jew. I was a Pole, a Catholic, by the name Irene Zahorska.

"Why were you trying to run away from Poland?"

"Because I am a Polish patriot." This was true. I always separated my feelings for the land I was born in from the revulsion for many of the Yahoos inhabiting it.

"You liar. You are a Jew."

"I am not. Here are my documents, and this is my identity card."

"We will send you to the Gestapo. There you will sing like a nightingale."

"You can send me wherever you wish, but this is my name."

This too was partially true, at least the first part of my statement.

This farce went on for a long time. Our interrogators, clad in freshly pressed, dark suits, sat on comfortable chairs and drank what appeared to be innumerable glasses of hot, dark, fragrant tea. They seemed to enjoy the situation. At the same time I, disheveled, feverish, on the brink of exhaustion, thirsty and hungry, stood facing them. Finally Syma, who did not have Polish documents, broke down and blurted out, "Yes. I admit that I am Jewish. My only crime is that I was trying to escape from certain death. Now my life is in your hands."

I was determined to stick to my story. "She might be Jewish, but I am not. I never saw her before meeting her on the border."

Syma, resigned, asked them in a low voice, "What are you going to do with us?"

"We will put you in prison, you dirty Jews. Afterward we will decide what to do with you. You will not get off easy. We know that all Jews are rich and carry diamonds and dollars. First you have to leave all your money and jewelry with us."

"We have no money and no jewelry."

"We will search you."

"You can search as much as you want. All I have is my pocketbook with my documents that you took already."

"We checked out the pocketbook. Now we are going to check you."

We looked at one another in mute despair. What did they mean by "checking you"? We were at the mercy of our captors. They could do anything they liked.

What "checking" meant we found out soon enough. It turned out to be a humiliating, painful body search. Mercifully, it was performed by a woman. She was a real pro. The only reason she did not find any jewels or golden coins was that we did not have any.

A whole day went by between the moment Kasia walked away in my shoes and the time we were taken from the police station into the prison. The dusk had already descended upon the small town, and all was quiet.

The dreaded prison was one large cellar room. Its only window, situated at the ground level, did not let in any light. It was dark outside, and in the cell it was even darker. In the prevailing blackness, we distinguished the contours of a wide bench along the length of the entire wall. There was a similar one along the shorter wall, which was broken by the door. A strong smell of urine and faeces emanating from one corner made us guess the location of the refuse bucket. Fresh straw was spread on both benches.

We were shoved in. The heavy door was closed with a grunt, and the custodian padlocked it. We heard his shuffling steps outside the window, and the creaking shutters coupled with a thud.

I felt lost and abandoned. The oppressive blackness seemed to press on my chest like a weight of a thousand tons. I had difficulty breathing. It felt like being buried alive. Since that night I cannot stay in a closed space without the frightening sensation of being choked.

Gradually my eyes became accustomed to the darkness, and soon Syma's familiar silhouette became distinguishable. After a while I realized that a woman was lying on the other bench. Her eyes were following our every move.

"So this is how the inside of a prison looks."

"Real comfort after the forest and the barn."

"At least we don't have to see Jasiek's and Kasia's faces. They would sell their own mothers for a few zlotys."

"Syma, we have company."

"Yes, I see."

"Let us ask her why she is here."

She was a young peasant girl. We tried to engage her in conversation, but she was not in a socializing mood. Anyway, she spoke only Czech, and it was obvious that she was not interested in us. From her curt answers we gathered that she was Czech, and her country at present proclaimed to be a Slovak republic. Between her monosyllables she whined and sobbed, so we let her be. How it felt to be a member of a despised minority we knew too well, except that even then we would have gladly exchanged places with her. My fatigue took over, and the moment we settled for the night, I sank into a dreamless, deep sleep.

It was morning when a loud knocking at the window woke us up. From behind the window a woman was smiling, waving at us and talking in German: *"Kinder. Kinder. hat kein Angst* [children don't be afraid!]!" We heard steps in the corridor, and the heavy door was opened.

I sat up on the bench, pulling straw out of my hair and rubbing my eyes. Sure that I was losing my mind, I closed my eyes again. When I opened them, I pinched myself to make sure that I was not hallucinating. I was not. The woman standing in front of me was real – a real Jewish lady.

Smiling broadly, she kissed and hugged us both and told us not to worry. She was one of the few Jews left in Nowe Miasto, and they were all taking part in the rescue operation, funded by money smuggled in from Switzerland. From now on we would be under their care.

Our arrest was part of the scheme, she explained, necessary in order to transport us safely to the Hungarian border. Tired and confused by all that had happened to us in the last forty-eight hours, we could hardly follow and understand the full meaning of her words: According to International law, or maybe it was the Geneva convention, a fugitive arrested in a frontier pass – which is any place within eight kilometers of the actual border line – has to be returned to the country he came from. It was to be arranged that Syma and I "came from" Hungary.

So, Kasia and Jasiek were not traitors, after all! Just venal, I thought, remembering my boots and the other pitiful possessions that the Czech police had seized. Ilona could not have known that her highly recommended guides would conspire with their Slovak counterparts to rob the people entrusted to their care.

We would have to go back to the police station, our benefactor said, where at a new hearing we would recant everything we had said before and "admit" that we were refugees from Hungary. The rest would take care of itself. We were not to worry anymore. She reassured us that the police were bribed, but they liked to play the Interrogation *Spiel* (game), and we must play along. After all, the men had not touched us – true – and even if they took some money, that was irrelevant. America was sending money! America wanted children! Great America was saving children!

"Children? What children?" Syma and I asked in unison.

"Jewish children!"

"There are hardly any Jewish children left to be saved," I said with bitterness. For a split second it seemed to me as if I heard the peels of laughter of Lalusia, my little cousin. I swallowed a salty tear, hoping that no one noticed. If I were to live, one lifetime would not be enough to encompass all the grief and sorrow that would become a survivor's lot.

"Yes, there are!" Syma broke in. "My sister has two children, and my family is taking care of a girl whose parents were deported. I hope they all make it." Our eyes met, and at the same instant we looked away. The image of nineteen-years-old Tuvia flashed in our minds.

Our Lady Bountiful had brought along a basket of long-forgotten goodies: a thermos with hot, fragrant tea, buttered rolls with jam and cheese – a feast fit for a king. We wolfed it all down in quite an unkingly manner. Our self-esteem and confidence were restored. We were among our own people, and all was going to be fine.

The first day of our prison stay went by quite pleasantly. We did not panic anymore when an officer led us to the police station for another hearing. Afterward we were escorted to the house of the Traurig family, where we were treated to a delicious lunch. The rest of the day we lounged in their garden. Our host's family had four sons, who kept us company. We talked, made plans to meet in Budapest, joked, even flirted a bit, just like young people do under normal circumstances. The ability to adapt at once to every situation carried us through those unbelievable times.

The town Nowe Miasto is situated in a most picturesque valley at the feet of the majestic Carpathians. It was harvest time, and the fields were already golden with the ripened stalks of wheat and silvery with corn. A benevolent sun shone over the lush meadows, brooks, and ancient forests. We seemed to have transcended reality. But when time came to return to jail, we instantly slipped into the role of obedient prisoners.

Next morning I woke up feeling sick. My body felt on fire and was covered with a red rash. I was sure that the dreaded curse had caught up with me, and I had typhus. The small community was put on alert. Not one Jewish physician was left in Nowe Miasto. The druggist, who had taken over the medical care, came to see me in the prison cell and reassured everybody that there was no reason to be alarmed. For precaution he recommended that I be placed in isolation. Our Lady Bountiful volunteered to take me in. All I remember was waking up in a delightfully clean bed, all to myself. I already felt better. Lucky for me and the entire rescue operation, it turned out to be just high fever with a benign skin rash. The most tender, loving care was bestowed on me, and after four days I was well enough to return to the jail. A day later my mother arrived in a group of four. It was a happy reunion and living proof that the "road" was still open and the rescue operation going on.

One ten-year-old girl came with my mother, and the local people were overjoyed: "Children, children, America wants children!" Bitter, painful resentment was rising in me. Who was America? Where was America? Where, when little children were tortured, starved, thrown out of windows, and smashed over the sidewalks? Our escape was a living proof that much could have been accomplished with outside help. Bribery was opening many doors, but while there was still time to act, America slept.

It was decided that we should be moved on. More people were expected, and it was not wise to keep a large group of illegals in a border town. Mother, Syma, and I were told that we would be sent to Hungary.

This part of our journey was hard to believe. Under official police escort, we rode the train to Presov, a town then on the Hungarian Border. (Today redrawn frontiers put it halfway between Poland and Hungary.) As was suitable for a trip to freedom, the day was brilliantly bright. We prisoners stood most of the time on the platform of the train, taking in the magnificent view. Hopeless captives only few days ago, we were today passengers on a train on the Slovak side of the forbidding Carpathian Mountains.

After a long ride, we arrived in Presov. At the station we were met by a representative of the Rescue Committee and a few of Bochnia's escapees, anxious to hear about those left behind. We were escorted to the Jewish committee, where it was decided that, because of the influx of refugees in the last few days, we would be sent over the border immediately.

The details of that memorable passage are blurred in my memory. All I remember is that our small group of three was joined by a young woman with a child. Mr. Schwartz, the president of the Rescue Committee, and the commandant of the border police, rode with us to the border, a few miles out of town. While we were in the car, Mr. Schwartz said to us in German: "I wonder what that goy [the commandant] is thinking when he sees us smuggling people in broad daylight." Apparently all the commandant was thinking about was how much he was getting paid for every person "repatriated" to Hungary.

The car reached the end of the road. Everybody got off. Mr. Schwartz kissed the child, we all shook hands, and he said "Go straight ahead! Behind those bushes is Hungary!"

Without a moment hesitation, without once looking back, we proceeded as we were told. A few minutes and a few yards later, our tired feet were treading the ground of the land of our dreams.

We were in Hungary!

27 · In Hungary

We were in God's country. As far as the eye could see there were gently rolling hills covered by lush greenery. Sounds of faraway church bells harmonized with the twitters of sleepy birds, getting softer and gradually lapsing into silence. An ensemble of frogs started a long, syncopated chorale. Last to be heard was the cacophony by the cricket minstrels. One by one their voices fell off. For a while a lonely cricket went on with his song till his weakening voice was not audible anymore. Swathed in translucent shadows and caressed by gentle breeze, Mother Earth was settling for the night.

The moment we came out from behind the Slovak bushes, a man emerged from behind the Hungarian bushes and motioned us to follow him. None of us understood a word of Hungarian, nor he of Polish, but when he pointed at a farmhouse at the bottom of the hill and gestured for us to sit down, we obeyed. He slid down the slope, and few minutes later returned, carrying a basket full of purple plums. As I greedily bit into the velvety skin, the sweet juice dripped over my chin and stuck to my fingers. The land of our hope received us with a manifestation of abundance – the luxury of feasting on freshly picked fruit!

The night was spent at the farmhouse. Early in the morning, we were taken to the town by a horse and cart. At the outskirts we got off and continued by foot. By side streets and narrow paths, we reached the back entrance of a small Hassidic house of prayer. But for the old sexton, the place was empty.

Deep under the lining of my pocketbook was a tiny scrap of paper with a message written by my uncle to a family friend in Kosice. The content of this little note mirrored the despair Mother and Uncle felt when I was leaving Bcchnia. It read as follows: "Dear Yosel, This girl is my niece. She is the daughter of Wolf Landerer. When she reaches you, please take care of her. Only a few are left of our family. Josef Horowitz."

Mother, emboldened by the fact that we were in "safe" Hungary, asked the sexton to inform Yosel Stern that the wife and daughter of Wolf Landerer from Krakow had just arrived. Her authoritative manner did not fall to impress him, and he obliged immediately. Few minutes later a tall, distinguished-looking man entered the place. Yosel Stern greeted us politely, but the enthusiasm we had encountered in strangers in Slovakia was missing. He told us that we were in an extremely dangerous and compromising situation. The police were alert for illegal aliens crossing the borders and for Czechoslovak Jews trying to pass as Hungarians. An entire family of Christians was deported to Auschwitz for harboring a Jewish infant. Mr. Stern begged us to understand that he personally could not take care of us but would see to it that we reach Budapest as fast as possible. He lingered few more minutes, asking for friends and family, and then sent us off with a young boy as a guide.

We wanted to be invisible, but it was a maddeningly bright morning as we sneaked through the empty streets of the sleeping town. Fortunately the widow who harbored illegals lived close to the synagogue, and the stealthy walk did not take long. Mother was very subdued, but Syma and I, excited by the prospect of going to Budapest, bubbled with joy.

In spite of the danger, the Jewish community of Kosice was actively engaged in the rescue operation. Yosel Stern proved to be as good as his word. As soon as we arrived at the widow's, he informed the community of our whereabouts. Before World War II Kosice was the seat of a famous Hassidic rabbi, the Stropkover Rebbi, whom my father visited often. Thus the name "Landerer" was well known in the community. The Rebbi's widow mobilized the Stropkover Hassidim, and we were given special treatment. Mrs. Friedman, the wife of one of them, brought us a most delicious, home-cooked meal. Seeing me hobbling in my uncomfortable shoes, she returned shortly after with a pair of brand-new shoes that she had bought for me. Mother paled. She had never thought she would see a day when strangers, out of pity, would buy shoes for her daughter. I accepted the gift without trepidation. After all, didn't the world owe me something? Didn't my acts of courage prove that human spirit was invincible? At the age of eighteen, I still believed in universal justice.

Mr. Friedman came to see us in the evening. I cannot emphasize enough how these people endangered their own safety. Just keeping our whereabouts secret was a highly punishable crime. Mr. Friedman informed us that Syma and I would leave for Budapest the next day. He gave us the address of his daughter where we would be able to stay for a while to recover from the ravages of the road, Mother would stay few days more.

Budapest! A magic city where people sit in coffeehouses and girls go to the movies! In my imagination it was an enchanted place where Tokay flowed from the faucets instead of water, gypsy violins sang of love, and on the streets people danced czardas. This dream city was now within my reach!

Brimming with excitement, I followed the Jewish woman, who led us to the train. My possessions were gone. All I owned was contained in my pocketbook. My old shoes landed in the garbage pail, and I, shod in my new ones, was marching to conquer Budapest!

In retrospect it is hard for me to understand how we made it at all. Illegal allens, not speaking the language of the land, boarding the train in a heavily guarded border town. No Hungarian male worth his salt would ever ignore the presence of two young girls, and as soon as we sat down, we were surrounded by men of all ages, trying to make conversation. We communicated by gestures, and it did not take long when even outside-the-compartment men, trying to get a glimpse of the curiosity, were crowding the corridor. That no detective was alerted, and the conductor good-naturedly ignored the disturbance, defies all logic. The only explanation plausible is that the Divine Providence rode the train with us.

It was dark when we arrived in the city of our dreams. We took the tramway to the Jewish quarter, where an impoverished family of refugees from Vienna was renting space on the floor. Tired but happy, we took off our shoes and slept soundly. Better a spot on the floor in Budapest than a whole bed in Bochnia, which I did not have there anyway.

Next morning we were on our own. Before registering with the committee, we did a bit of sightseeing. In daylight the city was everything I had ever dreamed of – and some more. From my side it was love at first sight. Budapest, however, did not take kindly to the refugees. But on that lovely August morning Syma and I walked on the broad Andrassy Boulevard, impressed with its architecture and the magnificent vista of the broad avenue, enchanted by the beauty and elegance of the women and fascinated by the dashing men.

The large restaurant we entered was almost empty. As soon as we sat down, a waiter in formal attire approached us and took our orders. To counteract my stomach's rebellion against the spicy Hungarian food, I ordered Mother's time-proven remedy: a cup of tea. Speaking German, I pronounced it exactly the way Hungarians say the word "milk" in Hungarian. Confusion arose when the waiter brought me a tall glass of cold milk while I craved tea. I was trying to explain that I wanted *Tea*, while he was trying to convince me that this was what he had brought me. Since in Budapest dapper young men seemed to materialize out of thin air, soon we were joined by one who fortunately knew some German, and he explained the misunderstanding.

Few moments later the waiter brought my tea, and I had my hour of bliss. It was real tea, not the *Ersatz* we drank at home. It was dark, fragrant, with lacey steam rising up from the cup nestled in a silver holder. The sugar dish was overflowing with sugar cubes, free for the taking, as many as I wished. Slices of lemon were gracefully arranged on a little plate. I stirred this dark, brown nectar with a little silver spoon, polished to a high shine that would have pleased even our fussy Jozia. Meanwhile Syma was attacking a large dish of ice cream. Overcome by temptation, I too ordered one. Afterwards I had to have more tea, but it was worth it.

After the libation we went to the little coffeehouse at Kiraly Utca 9. It was the Rescue's unofficial branch. We registered, received a money allowance, and went to find the daughter of the Friedmans' from Kosice. Her married named was Friedman too, and they lived on Hajos Street.

Next day we met with a delegate from Rescue, who went with us to KEOK, the headquarters of the secret police. All newly arrived refugees had to register there and have their stay in Budapest approved. Before we left, we bathed, washed our hair, and laundered the only clothing we possessed. When we arrived at the KEOK, we did not look like haggard arrivals straight from the border. The trained eye of the detective noticed the difference, and he suspected a trick. If it weren't for the man from the committee, who dealt with the situation, we would have been lost. Not understanding a word of what was said saved us from panic. Later we were told how close to losing our freedom we had been. People arrested at the KEOK rarely saw the daylight again. But on that hot summer day, with the registration papers in our hands, we believed that the worst was over and the future smiling at us.

A day in the life of a refugee in Budapest always began with a pilgrimage to Kiraly Utca. Inside or outside the tiny coffeehouse was the focal point for all Polish refugees. They all came there to find out what was going on in the self-contained world of displaced, homeless people.

For lack of something better to do, I explored the city. With friends, other young refugees, I used to walk for hours. Our starved-for-beauty eyes feasted on the magnificence around us. After the poverty and shabbiness of ghettos, Budapest's broad boulevards, parks, palaces, museums, the Parliament building, and the legendary Danube, flowing through the heart of the city, appeared like illustrations from fairy tales. At that time the Pearl of the Danube was still untouched by the ravages of war.

The biggest attractions for us, the homeless, were the coffeehouses. For a price of a cup of coffee or tea, all our meager resources permitted, we could sit for hours, rest our tired feet, and luxuriate in elegance and comfort. The larger houses had balconies with stages for gypsy orchestras, which used to perform during dinner services. For me the absence of musicians made no difference. In Budapest music was always in my ears.

When Mother arrived, I parted with Syma, and we rented a bed from a Jewish family, themselves refugees from Vienna, who supplemented their meager income by taking boarders. After our first night there, our host, an Orthodox Jew wearing a beard and dressed in traditional garb, took our documents in order to register us at the local precinct, as the law demanded. The anomaly of a bearded Jew harboring two Polish Christians awakened suspicions, and without wasting any time, two detectives accompanied him right back. We were ordered to pack up and follow them. It happened so fast that before we knew what was happening to us, we were at the Rombach

Utca Synagogue, which had been converted into a detention center. There we met familiar faces, even some from Bochnia. In those days detectives were on alert for Polish Jews. For the two weeks that we stayed at Rombach, new prisoners were brought in daily. Two weeks later, after the number of Poles swelled to twenty or more, we were shipped off to a Hungarian detention camp, Ricse. In Ricse we met refugees from Poland, who had been held there over two years already. But fate was kind to us and did not test our endurance. The Rescue operation, in concert with a Zionist organization and the Polish Committee, intervened, and after six weeks all Polish prisoners were released and returned to Budapest.

Coming back to Budapest we felt like conquerors entering a vanquished city. All truly believed that our misery was over. What a wishful thinking that was we found out much too soon. But on that unforgettable night on the train taking us out of bondage, the released prisoners were drunk with joy.

Because we had to change trains and wait for a number of hours at a railroad junction, this "freedom ride" lasted a whole night. A group of gypsy musicians came by. We pulled together our resources and ordered a round of drinks for them. Soon they began to play for us. More drinks and food appeared on the table, and we joined them in a song. First the Hungarian songs we knew, then Polish, Yiddish, and Hebrew. The musicians quickly picked up the tunes and accompanied us with fervor. What a splendid reception it was! This was the celebration of our lives.

After midnight we boarded the train to Budapest. Many were dozing, but I remained awake. This night sleep did not come to me. Serious thoughts replaced the euphoria of previous hours. Where would we go once in Budapest? What would I do? The idea of relying on committees for support did not appeal to me. Up till then, thanks to Mother's clever management of our resources, we never had money problems. Now we had become destitute refugees, just like the people without names we had fed, clothed, housed, and given aims to just a while ago. The reality of not having anything was staring into my face, and it was scary. I remember taking a scrap of paper and scribbling a note to myself: "No matter what is in store for me, I will never let myself be defeated by life." I carried it with me until the paper disintegrated. Experience soon taught me that, at times, keeping a promise made to oneself at the age of eighteen could become quite difficult.

It was fall of 1943 when we returned to Budapest. The end of our wanderings did not come yet, by far not, but we did not know it then. We registered at the Polish Committee as Madame Sophie Zahorska and daughter Irene. Like the rest of the refugees without means, we were sent to live in the provinces. Our lot fell under the jurisdiction of the court in Kalocsa, a provincial town in the Danube valley. From there we were dispatched to Dunaszentbenedek, a village about four hours distant by horse and cart from Kalocsa. There a group of Polish refugees lived scattered among peasants. Our representative was appointed by the authorities, and he was a genuine Catholic Pole. We were not allowed to leave the county, but otherwise we were free and could walk to neighbouring villages and Kalocsa. A few of the local Jewish families befriended us and we visited with other refugees.

It appeared as if we had finally found a safe corner to stay in till "after the war."

28 · Among Hungarian peasants

Our fantasy about being safely tucked away at the end of the world seemed to have become reality in the winter of 1944. Europe was in flames, but in the village of Dunaszentbenedek in the Danube valley, farmers were getting ready to plant summer crops.

Grateful to be alive, we fancied ourselves in paradise. Mother and I were assigned one bed in a room shared already by the old farmer and the grandmother. The rental included the use of one drawer in their dresser and a nail on the door to hang clothes on. For what we brought along, it was more than adequate. The floor was made out of compressed mud, the outhouse a short walk to the back of the house. Wooden floors and modern plumbing seemed like prehistoric relics. It was geese country, and we were given big, fluffy pillows and a comforter. To aspire to a bed of one's own was a luxury beyond our dreams. The hut we lived in consisted of one room and a kitchen, which doubled as a sitting-family room and an additional bedroom at night. The iron stove in the kitchen gave warmth, the oil lamp light was sufficient for reading and writing. The food was abundant and delicious. Mother performed her culinary magic in a little pan on the corner of the stove, and I licked the plates clean. Lici Shuffeld, who befriended us during our short stay in Budapest, sent us books to read. My evenings were spent reading and writing. What more could have been asked from life? I loved it all – the barefoot, bare-bottomed baby Lacsi, even the ugly, brown stripped tabby playfully rubbing against my legs under the table.

To be able to breathe free, to run against the wind, to touch and smell the freshly plowed earth, to follow the even rows of just turned soil, and plant potatoes for early crops – that meant to be alive with every inch of my body.

The village of Dunaszentbenedek was officially assigned as an open internment camp for legal aliens, and a sizable group of Polish refugees lived there. Our group consisted of two subgroups: the Christian and the Jewish Poles. Every Sunday, ignoring the hostile stares of our gentile compatriots, the Jewish contingent marched dutifully to the church, where we followed the motions of other worshippers. Following the instructions of their government-in-exile in London, the Poles were trying to curb their hatred of the Jews, but, still, we did not trust them. The fear of Polish police and informers was fresh in our memory, but for the outside world we presented an image of unity. Our common destiny, the longing for home, the worry about families left behind, and the hatred of the Germans created an illusion of solidarity among all refugees.

The beauty of this hospitable land became a unifying force for all. It seemed as if the entire countryside had rearranged itself to please us. Shortly after the celebration of a snowless Christmas, the flatlands begun to burst with new life. Farmers were busy in the fields and vineyards, women doing laundry at the river bank, children playing in the streets and courtyards. Man and nature were rising from the winter's inactivity. At the horizon, Heaven and earth met in a perfect line. Bochnia, ghetto, Actions, and deportations were things that happened to other people on another planet. By an unspoken agreement they were not mentioned. The most popular subjects of our conversations were remembrances of the life we had had and our hopes and dreams for "after the war."

In March of 1944 the German army occupied Hungary, and our magic bubble of serenity burst with a thunder that shattered our little world. The unthinkable had happened. Our rustic paradise had become a death trap. We could not trust our compatriots anymore. And the local people? After they find out that the "Catholics" they took in were devious Jews? Their reaction was easy to imagine. We had to plan our escape!

A frightening episode took place few days after the invasion. A garrison of German soldiers was stationed in Kalocsa, and one sunny afternoon a few of them decided to take a ride through the countryside. Among our group were three young women, recently widowed, with small children. One of the children, five-year-old Mina Bornstein, was playing in front of the house when the car with the German soldiers whizzed by. At the sight of them the child fainted. It took a while to revive her. Afterward the usually cheerful little girl went around asking everybody, "What do we do now? The Germans are here. Where do we go from here? What will happen to us now?"

Romania, especially the capital, Bucharest, now became synonymous with salvation and hope.

People have asked me why. The Romanians were an ally of Nazi Germany with a Nazi-dictated premier running the country. Persecution of the Jews was widespread and often bestially cruel. What's more, the counterattack of the Red Army was heading straight toward the heart of the country.

All I can answer is that such facts paled into insignificance in comparison ... Romania's position as gateway to the Near East – to Turkey and the Jewish National Home (as it was called) in Palestine. Moreover there was a large Jewish community in Bucharest, well organized and comparatively well financed, and offices of the Jewish Agency. In Bucharest, we felt, baksheesh, the neverfalling door opener, would enable us to escape from Europe altogether.

Bucharest became for us the New Jerusalem.

But first, how were we to get out of godforsaken Dunaszentbenedek?

How does a group of over twenty adults and five children disappear from a village without attracting attention? The Hungarian government had treated us as friendly aliens on condition that we stay put in places assigned to us by KEOK. Our group was permitted to live in Dunaszentbenedek, and according to the law we should have remained there until new instructions. This was an impossible situation!

How to get out and which route to take? We knew too well what to expect if we stayed. To wait and see what the next day would bring was out of question. There was frequent controls on the trains and roads. Our documents were perfect as long as they were not closely examined. But nothing could have held us back. Eventually the whole group of Polish Jews trickled out of the village.

Right after the German invasion Syma Schiff, who had a permit to live in Budapest, moved to Nagyvarad, a town on the Hungarian-Romanian border. We decided that Sianka Englander, her sister, who with her two little children escaped from Bochnia and was with us, would leave first and with my mother go to Nagyvarad (now Oradea, Romania) via Budapest. Once the "road" to Romania would be established, I would follow together with my girlfriend Celina. From the perspective of time gone by, this arrangement might seem unreasonable, but at that time both Celina and I were nineteen years old and felt invincible. Let the women and children be taken care of first! We would always make it, one way or another.

We planned the departure in secrecy. In the middle of one night Sianka's gallbladder cooperated by staging an attack of violent pains. Her moans and her children's frightened cries woke up her landlady, who in turn woke us up. After that there was no doubt in the minds of the entire village that she must go to Budapest to seek medical care, and Mother must accompany her. Their journey was a small epic.

The logistics of transporting from Dunaszentbenedek a group consisting of two women with two children, one of them a circumcized male, were complicated. In order to arrive in Budapest during the day, they had to leave Kalocsa on the early morning train, but it was not possible to leave our village before dawn. The country was infested with soldiers, *militzia*, gendarmes, military police, and marauders, one more hostile and dangerous than the other. They would have to stay in Kalocsa overnight, but there was not one hotel available to civilians – certainly not for those running away from the law. Our farmer's sister Berszi worked as a domestic for a high court official in Kalocsa, and he advised us to ask her for help. When we arrived unannounced in the late afternoon, her patrons, charmed by the kids chattering in fluent Hungarian, would not hear of our going anyplace else. Next morning Berszi directed us to the train station a few blocks away from the house. Their departure was uneventful. After the train left, I turned back and walked into town.

I returned to Dunaszentbenedek, hoping that the time left for me there would be restful. For the last four months it had been home – meaning comfort and security. As it turned out, I was in for a big surprise.

During the twenty-four hours I had been absent, things had changed. The Dunaszentbenedek I returned to was different from the one I just left. No more giggling, festively dressed girls gathered at the artesian wall, no more housewives gossiping at the bakery, the unofficial exchange of village gossip. The cheerful sound of the customary greeting *"Jo Napod Kivanok!"* seemed to have shrunk and lost its cheerfulness. The last of the young men still left in the village were being called up for military service. War had finally caught up with Dunaszentbenedek, and it was scary.

The refugee grapevine informed us that General Koliontaj, the Head of the Polish Committee in Hungary, had been executed by the Nazis. It wasn't so good to be a genuine Polish Catholic anymore, but too be a Polish Jew living under a false identify was outright hopeless. But hardened by our suffering, we absolutely refused to give up. The call of the hour was to act fast.

It was not for the first time that we, the fugitives from ghettos and concentration camps, felt the ground under our feet crumbling, but our gentile compatriots were visibly shaken. The brutal murder of their leader had destroyed their complacency. They did not know where to turn and what to expect. While they groped in murky insecurity we, the handful of Polish Jews, saw the situation all too clearly. The moment our real identities were known to the authorities, our fate would be irreversibly sealed.

I did not go back to our corner of the room. The luxury of having the whole bed for myself did not appeal to me anymore. My girl friend Celina, who lived alone in a little shack at another farmer's backyard, gave up her hard-won privacy too. Mindless of the indiscretion, we both moved in with the only Jewish family in the village. They had a large house, and some of the single refugees roomed with them. It was hard to be alone in times of acute danger, and we became like one extended family.

The main event of our day was the delivery of mail. I had already received one letter from Mother, informing me that they had arrived safely in Nagyvarad. There she met the son of the Koloszycer Rebbi, who was connected with the rescue operation. I was to be ready to leave at a moment's notice.

Thus waiting for the crucial letter, Celina and I pretended to enjoy our leisure and the company of other young people. Acting like any teens with a lot of free time on their hands, we used to walk in a large group, all the time scouting the roads and paths leading out of the village. Should the letter come, it would not be feasible to leave through Kalocsa. No farmer could be trusted to deliver us there in the deep of the night. Anyhow, the few horses still left in the village were being conscripted together with their owners. We had to find another way out – and we did. The afternoon train to Budapest passed through the neighboring village. Getting there without attracting the attention of the villagers and the Poles required foresight and elaborate planning. The country was as flat as a table top, and there were no buildings along the way, only a few naked, far-apart-growing trees and the freshly planted crops on both sides of the road just beginning to sprout tiny leaves that made any movement on the highway visible for miles.

Our daily ritual of walking in a group to the neighboring village was born out of necessity. Soon local people became accustomed to seeing us on the road every afternoon. We never once missed going to the train station at the time of "our" train's arrival. There we stood on the platform, waving to passengers, laughing, talking to people in our broken Hungarian. A bunch of seemingly carefree youngsters, we became a permanent fixture in the otherwise deserted train depot. The station manager even stopped counting the people entering and leaving after the train's departure.

What should have been a relaxing interlude became a nightmare. The highly developed Hungarian police apparatus was terrorizing the entire population. Fortunately for our village, hardly any uniformed law-enforcers were seen there. The city hall housed, in addition to the town clerks and village elder's offices, the court, the post office, and the jail. All these were located in an unprepossessing, one-story-tall white-washed building on the main street. An elderly man, called by everyone Bacsi ("uncle" Hungarian), carried out the duties of a beadle, information officer, and watchman, according to need. Otherwise the county was under the jurisdiction of a special branch of gendarmerie whose task was to patrol the roads and railways, and generally maintain order in the countryside. Their uniforms were sombre black, but their headgear, adorned by luminous and large clusters of rooster's feathers, made them stand out in the largest crowds. They were nicknamed *kokoshes* ("roosters").

One day, as Celina and I were passing by the courthouse, two *kokoshes* apprehended us. The street was deserted, as the two led us straight to the empty police station. Our desperate attempts to convince them that we were Polish and not under their authority were in vain. Both men were drunk, and the legality of our documents was the last thing of their minds. Heaven only knows how it would have ended if it were not for old *Basci*. He saw them coming with us, alerted our Polish commandant, and we were immediately released.

This seemingly minor incident might not stand out among my war experiences, but it became like the proverbial straw that broke the camel's back. My long-suppressed fear of the police, the feelings of vulnerability and helplessness became unbearable. I felt trapped and was afraid to leave the house alone. Our friends kept urging me to forget this minor incident, but whenever I saw a headgear adorned by black, shining rooster's feathers, I went limp with fear. No argument or persuasion could convince me that all *kokoshes* in Hungary were not out searching for me. Once the fear took possession, I could not shake it off. We decided that regardless of news from Mother the two of us would leave immediately. Celina, whose boyfriend was in Budapest, was to leave first, I was to follow a day or two after. We hoped that the coveted letter from Mother might come meanwhile, and all would work out as planned.

My friend Celina left, and with her, two young men from our group. I felt lonely without her and decided to leave two days later, letter or no letter. Again, like every afternoon, our group walked to the neighboring village and its train station. We didn't meet anybody on our way and boarded the train unnoticed. The ride was uneventful, except that I was petrified. Every station was patrolled by *kokoshes*, and no matter how hard my gallant companions tried to turn the whole matter into a joke, the horror was overpowering. We reached Budapest without incident and went to look for Celina but she was not there. She and the whole group from Bochnia had left for the Romanian border.

By the time we found the address we had been given and learned that our friends were not there anymore, it was already evening. It would have been very unsafe to roam the streets looking for a place to stay, and we were greatly relieved when the owners of the apartment invited us to stay overnight with them. It turned out that we were not the only illegals they were harbouring. Other people stayed in the room that used to be occupied by the refugees from Bochnia. Every-

242

body bedded on the floor. I, together with Mrs. O. from Krakow and her little daughter, shared the only bed in the room.

Next morning I parted company with the people from my village and went to stay with the Shuffeld family who had befriended us after our release from Ricse camp.

29 · *Back in Budapest*

It was spring 1944. Budapest's merry shine was rapidly wearing off. The Hungarian Jews had been rudely awakened to the bitter reality that they, too, were doomed, as we refugees had suspected all along they would be.

The majority of Hungarian Jews had always mingled with the general population. The sudden expulsion from their position in the Hungarian social structure, which had been handed down from one generation to another, came as a shock. Proud of their roots in the cultural heritage of the Austro-Hungarian empire, they had believed themselves to be immune to the fate of East European Jewry. Faced with brutal and irrevocable change, they were stunned and helpless. The end of the war was approaching and with it the anticipated German defeat, but Hungarian Jewry, renowned for its compliance to the law of the land, accepted the new status with resignation.

The only organized resistance came from the Zionist organizations, mainly youth groups. Sporadic cases of people surviving in hiding or with false documents were few. The spirit of rebellion and the organized effort to help people to escape from ghettos, prison, or concentration camps was instigated by Zionist youth. (In order to give justice to one of the greatest heroes of resistance to the Nazi regime, the incomparable Raoul Wallenberg, I must add that I was not long enough in Budapest to become aware of his incredible rescue operation.)

The return to Budapest brought back my old spunk. The Shuffelds took me in like one of their own. Their daughter Lici opened her closet and let me pick out any dress I wanted. The fact that I was living in an elegant home, was well dressed and fed, boosted my self-esteem greatly. And thus out of a chance meeting grew friendship lasting till the present day.

244

Ours is a timeless, often-repeated tale. War, bombardment, deportation, escape from death. A homeless girl is befriended by a prominent family whose daughter accepts her as a friend. Then invasion comes, destroying stability; hate, vengeance, and cruelty stir new turmoil. Overnight the tables are turned. The once-sheltered girl becomes a refugee in a foreign land, and now it is the new friend, an expert in the art of survival and adaptability, who guides and protects. In that macabre reality an understanding develops between two minds. Hand in hand the girls struggle on through difficult times. The knowledge that there is always one person to go home to reinforces their self-confidence and faith in the future. At present our friendship is stronger than ever.

A few families among the large Jewish community in Budapest opened their homes and hearts to Polish refugees. My adopted family, the Shuffelds, was one of them. In the presence of Berta Shuffeld's charm and sincerity, the loneliness of the hunted people waned as if touched by a magic wand. Their apartment became an open house, where the elsewhere-shunned people were always welcome.

The constant tension and feeling of transience that had become second nature for a refugee gradually infected the Shuffelds, preparing that family to act when faced with deportation. Because of that, the Shuffeld family survived the Holocaust. Lici, after having escaped to Romania, reached Palestine in the summer of 1944. Ibi, the blond blue-eyed girl, remained in Budapest, using false papers provided by the Rescue organization. The parents were taken to Bergen-Belsen concentration camp, where they were liberated by the allies in April 1945. After the war the family was happily reunited in Israel.

My friend Lusia, who miraculously escaped from the transport train while it was actually standing in the Auschwitz station, arrived in Budapest during the winter of 1943, and we became inseparable. Our day in Budapest began with a stop at the Kiraly Utca coffeehouse. There we sat in the dingy, smoke-filled, crowded room, sipping the tepid nondescript beverage, and straining our ears and eyes. There was more to the little place than met the eye. This gathering point of Polish refugees became an unofficial branch of all illegal organizations dealing with refugees and rescue. A large part of their underground work was conducted in this place. The utmost secrecy was imperative, and thus "office hours" were erratic and unpredictable.

After our morning call at the coffeehouse, we used to linger in the vicinity – walking up and down the block, exchanging information, but mostly watching who was still here and who had already left the doomed town. At the same time we kept a lookout for the secret police. They knew where the Polish "outlaws" congregated, and *razzias* (an italian word but used by the Hungarians as the equivalent of *oblavy*), were frequent. To the lucky person who has never lived through the misery of being a refugee, our hanging out every day on the teaming Kiraly block might appear as folly. Only the one who has lived through it would understand why we returned to this place day after day. Somehow, the sight of other people with nowhere to go, the familiar faces and the sound of our own language was greatly reassuring.

A tiny park at the end of Kiraly Utca became a favorite meeting spot of young people. Whoever was in Budapest was sure to show up during the day in "our" park. Families and couples did not frequent this place. They had each other and had no need to search for the comfort of company. Those who came there were mostly the young and unattached, and a feeling of loyalty and camaraderie developed quickly. We all lived scattered over the large city, and it was good to start the day – a day with nothing to do and nowhere to go – by seeing well known friendly faces.

The situation was becoming gloomier with every passing day. I made a habit of checking in with the Shuffelds, my hosts, during the day, so they would know that nothing had happened to me – yet. As it was, they had enough worries of their own. One day, while I was out, they had been tipped off that KEOK was preparing a *razzia* on all Jews born outside Hungary. Jacob Shuffeld was born in Poland; his family had settled in Hungary while he was an infant, but, still, the stigma of his birthplace could become a serious handicap.

I realised that I could not stay with them anymore. As it was, the ever-watchful concierge had commented already on the unusually heavy traffic on the floor where the Shuffelds lived. Their harboring of a dubious Polish-Christian with a permit to live in Dunaszentbenedek, Kaiocsa, could hardly be explained. (Since I had no right to be in Budapest at all, no attempt had been made to register my arrival at the local precinct, as required by law.)

Downcast and discouraged I walked out. Lusia, waiting for me downstairs, did not fall to notice my worried look.

"What happened?"

"I can't stay with them anymore."

She did not ask why. Lusia would have been happy to share her corner with me if she only could. Once I spent the night with her, and in the morning her concierge demanded that I register at the precinct. For want of something better to do, we went to the park. Our habitual benches were as usual occupied by our friends.

"I have no place to sleep tonight!" I had hardly finished the announcement when the group began to disperse. Nobody could offer me shelter for one night even. Vulnerable to danger as we all were, these young people could not afford the luxury of compassion. Ashamed of their own helplessness they could not face me.

Defeated, with no one to turn to, I sank on the suddenly vacant bench, covered my eyes with one hand and stuffed the other into my mouth. My eyes felt dry as I tried to suppress a sob rising in my throat. Only nineteen years old, and it felt as if my lifetime's allotment of tears was used up already.

"Lala, how are you? What are you doing here? How is your mother?"

It was Mr. Gletzel from Krakow. Having escaped from Poland with a considerable amount of money and valuables, this family resided in Csillaghead, an affluent suburb of Budapest where many of the prosperous refugees lived.

"My mother is in Nagyvarad. I am staying with a Hungarian family, but tonight I have no place to sleep, because they were tipped off that there might be a *razzia* tonight."

"I will be going home on the six o'clock train. Meet me at the station, and I will take you home with me," he said.

Hallelujah! I felt reborn. Lusia too was greatly relieved. She had been in a dilemma – could not help me and would not leave me alone with my fears. Once the problem appeared to be solved, at least for this night, we parted in a state of euphoria.

That day my moods changed rapidly: despair, fear of the approaching night, worry over the Shuffelds fate, then unexpected deliverance.

Before leaving for the train station, I walked over to the Shuffelds again, to share with them the good news, so they wouldn't worry when I failed to return.

When Mrs. Shuffeld saw me, she exclaimed, "You are not going anyplace!" "Let me see your feet."

One look at my bruised feet, and she clucked reproachfully. "You poor child, you can hardly move. You're staying, and that's that. Der Lieber Gott will watch over us all."

After dinner my feet were soaked and dressed, and the three girls, Lici, Ibi, and I, prepared a contingency plan for the night. Should the detectives be heard coming, I would run from my bed and hide in the storage chest under Lici's bed. Having promised myself to be on alert the whole night, I sank into a deep sleep the moment my head touched the pillow. Needless to say, if there had been a *razzia* that night, or any of the nights I spent in that house, I would not be writing these lines today.

A few days later I met Mr. Gletzel, and was he happy to see me! He told me how he had looked and looked for me and waited till the last possible moment before boarding the train, worried over what could have happened to me. A few minutes and some miles away from Budapest, he was relieved that I hadn't come. A major *razzia* was conducted on the train. The passengers who could not prove that they lived in Csillaghead were arrested and taken off the train. Berta Shuffeld's loving kindness had saved me from imprisonment, and who knows what else?

It was time to move on and join Mother. The Rescue Committee received funds from Switzerland, which was then disbursed to people fleeing Budapest. One of the persons in charge was David Rosenfeld, a writer from Krakow. I will always remember what he said to me after I approached him in the Kiraly Utca coffeehouse: "The daughter of Wolf Landerer should not have to come to the committee. We will come to you." Few days after he and another gentleman came to the Shuffelds and handed me a stack of banknotes, the equivalent of $150 on the black market, a sum beyond my wildest dreams.

After they left Mr. Shuffeld closeted himself with me and handed me a hundred dollar bill, saying "Soon you will be leaving my house to travel to Romania. I have inquired about the conditions there and calculated how much a person would need in order to live in Bucharest comfortably for six months. This money plus what you have received from the committee should carry you through this period of time. By then, we hope the war will be over, but in any case I have confidence that once you become familiar with your new surroundings, you will manage on your own. Your father will pay me back after the war."

(I must add as a footnote that after the war the Shuffelds refused to accept the money back.)

I felt as rich as Croesus. My self-confidence was restored, and I felt invincible. I had an enormous amount of money at my disposal, and my mother was waiting for me in Nagyvarad.

The next day was Wednesday. As was his habit, Mr. Shuffeld went down to buy newspapers and returned with a long face.

"Lala," he said, "I am afraid that the news is especially bad for you."

"What has happened?"

"The ghetto in Nagyvarad will be sealed off this coming Friday noon."

That was very bad news indeed. Tragic for the Jews of Nagyvarad, of course, for "sealing off" – forcing scattered Jews into the ghetto, then guarding the entrance – was only the first step; next would come deportation to concentration and extermination camps. But bad for me, too, because the Jews there – anonymous friends, advisers, and translators for refugees – were my only hope of contacting Mother, who had been staying with a Jewish family outside the ghetto.

I would have to reach Nagyvarad before Friday noon, before the Action began. But how? The only train for Nagyvarad left Budapest in the evening and arrived at this border town at midnight; only the passengers on the sleeping car were permitted to stay aboard the train till morning, and those tickets were sold out two weeks in advance. This meant that we would be debarked from the train in the middle of the night – in an unfamiliar border town, probably swarming with suspicious officials and rough soldiers.

We were aliens, without permission to leave our assigned locations – Polish Jews, thinly disguised as Polish Christians. Our false documents would not stand up to a rigorous examination. People like us had as much chance to escape arrest, wandering through Nagyvarad at midnight, as if we had gone straight to the police station and said, "Ship me to Auschwitz."

As I was pondering this dilemma, I noticed that two young men had taken to following me every day. "What are you doing? When are you going to your mother?" they asked repeatedly. They believed that I had all the necessary information about the "road to Romania" in my pocket. They knew my mother and were convinced that all was ready and just waiting for me.

"What do you mean?" I asked finally, on that vital Wednesday.

"Well, we don't know anybody in Nagyvarad, and you can lead us to your mother's smugglers."

I tried to explain the problem about being stranded at the border town in the middle of the night, but that did not put them off. "Listen," they said, "If you promise not to leave us in Nagyvarad, we will get sleeping car tickets for tomorrow."

It was the answer to a prayer – if they could pull it off. But I wasn't sure I could be of much help to them. "Well," I said dubiously, "I want you to know that it is over a week since I had my last letter from Mother. I'm not sure where she might be."

"All right, all right. Just promise that you will not run away from us in Nagyvarad."

"Good, I promise!"

The truth was that I was not sure I could find Mother even if I did make it to Nagyvarad before Friday noon. Nevertheless, I decided to accept the young man's offer. Calina and the whole group of young people from Bochnia were there.

Lusia became very upset. There I was, supposedly her best friend, going to Romania and leaving her behind. There was nothing I would have liked more than to be with her, but I could hardly ask her to share with me the unpredictable. She had gone already through the liquidation of Ghetto Bochnia, concentration camp Czebno, transport to Auschwitz, her escape from there, hiding in empty trains at night, and the passage to Hungary. But when she said that, no matter what, she did not want to stay in Budapest without me, I was overjoyed. It was too late to get a ticket for her, but we were told that for a sizable tip the conductor would permit another passenger to occupy the sleeping compartment.

The young men were as good as their word. Somehow they produced the all-important sleeping-car tickets, and on Thursday evening, we departed from Budapest. In order not to appear like new arrivals in town, we took only our pocketbooks. The lady who shared my compartment had no objections to Lusia's presence. She even suggested that, since she would be leaving the train before us, Lusia would be able to spend the rest of the night in her berth.

Too excited to sleep, we went to see how our traveling companions were doing in another part of the train. To our amazement we found other refugees sitting with them. In order not to think what the next day would bring, we talked and joked, and the evening passed quickly. When a knock at the door reminded us that it was time to make up the berths and turn off the lights, we reluctantly left.

Lusia and I returned to our compartment. Our Hungarian lady was already asleep, and as quiet as a mouse, I climbed onto the top berth. Lusia and I had agreed that, since we would not be able to close an eye anyhow, we would alternate, every hour – one would lie on the berth while the other sat in the corner, then change positions. At least we would get some rest.

The train was moving at a considerable speed and the sounds of the rolling wheels had a hypnotizing effect on me. When a sharp knock at the door woke me up, it was morning, and the porters were urging the people to leave the train.

30 • Over another border

It was early morning when our group left the train station. Under an overcast sky, a gloomy town was awakening to the last day of freedom for its Jews. Impersonating young people on a leisurely stroll, we all walked arm in arm on opposite sides of the street. As we proceeded along what seemed to be the main artery of the town, the scenery begun to change and noises to intrude on the quiet of the half-asleep town: the lamentlike whining sounds of ungreased wooden cart wheels and the harsh clatter of horses hoofs clapping over the stony road. Soon enough we were greeted by familiar sights: peasant carts loaded high with household goods, little children and old people seated among the makeshift bundles, silent men and women, each with a yellow star sewn on their clothing, walking alongside the moving carts. Country Jews arriving in Nagyvarad to be "sealed off." On every cart, seated beside the driver, a bored-looking policeman was nodding sleepily.

More carts turned in from side streets, and the road was becoming crowded. Occasionally we heard a child weeping, the wistful barking of a dog following his master, or the coarse voice of the peasant prompting his horse. Stealthily we squinted at the passing people, but there were no familiar faces, and we slowed our pace. We did not want to be mistaken for escaping Jews!

The sorrowful caravan left us behind, and we walked on the main street till we reached a large marketplace. It was unlike any we had ever seen. The entire space was taken up by countless small wooden booths, all securely bolted. The center of the city was deserted and all stores closed. As we were walking in circles among the scattered booths and trying to make some sense of the situation, I spotted two young men from Bochnia and ran over to them.

Hardly a year had passed since we were all prisoners in Bochnia, and we were overjoyed to see each other.

"What are you doing here? When did you come?"

"Just this morning. Where is Celina?"

"She is with us. We rented a little house on the outskirts."

"Great. I am not alone. Lusia Steinfeld is with me and two other people from Dunassent –" I froze in midsentence. Two massive hulks of men in black uniforms, on their heads clusters of the largest rooster's feathers I have ever seen, accosted us.

"Your papers?" It was a command. While the men who were equipped with genuine looking but homemade documents and permits to live in Nagyvarad were handing over their papers, I ducked in between the booths and ran. Before the ghoulish enforcers of the law realized what was happening, I was nowhere to be seen. My companions saw this from afar and caught up with me at the other end of the marketplace, where I hid behind a booth. I was wearing a bright green suit and was easy to spot from far away.

"Did you ask them where they live?"

"Nope. Had no chance."

We entered a little bodega, where we had breakfast. Once we had eaten, the situation did not seem so bleak anymore. Over the coffee we comforted each other. After all we did not come to Nagyvarad just to see Celina and the Bochnia people, but my Mother.

As it turned out, she was staying close by, and we walked over. In front of the house stood a group of people. In spite of the warm weather, all wore overcoats with a large yellow star sewn in front. It was obvious that they were Jews waiting to be taken into the ghetto. Having made sure that we were indeed at the right address, I asked for Mother. They looked at each other, then at me, and finally one of the men told me in broken German that my mother, together with the group of Poles, had crossed over to Romania. Another asked if I was the daughter of the lady who cried so much, because she had left a letter for me. I was handed a piece of crumpled paper. The ink had run, blurring the letters, and the page was full of round spots, my mother's tears, making it difficult to read. Still, I was familiar with mother's handwriting. The message read: Dear Lala, I am desperate. The whole group is leaving. I refused to go with them, but everyone claims that this would be suicidal. If I stayed, I would at best be taken into the ghetto. Because of my documents saying that I should be living in Dunassent most probably would be handed over to the Gestapo. All assure me that I have no need to worry about you because they know how brave you are, and how well you always know how to get out of impossible situations. May God protect you, my precious child, because your own mother can't. Forgive me. Your heartbroken mother.

It was a bit unexpected, but at least my mother was safe, and I did not have to worry about her. My companions were looking askance at me. Not knowing what to say, I handed the letter to Lusia. She had just started to read it when she was interrupted by the German-speaking man, addressing his friends. I will never forget what he said.

"Those poor children, those poor Poles. Came all the way here, and again they have to run. But where should they go now?" After a few moments he turned around and told us that this morning, soap smugglers had arrived from across the border, and because the people they did business with had already been taken away, they were ready to go back with a "cargo" of Jews. Nobody knew them, because they had never led people before, but if we were willing to take the risk, we could go with them.

I had not one change of clothing, no place to go, nowhere to return, nobody to ask advice. But the unexpected encounter with the *kokoshes* had stirred my dormant fears of people in uniform. Afraid to be seen on the street lest the entire population was on the alert for a girl in a green dress, I was ready to run to the forest right away.

We all decided to go, but had to wait till nightfall. To our delight, we discovered that already two other people were waiting to go with the smugglers: a woman from Nagyvarad, whose husband crossed the border a few days ago, and a man, an escapee from the *munka tabor*, the Hungarian counterpart of Nazi forced-labor camps for Jewish men. Dressed as a peasant in a regional suit of homespun, coarse linen, white pants tucked into black leather boots, and a collarless, loose shirt tied at the waist by a piece of rope, he looked the perfect country yokel. Fluent in three languages, Hungarian, Romanian, and Yiddish, he became the guiding spirit of our group.

Every hour seemed to stretch into an eternity. Noon arrived and with it the dreaded deadline (what an appropriate expression). Silence and desolation spread over the abandoned streets, occasionally disrupted by loud, angry commands barked in Hungarian and the hubbub made by the rolling carts. Like a funeral march created by a composer gone berserk were the sounds accompanying the Nagyvarad Jews into exile.

The entire town of Nagyvarad and vicinity had become *Judenrein*. The deserted Jewish streets had acquired the lifeless look of a ghost town. After an emotional farewell from the people we had just met and who had shown us so much love and compassion, we felt bereaved. Their little house and the gravelike silence of the narrow, dirt street, seemed foreboding. We could not face the empty stoop, where the footprints of the inhabitants were still visible in the dust. This morning the tidy housewife did not sweep in front of her house. One window of the abandoned building was left open. A slight breeze moved the curtain in and out of the window like someone waving good-bye.

I remember what they said, their concern and pity for us, but not their names, not even the street they lived on. I will never forget them because these anonymous people personified all that is good and noble in a human being. May their memory, and of many like them that I have met during my wanderings, be blessed forever!

A long afternoon stretched ahead of us – six people who didn't know how to pass their time or where to go. To linger in town was not advisable. Sporadic checks by eager police and looters were to be expected. We had seen it all before and did not think that the Hungarian police would behave any better than their Polish counterparts.

Where could we hide till dusk came? I was getting jittery. I imagined an entire division of *kokoshes* searching methodically through the entire town just for me. Falling into their clutches just a few hours before the scheduled "departure" to Romania was unthinkable.

Izsak, our "peasant," was a born leader, and in the most natural way he assumed the responsibility for our group. Familiar with those parts, he told us that over the town's boundary was a river, where we would be able to stay for hours without attracting attention. Relieved to have someone tell us what to do, we would have followed him anyplace.

It was early afternoon when we set out for a leisurely outing at the river bank. Izak, our guide, went first. A short distance behind him, Mrs. Shapiro, holding a small wicker basket over her arm, rambled over the unpaved road. Then Lusia with one of our companions, myself with the other, each pair trekking apart from the others. We reached the expanse of the fields in no time. Everything around was peaceful and quiet. In the pale afternoon light the river moved lazily toward its destination. Occasionally an isolated fisherman was seen, throwing his bait, or a peasant, looking like a carbon copy of our Izsak, walked by. As we begun to enjoy the walk and even relax a bit, we reached the bend of the road. Suddenly, a sentry booth with two threatening-looking *kokoshes* appeared just a few hundred meters ahead of us. Because of the booth's location behind the bend, they saw us before we could have seen them. I felt myself going limp with fear, when Mrs. Shapiro's loud voice cut into the silence. In her purest Hungarian, the only language she knew, she demanded, "What should I do now with the Jewish Star on my dress? There are police ahead of us!"

As if this were not enough, she opened her coat and pointed to her yellow star pinned to her dress. While escaping the ghetto in order to steal across the border, she was careful not to break the law by discarding her yellow patch.

"Just button the coat and keep on going after me," Izsak mouthed with anger. Without changing his pace, he reached the sentry and passed undisturbed. Clutching her precious basket, Mrs. Shapiro hobbled by next, and she too was ignored. We, the two girls with our "dates," walked by, and no one paid attention to us either.

We continued ahead until we saw Izak going down to the river bank where he stretched out under a tree. Following the lead, each couple sat under a separate tree with Mrs. Shapiro someplace in between. And there we sat, waiting for this long day to end.

We thought the sun would never set, but at last it did, signaling that it was time to meet the smugglers. The walk back was uneventful, and at the appointed place, we met our guides.

There were three of them, big, husky, ferocious-looking fellows, talking fast in an incomprehensible language. But they took to Izsak as a long lost brother, and he told us not to worry.

Us, worry? What did we have to worry about? Our other options were to be arrested and taken over by the Gestapo or imprisoned in Hungary, to be executed on the spot or tortured in order to denounce other people, to be deported back to Poland or, with the best of luck, to land in a sealed ghetto with the Nagyvarad Jews. Better to take a chance on people who claimed to lead us out of Hungary.

Izsak explained to us that crossing the border would take three days and three nights. First we would pass over Hungarian territory. Our road would lead across an established path of the armed border patrol. It was well known to all smugglers that the patrol kept regular hours, and the place was considered safe before midnight. Excited, we were eager to start immediately, but we had to wait till full dark. Once we had started, no rest would be allowed till safe territory was reached. We would walk during the nights and remain hidden during the days.

As soon as the twilight spread over the deserted town, we sneaked through the empty streets and in no time were climbing up through the dense forest. Silence and tranquility enveloped us. Our silhouettes blended with the shades and shadows of the dark forest. We marched fast till we came to a field of tall, ripe-for-harvest oats. Afraid of leaving traces, we carefully traversed the verge of the treacherous terrain. A large bald field skirted by few lonely scrawny pines loomed ahead.

"Psst." We stopped. The smugglers whispered to Izak, and he told us that so far we had made excellent time and would be passing "the strip" an hour before the border patrol. Thus encouraged, we were ready to race the wind, but there was no wind that calm night. Nothing was moving, only the dewdrops shimmering on the grass reflected the moon's cool shine.

We were getting ready to start when Izsak's urgent whisper cut us short. "Fall to the ground!" In a split second we flattened ourselves in the tall grass. We didn't know what had happened. An eternity loaded with fear passed before I dared to open my eyes. No more than a hundred yards from where we huddled on the ground the border patrol was passing the field.

There were two of them. Bayonets gleamed above their heads as they inched their way ahead, stopping occasionally and looking around. We heard their voices as they talked, and we silently prayed that they would not hear our pounding hearts. It took a long, long time till they had crossed the field and disappeared behind the trees.

What had happened? Were we being led into a trap? Was it a reinforcement of border control, because of the situation in Nagyvarad? Or just a chance occurrence? We left it at that. . . .

Long time after the patrol passed, we remained afraid to move, even to take a deep breath. The damp grass and the night's cool air made us uncomfortable, as we lay there, stiff and miserable. But when given the signal to run, we broke into a gallop fit for Olympians.

Entering another forest felt like being embraced by a trusted friend. We trotted after our guides and Izak under a canopy of intertwining branches. Our next stop, a farmhouse in the clearing, was reached before dawn. We were sent up to the attic above the barn, and thus ended the night when the border patrol decided to change its regular schedule.

Gray morning light was seeping through the crevices of the roof as we settled for a day of waiting. I stretched out on the fresh hay and for a few peaceful hours dozed off. When I woke up, the sun stood high. Golden beams crossed the garret in a lopsided, geometrical pattern. Muted voices were heard from below – another working day on the homestead had begun. The rooster's shrill voice awakened his harem of obedient hens, and they were clacking excitedly. Steps were heard from below – somebody coming in to milk the cows. Streams of milk released from heavy udders hit the empty bottom of the tin pail in a steady musical stream. As the pail filled up, we heard the whisper of the milking woman, apparently praising the patient beast. A man's loud voice merged into the harmony of the sounds. The farmer's daily chores, as predictable as sunrise. Simple, unpretentious, close to nature – this was life in its purest form.

The farmyard quietened down. Our attic was getting hot, and the insects were up in arms against us, the invaders. The discomfort made us restless. Since sleeping was not possible anymore, we talked. First to have the floor was Izak. He showed us the photos of his family, which he carried in a worn, otherwise empty wallet. When his platoon of slave laborers was preparing to be sent to the Russian front – they always reserved the most dangerous places for Jews – he decided to beat it. The tattered clothing he bought from an unsuspecting peasant. First he returned to his home town, but unfortunately it was too late; all Jews had already been deported. Having lost hope of finding his family, he decided to go over the border to Romania. The faded, precious snapshots were passed from hand to hand. Facing us were two little girls and a young, smiling woman. Tears rolled down Izsak's dark, weatherbeaten face. All were quiet until Lusia interrupted the silence. "Izsak," she said, "you are still luckier than the rest of us. At least you do have some photos left." Like a real peasant Izsak wiped his teary face with his sleeve and returned the photos to his breast pocket, where they remained close to his heart till the end of the journey.

It was evening again. We heard steps climbing up the ladder, and someone placed our supper on the landing. It was dark, coarse peasant bread, butter and milk, and a jug of spring water. Refreshed, we put on our shoes and were ready to go. When the disheveled head of the smugglers' leader appeared at the top of the ladder, Izsak bent down and held a lengthy conference with him. All smiles, he happily translated the instructions for part two of our escapade. We would be leaving as soon as it got dark. This time the march would be long and strenuous; because of a hostile village on our route, we would have to circle around it a bit. Circles, triangles, quadrangles – nothing could have held us back.

It was another cloudless, moonlit night. Following Ali Baba, as we had nicknamed the head smuggler, in a single row, we entered a dense forest. Walking through the thick underbrush was tiring. Our legs felt heavy. The only sounds heard were those of twigs broken under our feet and occasional hoots of an owl. High above, glittering stars were sprinkled over an expanse of navy blue velvety skies. Between the galaxy of merrily blinking lights, a lonely moon was sailing. The spectacle of mute shadows racing the cosmos was awesome.

We had lost all concept of time. The underbrush was getting thinner, the trees less dense, and we felt grass under our feet. A clearing in the woods was near, and the hope of rest and maybe even of finding water to drink boosted our endurance. Suddenly Ali Baba stopped and remained motionless. Instinctively I held my breath and looked ahead.

I blinked, rubbed my eyes, closed them tight and opened again, pinched myself, but the Fata Morgana did not disappear. It was not a figment of my feverish imagination, or a case of group hysteria. In front of us a silvery white road cut through a sleeping village, the very same one we had so laboriously tried to avoid. We had lost our way in the woods, and there was no going back. The group retreated into the forest, and after a short consultation with the smugglers, Izsak reassured us that the solution was simple. All we had to do was to pass through the village unnoticed. Very simple indeed!

Lighted by a bright moon only, the slumbering village resembled a stage set for a surrealistic play. On one side of the white road, a group of people, bent low, was moving up the hill. The village dogs picked up our scent and began to howl. We were crawling on all fours when we saw a farmer emerge from his house on the opposite side of the road. He held a lantern and searched around his yard. We heard his voice as he talked to his dog. Confident that there were no prowlers nearby, the farmer returned to the house. But the dogs would not stop barking. Whenever we saw lights appearing in a window, we flattened ourselves and remained motionless. How we traversed along the village road without being discovered, I will never understand. When Ali Baba signaled, we darted across the road.

Hanging over the village, like a bowl of liquid gold, was the moon, in whose magnetic glare the green of the grass and leaves melted into a nondescript shade. It made the white-underwear-clad farmers appear like spirits entering and exiting the stage on cue – a perfectly staged and executed play. Except that this was not a midsummer night's dream, only one event out of the tragicomedy our lives had become.

We crossed the road at the outskirts of the village, close to the top of the hill. How we accomplished it without being discovered is beyond me to explain. The only spectator was the man on the moon, and he must have been doubled over with laughter.

We made it! We made it! We galloped up the hill. When we reached the peak, everyone rolled down. Once at a safe distance, we were allowed to rest, and then the tension of the last hours exploded. I don't remember who was the one to start laughing, but it was contagious, and soon we were all laughing uncontrollably.

"Did you see the farmer with the gun?"

"Never saw such dumb dogs, God bless them!"

"Never saw such dumb farmers, God bless them double!"

"This was the funniest imaginable!"

Having gotten high on danger, we were able to ignore it completely, but our guides were practical. They wanted to get the trip over with and collect their money, and they made us move on. It was dawn already when we reached our next stop. We climbed a ladder above the barn and settled for the day.

The only one of our gang carrying something was Mrs. Shapiro. It was a small wicker basket tightly covered, which she watched over jealously. In response to our constant nagging, she informed us that she was carrying in it something for her husband. It was Izsak the joker who solved the mystery of the basket. When she dozed off, he quietly slid close to her and sneaked his hand into her basket. And what was it he pulled out? A cookie! All this woman could think of, while facing deportation and leaving her home forever, was to bake once more cookies for her husband.

That day, hidden in the middle of nowhere, deep in the forest on the Hungarian-Romanian border, we were in no mood to discuss human behavior under stress. But for Izak, the caretaker of our group's morale, this was great material for his jokes. He teased her about it good-naturedly until we parted.

And thus the third day went by. We joked, ate some of the cookies, and were in high spirits. There was not the slightest doubt in our minds that in a number of hours we would be in Arad. Mrs. Shapiro laughed with the rest of us. She understood that no offense was meant, but that, in order to survive another day under a barn's roof and be ready to tackle the last part of our wanderings in the wilderness, we could not permit ourselves to become serious. Whenever Izsak tried to reach into the pocket holding the wallet with his family pictures, one of us immediately distracted him with a joke or one of Mrs. Shapiro's cookies. Thus time went by fast, and when evening came, all were ready. This time we left later than usual because the border was not far away. Once we crossed it, there would be no more running! Never!

And it came to pass. It was morning, it was evening, the third night of our "going to Romania." We set out in joyful anticipation of a happy ending. This time it would be just a short, leisurely walk. When we reached the foot of a hill, the smugglers begun to talk animatedly and point their finger toward the space ahead of us.

"Children" Izsak called. "There, over there!"

"What is there?"

"The border!"

No prompting was necessary. We raced, each wanting to be first to reach the Promised Land. Long-legged Izsak was first. He fell on his knees and sobbed. "Children, we are free! We are saved! Kiss the ground!"

Bang! bang! bang! bam! A salvo of shots resounded in the valley and was repeated by the echo over and over again. Like demons possessed by supernatural force, we ran and ran until the cursed sounds were heard no more. Drained of all energy we gathered together and in disbelief looked at each other. It was true indeed.

We were in Romania!

31 · In Romania

The antiquated train chugged over the narrow track, all the time panting heavily, like a tired old man. Occasionally the shrill whistle of the locomotive interrupted the grunts of the turning wheels. We were crowded into one compartment, together with an assortment of peasants and labourers in soiled work clothes. The shabby, filthy train appeared to us, the six fugitives, as glamorous as the legendary Orient Express. Our clothes, slept in during the last three days, were crumpled and stained, our hair tinted gray with the dust of the attics. For good measure dry pine needles, mementoes of our underbrush crawls, stuck to our garments. Nevertheless, the bizarre spectacle we presented failed to attract attention. We were among the poorest in the land of riches, where plenty existed alongside abject poverty.

Oblivious to the loud, unintelligible conversations around us, ignoring our bruised feet and sore muscles, we were mesmerized by the sounds of the moving train. It seemed to be repeating endlessly the magic words: Romania, ROMA-NIA!! We-made-it, we-made-it, WE-MADE-IT!!! – and it was not a dream. A Romanian train rolling over the Romanian land leaving the Nazi kingdom behind. And I was on the train, and my best friend Lusia was with me. The nightmares of all the yesterdays were left far behind. Transfixed, I watched as a new day, brimming with light and hope, emerged out of the pale morning mist. Through my half-opened eyes I saw the enchanting countryside slide by, but my mind was already projecting plans for the future. I felt calm and serene as never before. It was spring 1944 when I, a nineteen-year-old, had arrived in the land of peace, believing that my race with a cruel fate was won. Was it any wonder that I was falling in love with life all over again?

A long, loud whistle and a strong jolt shook me out of my reverie.

The train had come to a stop. Izsak, still the leader, informed us brightly that we had reached our goal.

"*ARAD*"-large, black letters over the whitewashed wall of the station assured us that we were not dreaming. As we followed Izsak, I noticed some familiar faces strangely turning away from me, but as we were met by a representative of the Jewish community, I did not give it a thought. Yet, I had hardly introduced myself to him when a tap on the shoulder made me turn around. Standing there and looking at me sadly was an acquaintance from Krakow, Tonka Poser, who said, "Miss Landerer, I am sorry to inform you that your mother, together with the little Englander girl, was captured at the border and sent back to Hungary."

It felt as if the ground had caved in under me. Mother, my mother, the infallible one, let herself be caught at the border? How could it have happened? Wasn't she supposed to be waiting for me in Arad? Weren't we going to meet Father? and the boys and my sister and the rest of the family? Start a new life "after the war." No! No! No! It could not be true! But it was.

As I stood there downcast, disbelieving and rejected, I was approached by Mr. Berl Frankel from Bielitz (Bielsko), who in Bochnia had worked in the same building as we did. He must have watched from afar, because without even greeting me, he said, "Miss Landerer, you must stay in Arad till you hear what has happened to your mother." As I looked at him, bewildered and uncomprehending, he turned around and returned to the woman accompanying him. Shortly afterward, his strange behaviour was explained to me.

The lady companion was his sister, and together with her the distraught man was meeting every train coming from the border, hoping to find his young sons aboard. While the Frankel family was crossing the border, the two boys, one eight, the other ten years old, strayed from the group and were found by the Romanian border police. As illegal aliens, the two children were arrested, processed according to the international law then prevailing, and returned to Hungary. (We had met with this law before in Slovakia, where, thanks to clever bribery, it had become a useful tool in transporting fugitives from one end of the country to the other, but in Romania it proved to be a disaster.) The Rescue Committee was unable to deal with the situation because the border police were under the jurisdiction of the ministry in Bucharest.

The two Frankel boys were taken to the forest path leading to Hungary and ordered to go there. At night they lost their way and miraculously were found the next day wandering on Romanian soil. The community was alerted by informers, but again, there was nothing they could do. A day passed as the desperate parents waited and prayed, but their children were once more turned away into the wilderness. Mrs. Frankel had given way under the tension and was closeted in the house where they were staying. The entire Jewish community watched helplessly as this charade was cruelly replayed during the ensuing fortnight. For over two weeks those children were repeatedly abandoned in the forest, and each time, they returned to the place from which they had been chased away. By the eighth time, "justice" was felt to have been satisfied, and the exasperated authorities permitted the two little "perpetrators" to enter Romania legally.

Later on, on the train to Bucharest, I asked the younger of the boys if he was afraid during the ordeal. Didn't he lose hope during those days and nights alone in the forest?

"Afraid? Who? I? Never. A *Yid* must have faith. I knew all the time that, no matter what our enemies would do, God would not abandon us. You see, I was right."

Forty years later this child's affirmation of faith still rings in my ears.

While this nightmare was going on, I was too wrapped up in my own problem and too exhausted by the latest happenings to be able to follow it closely. Lusia and I were assigned quarters with the Farkas family, because Mrs. Farkas had requested "pretty girls." Disheveled, dirty, and depressed, we hardly fitted her qualifications, but when she saw us, two orphaned girls in need of mothering, the kind woman responded with feeling. "Tante Roszi," as she asked to be called, was a jolly, kind soul, who made us feel right at home. She put ointment on our bruised feet, fed us choice morsels, and our strength returned quickly. My sagging spirits were lifted by her reassurances that as soon as Mother arrived, she too would stay there.

A special messenger, with instructions to trace my mother and the Englander child, was immediately dispatched over the border. A few days later he returned with the sad news that they had already been sent to the fortresslike prison in Budapest, the Tolonzhaz.

My vigil at the border was ended. Even Mr. Frankel agreed with the committee that I should move away from the border, go on to Bucharest, and stay there till the end of the war.

The three Schiffs, Syma, Sianka, and Naftali, remained in Arad, where they vowed to move heaven and earth, if necessary, to free Sianka's little girl and my mother. To their amazement they found out that every committee they approached gave them preferential treatment. Later they learned why. When their name was spotted on the survivors' list, it was assumed that they were related to the famous philanthropist Jacob Schiff, and they were treated as befits members of this illustrious family. Nobody in their native Brzesko had ever heard of Jacob Schiff (a German-born American-and not Polish-and long since dead by then anyway, as I have since learned), and neither was related to him, but during the ensuing complications, this mistake proved to be a real blessing.

Eventually this story had a happy ending. Mother told me later how, after they had crossed the border and were waiting in a shack in the woods for the Romanian smuggler, the little girl fell asleep. Someone suggested that since Mother was the oldest in the group, she was probably tired too, and when the smuggler came, the whole group departed, leaving Mother with the child to follow with the next group. Before she realized what was happening, they were gone, and she was left alone in no-man's-land, with the sleeping child as her only companion. She became frantic. Her sole consolation was that Sianka would realize the foolishness of separating herself from her child and would send the guide back.

It did not take long before a stranger appeared and with gestures motioned her to follow him. Full of misgivings but forced by circumstances to obey, she dressed the child and did as she was told. As soon as they started on their way, she realized that they were going back in the same direction from which they had come. The sad march was soon over. When they were handed over to the Hungarian police, she knew that her intuition had been right.

My mother was put into a prison cell with a Hungarian Jewish woman. Thrown together by common destiny, the two jailmates became friends in no time. After one day together the woman confided that she had hidden jewelry in her bread ration, which was already crumbling, and she was afraid lest it be discovered and taken away. If that happened, then not only would she lose her entire fortune, but she would be severely punished for trying to hide it in the first place.

After the war Mother met her former cellmate. She, with her entire family survived, and settled in Israel. It was a most happy reunion. This lady told us that the jewels Mother concealed in her loaf of bread, helped her and her family to survive.

After a few days in Nagyvarad the Polish prisoners were transferred to Budapest, where it felt almost like home. A large group of Polish Jews were incarcerated there, rounded up during numerous *razzias* in Budapest and different towns on the Romanian border. The Rescue Committee was alerted, strings were pulled, and after four weeks the prisoners were released.

When Mother was set free in Budapest, I was already in Bucharest. On top of the precarious freedom she did not know what to do with, she had to care for a ten-year-old girl. The Schuffelds were still living in their apartment, and that became Mother's base. The situation of the Hungarian Jews was desperate. The Russian front line was coming nearer and nearer, and the possibility of Budapest becoming a city under siege was real. Under such circumstances Mother had to plan for her own survival and that of the child she had involuntarily become responsible for. Lucky for all concerned, her indomitable spirit never left her. Hunting around, she found an exclusive convent school for girls whose headmistress spoke German. Thus, relying on her own intuition, her Aryan looks, and her aristocratic bearing, she became acquainted with the prioress, and soon she won the woman's consent to shelter the child in the convent till the end of the war.

Meanwhile, the Schiffs, elated by the happy news that not only was the child alive, but both she and her protectress were free, pressured the committee for help in reuniting the child with her mother. Sure enough, the magic of the Schiff name worked again, and a special smuggler was dispatched to Budapest to bring back the lady with the child. In a tragicomic twist, the messenger arrived only a few days after Mother had placed the girl in the convent.

But leave it to my mother. She somehow got the child out, and a few days later they were reunited with the Schiffs in Arad.

Little Mirlam survived the war, together with her mother and brother. At the moment she lives in Haifa, happily married, a mother of three daughters herself. For Pani Zahorska ("Mrs. Zahorska!-Mother), her past guardian and companion, she retains a special spot in her heart and memory.

32 · At long last free

Bucharest, a wonderful, wonderful town, so fondly remembered by all who lived there during the unforgettable summer of 1944. A mixture of tolerance and bigotry, piety and profanity, old and new. Narrow, crooked streets alongside broad, tree-lined boulevards. Tall, modern structures crowding out dwarfish, old buildings. Romanians are great lovers of nature, and their capital has many large parks and small, beautifully landscaped plazas. As clean and well kept as the parks, lawns, and plazas were, the streets were neglected and dirty. And cats, cats, cats everywhere. The flowers, the pigeons, the dirt, and the cats, combined with the friendly people, added up to the unique, slightly exotic charm of this great city.

In spite of total blackout, Bucharest's night life went on as usual. Sleep in the crowded, noisy apartments was hard to come by, and people took to the streets. We, the young refugees, fascinated by people not afraid to be outdoors at all hours, used to wander around in groups. The restaurants and coffeehouses spilled outdoors. Our favorite pastime was to watch people. Entire families crowding around a single table. Dark-skinned men sipping wine, sleepy children propping their nodding heads on dirty hands. Women in colorful dresses, a wineglass in one hand, the other holding a baby sucking at a bared breast. Pungent smells floating in the air and the cacophony of loud talk, laughter, and often drunken singing. It soothed us, made us forget reality. The radios blared popular music. The French song "J'Attendral" was an international hit from before the war, and the lilting voice used to touch a raw nerve. The sad, full-of-expectation lyrics, about somebody waiting the return of a loved one, carried a special meaning for us. The radio broadcasts were often interrupted by warnings of impending air raids, turning the peaceful scene into pandemonium. The warnings were signaled as soon as the

269

planes, leaving their bases in North Africa, were picked up by the radar in Italy. Quite often the alarms proved to be false, and in no time life returned to normal. Unfortunately for the partly devastated city, most of the time they were real. Usually ten minutes after the alarm was sounded, cadres of menacing planes followed.

No one who has not lived through an air raid had seen such a spectacle. No fireworks can duplicate the dramatic display of a burning city, especially at night. Many times the streets became so illuminated by the burning buildings that it would have been possible to read a book in the middle of the night, should one have wished to; but the only desire felt after leaving an air-raid shelter was to find out who was missing and who was spared. Every raid had the semblance of the Day of Judgment, except that it felt as if we were in Hell already.

In Bucharest it was possible to ride the tram for hours through whole sections of the city entirely destroyed. I will never forget the picture of a house torn in two, on a street totally in ruins. This was the only skeleton of what used to be a human dwelling. One wall of this house with a part of the floor still attached, remained intact. A picture was hanging on the pink painted wall; under the picture was an empty crib. It stood there among destruction like a sore in the flesh, like a gravestone of all shuttered nurseries, like a monument to human cruelty.

These air raids have to be considered a new barbarism in the history of Western Civilization. Any mass destruction that happened before the World War II came as a result of natural disasters like epidemics, earthquakes, floods, and the likes. The massive bombardments of open cities were the first of many acts of mass annihilation by technological means.

It happened one unforgettable summer night. The regular radio broadcast was suddenly interrupted. King Michael of Romania proclaimed Romania's secession from the Axis and its joining of the Allies. The whole city went wild with joy. It was after midnight when Mother and I went out to the street. That night nobody slept. People danced, sang, laughed; strangers embraced, young and old shouted in unison: "Pace la Romania! Pace la Romania!" The coveted peace had finally come.

The rejoicing did not last long. The German Luftwaffe, which occupied the airport, issued an ultimatum for unconditional surrender of the city. The deadline was set at ten o'clock next morning. Refusal was to be met with total destruction.

At ten o'clock in the morning the walling sirens signaled the approaching German planes. After joyful celebration of the promised peace, which went on until morning, people seemed to be drained of all emotion. Equipped with blankets, food, bottles of water, all went rushing into shelters, resigned to whatever might happen.

After forty-eight hours of continuous bombardment a strange quiet pervaded the space. Fearing new German treachery, we all huddled in the cellar for a long time. Finally, a few brave souls ventured out – and moments later returned jubilant. The entire city was calm. The Red Army had entered Bucharest!

The city received the Russians with open arms. Overnight the exuberant Romanians recovered from the shock of the bombardment, and the city once again teemed with life. But it did not take long for the people to realize that the liberation by the Red Army meant only a change from one occupation to another. The Russians descended upon the city like a swarm of locusts and ravaged it like one. The fear of sudden arrests and executions disappeared (it was years before the world acknowledged the existence of gulags), but nevertheless people realized that things would never be as they had been before.

Two days after our liberators entered the city, I witnessed scenes beyond my wildest dreams. German POWs – the SS elite troops – transported on trucks, as befitted the criminals they were. Entire German families being deported to detention camps or, even better, "relocated" someplace deep inside the U.S.S.R., leaving their possessions behind. Familiar scenes, but this time I was the gleeful spectator.

Rabbis can preach forgiveness, the priests Christian mercy, the philosophers that evil acts do more damage to the perpetrators than to the victim. But I attest what my own experience taught me. Revenge for the death of little children and the murder of entire families is nectar of the gods. Happy is the one who has tasted it!

The war was still raging in Europe, and even though the outcome was assured, there was no security in our future in Romania. Poland, the land where we were born, the place considered ours through generations, would never again be home for us. During the many idle hours spent in hiding or in prison or in camp, when we spun our tales about home, we referred to our hometowns. In our simplicity, or just the need to hang on to something very tangible and familiar, we all planned out triumphant returns. For me "home" had always been the building on a corner in Krakow with an open gate, where I hoped to pick up again the threads of my life, cut abruptly when I was fourteen years old.

Together with the awareness that "after the war" had arrived for us, came the realization that we could not go back. The Poles had achieved their dream of "Poland without the Jews." For us Palestine, always a dream, was our new home.

The offices of the Jewish Agency were besieged by people applying for certificates for Palestine. The Polish refugees were joined by newcomers from Bucovina and Transnistra. As more and more people wanted out, new faces appeared every day. My mother and I and some of our friends were among the lucky receivers of the first certificates awarded by the British to refugees. A group of young people from Poland, who had survived under different disguises, congregated around us because of my mother. She symbolized all the mothers that had perished. Sometimes they just enjoyed the sound of the word "mother," which they had been forced to eliminate from their own vocabularies forever.

In December 1944 we boarded the train in Bucharest, the first group of survivors to leave for the Promised Land. The trip that was supposed to last four or five days took six weeks. It was the middle of January 1945 before we reached Haifa.

The picturesque trip through the magnificent Romanian country-side went smoothly, but in Bulgaria we were abruptly stopped at the city of Stara Zagora. The Soviets, who were already occupying Bulgaria, put the whole train under arrest, and we were confined to the station. But after a few days the local people intervened, and we were allowed at least to go into town. The first visit was to the public bath to try to deal with our thriving colony of lice. Then we looked about for friends. With few exceptions, the flourishing prewar Jewish community of Stara Zagora had been wiped out. Nevertheless, the few Jewish families who somehow survived did their utmost to ease our situation. As we began slowly to adjust to this unexpected situation, we were joined by a second trainload of bewildered survivors. Thus, the impoverished skeleton of a Jewish community found itself burdened with a group of six hundred people, who had to be fed and taken care of. Despite all the odds against them, the community was wonderful and provided all possible assistance.

During our stay in Stara Zagora we witnessed a scene of justice being administered in totalitarian style. Three alleged collaborators with the Germans were brought to the public square where a large crowd was gathered. There were no courts, no judges, no witnesses testifying. The accused were brought in blindfolded, and the public was asked to give the verdict. The whole crowd begun to shout: "Death! Death! Death!" A few moments later, the same motorcycles that brought them there took them to execution.

While we were detained in Stara Zagora, international pressure was exerted in order for us to get a free passage. After nearly three weeks, we were loaded aboard once more, and the train moved. The ill-fated train had hardly managed to gain full speed before we were stopped again at the border of Turkey. It took the Bulgarian officials "only" two weeks to clear the matter with Sofia. Meanwhile we were stranded in the middle of nowhere, without any local Jewish community to be of help and provide contact with the outside world. When the ghost train was finally allowed to cross the border to neutral Turkey, we were carried to Istanbul, where we had to spend two days on a quarantine ship. It was sent out into the bay a few miles from the harbor, flying a yellow flag as a warning to other ships. From there we witnessed one of the most beautiful sights in the world, sunrise on the Bosphorus – except that we were hardly in the mood to admire nature. After two days our ship moved to the Asian shore of Turkey where we boarded a train that took us through Turkey and Syria to what was then Palestine.

As the train neared Rosh–HaNiqra, the Jewish border settlement, excitement mounted. In the first car was a group of youngsters from Transnistra, all members of the Zionist Youth Organization. They brought along a large white and blue flag, and attached it to the platform. It was only after the train crossed the border, and we saw people standing on both sides of the tracks, crying and laughing, throwing flowers, waving and calling greetings, that we realized the significance of our arrival.

The scene repeated itself through the entire ride from the Syrian border to Atlith, an old army camp. The war in Europe was in its final throes, and we were the first survivors from the Nazi hell to arrive in the Holy Land. It was one of Israel's beautiful, sunny January days when a cloudless expanse of blue skies stretches over the land in the first bloom of spring. All of working Palestine had come out to greet us. Mothers with babies in their arms stood at every stop the train made, showing us those beautiful babies and pointing us out to the children, all the time telling them "Maapilim, maapilim (Survivors)." Farmers signaled from the fields, drivers stopped their cars on the highway, schoolchildren, people young and old, ran and waved to the slowly moving train. We were crowded at the windows, trying to take in the scenery and to have it imprinted in our memories forever.

When the train finally arrived in Atlith, the station was crowded. The refugees were greeted by the representatives of the Jewish Agency, photographed by the mob of press people, embraced by friends, and besieged with questions by anxious strangers who had not heard for years from their families in Europe.

We all were so happy to have reached the end of our wanderings, that we even delighted in our stay in that old army camp, during the two weeks it took the British bureaucrats to process the newcomers.

The anticlimax came only when the refugees entered regular society and the struggle with everyday problems began.

And here the survivor's story ends. I would like to ask the reader to remember that mine is only one family's tale of suffering and survival and brushes with danger. Millions of others could be told. How many were killed while attempting to escape? Who knows the names of those who were lost along the way to freedom? Thousands upon thousands perished on the Aryan side, during armed resistance, fighting with the partisans, and in jails all over Europe.

Each life lost is a story untold.

Part Three • New life begins

33 · *Tel Aviv*

In January 1945 Mother and I arrived in Tel-Aviv. Through the good offices of Oleh Polania (society of Jews from Poland), we were assigned one room in the rooming house they had recently acquired. It was an old, dilapidated office building at Rothschild Boulevard 2, bordering Yaffa, the Arab quarter, hastily converted into dwellings for immigrants. The second floor was divided into six rooms, each the size of an average New York bathroom, and those were assigned to couples. Thanks to the magic of the name "Landerer," we got one of those rooms. Furnishings provided by the Jewish Agency consisted of an iron bed, a small table, and two stools. One room on the floor was converted into a kitchen. There was one cold water sink and a bench on which each family kept her petroleum-fuel Primus, a fast cooking lamp. One toilet was situated on our floor as well. On the main floor were rooms for single men, who boarded 3 or 4 to a room, and there was a cold water shower room, servicing the entire building of thirty occupants.

The euphoria we felt after having settled in our "apartment" is hard to describe. We were alive, each had her own bed, and we could close the door of our room whenever we wanted to.

And then the end of the war came, and we had to face reality. Lists of survivors were published daily – but to us they did not bring good news. From hearsay we learned that the deportees from Siberia were transferred to the south of the U.S.S.R. With fear and trembling we waited for news from ours. When finally letters from Father started to arrive, we relived our tragedy.

The letters from my father, and the PS. from my brothers and my Aunt Dina Anisfeld, whose husband Szymon was murdered in Tarnow in 1942, don't need introduction. In these few pages that my mother kept among her things is contained the tragedy of the Polish Jewry.

They are self-explanatory.

Marx [a town not far from Saratow] May 7, 1945

Chaciu and Laluniu,

Finally I received your address from Rand's sister in Palestine, and Osiasz Grossfeld in New York. Where is my Lelunia, Sala with Bubek and Eva? What happened to Szymon Anisfeld, Hirsch with family? We heard that all Jews from Nowy Sacz were saved, but know nothing about those in Sambor, Sanok, and Przemysl. The news coming from Poland is tragic, however everybody hopes that his nearest and dearest were spared.

We heard about you first from Rabbi Kanner who had a letter from Aron Eberstark from Bucharest. I assume that Siolek and Escia Frelfeld (Ruchcia's Beer daughter and son-in-law), who were in Tarnow, survived. Are they with you? Please, do cable immediately!

We, thank God, are alive and well. In 1942 we left from Minora and came to Yakutsk, and in 1944 were allowed to move to Saratov. I am with Benek and Moshe, Dina and the children. Haskel, Ruchcia with Moniek, the Reifers (Ruchcia's married daughter), Rottenstreichs live in Engels. In the next letter I will write more, meanwhile I am waiting for news from you.

Love
Wolf

Dearest Mother,

I am happy to hear that you and Lala are in Palestine. We live in Marx, together with Aunt Dincia, and we doing very well. However, we are very worried that you did not let us know where is Lela. What with the rest of the family? I hope that soon we all will be together. Your loving son,

Moshe

278

Marx, May 13, 1945

Chajciuniu and Laluniu,

I'm beginning all over again because I don't know which one of the letters will reach you first. I'm overjoyed that you are in Palestine: on the other hand, I'm very alarmed about Lela, Sala, Eva, and Bubek. Why are they not with you? If Aron Eberstark is in Bucharest, then it is to be assumed that all those who were in Tarnow escaped to Bucharest, but we did not hear from them yet.

As for us, after two years in Minora we left for Yakutsk, and in summer 1944 we came to Saratov. Myself, Benek and Moshe. Dincia Anisfeld and her precious children are with us in Marx. Haskel, the Rottenstreichs, Beers, Reifers are in Engels, fifty kilometers away from us.

Chajciu, you will not recognize our sons. Thank God, they matured beautifully. Benek is fluent in six languages, and Moshe performs as a cantor. You cannot imagine how beautifully he davens [recites the prescribed prayers of the liturgy] and sings; whenever he performs he creates a real sensation.

I'm longing for a letter from you, confirming the wonderful news that you are alive and in Palestine. All I know about you so far is from hearsay.

The war is over. [Germany surrendered May 8.] Most probably we will be able to return to our homes, and then what? I haven't made any plans for our future as yet. Ask the advice of my sister, Gela Brandt and her children. At any case our boys got a good training in the Soviet school of life, and they will always be able to take care of themselves. Meanwhile the future is of no concern to me. The destiny of our most beloved is foremost on my mind. I'm full of hope, but at the same time not knowing what happened to the rest of my family is a constant nightmare.

All my love,
Wolf

Dear Mommy,

The news that you and Lala are in Palestine made us most happy. What worries us greatly is that we haven't heard about Lela. Write us in detail how you managed to get into Palestine. Where is Lela and the rest of the family? We are all, thank God, well and alive, but most anxious to find out when we will be leaving Marx for home. We all hope that by the time this letter reaches you, we will be on our way back to Krakow.

With best regards and love,
Moshe

Dearest Mother and Lala,

We wrote already once, but in order to make sure that you hear from us, we are writing again. We are all well. You will not recognize us. Father dear exaggerates a bit, as usual when his children are concerned. I did not master six languages yet, but he probably counts those I hope to learn in the future, but Moshe has become a really good cantor. I can't wait for you to see for yourselves.

With hugs and kisses,
Benek

Dear Chacia and Lala,

We are waiting for news from you with great trepidation. Every day seems like a millenium. We write every day. Why is Lela not with you? Chacia dearest, write me where is my dear husband Szymon and the rest of our precious family. From the very beginning I was together with Wolf and the boys. I take care of the household. You will not recognize my children. They are big, and Rachel is a real beauty.

With all my love,
Dina

Translated from Polish by S. R.

Marx, June 17, 1945

My very dear ones,

A month has passed since we received a cable from you from Tel Aviv. I can hardly wait for the letter bringing answers to all the

280

questions that occupy my mind day and night. Where is my darling Lelusia? Haskel's family, Szymon Anisfeld and Hirsch? You were all together in Tarnow, most probably they survived the same way that Aron Eberstark, who is in Bucharest now. I don't permit myself any doubt and live only by the hope that they survived Hitler's hell.

I don't know anything about the rest of the family. The gruesome news from Poland that reaches us here freezes the blood in my veins.

We hope to be going back to Krakow soon. I can hardly wait to be there with my boys and Dincia and her children. Haskel lives in Engels. He is very depressed and pessimistic, just the opposite of me. My incurable optimism and faith are of great help.

We are very well off here in Soviet Russia, and we don't lack a thing.

Stay well. God willing, we will meet soon.

With all my love,
Wolf

Dear Mother,

I wonder why there is no news from you and hope that you are well. We thank God are well and doing well.

Love,
Moshe

My most precious mother,

A number of weeks went by already since the first sign of life from you, and nothing more. By us all is well. We are healthy, have good appetites, and plenty to eat, but no more patience to wait for news about Lela and the entire family.

Benek

Chacia dear,

Every day I wait for a letter from you, but in vain. Over a month passed since the cable, and no more news. Chaciu, when will I see you? I do not understand myself at all. How did I go on living for over six years without a word from Szymon and the rest of ours? I live with hope but my hope is coming to an end.

How is your health? And you, Laluniu, are probably a real young lady by now. My children you won't recognize at all, they grew so. I hope to God that soon we will be together. The entire family!

Hugs and kisses,
Dina

Translated from Polish by S. R.

Marx, August 13, 1945

My dearest Laluniu,

I received your letter of January 15, containing the picture of your dear mother. Although I'm not sure whether you understand English well, I'm compelled to write to you in a language not understood by your Aunt Dincia in order not to break her heart.

You, my dearest child, did not describe under what circumstances you parted from Lelunia, and at which date. Further, whether at that time she remained in Tarnow together with Aunt Sala, whether Aunt Sala also had Aryan documents for herself and her children, especially whether Bubek remained together with them. Whether in Tarnow was the possibility to escape the way Mr. Eberstark did, whether your Uncles Szymon and Hirsch tried to do the same? Why do you mention nothing about them? If you were in contact with them until the end of 1943, then the hope that they saved themselves would be justified. You also failed to mention whether you were in the camp [Arbeitslager Bochnia] together with Uncle Josef and his family, if he was alone and what happened to his family. I'm shocked thinking what you must have gone through during the flight from camp.

I'm very heartbroken about not hearing from my Lelunia. Three and a half months have expired since the war ended, and how is it possible that she did not try to contact me through New York or Moscow? This alarms me greatly. Each member of our family, each one is a part of my heart.

Our repatriation is being postponed all the time, but most likely the next month or at the beginning of October we shall journey home. I hope that at my return home I will find mail from you. I did not tell Dincia about your letter and the postcard because you did not mention her husband at all.

I hope and pray to God Almighty that He immediately restores our ruined nation.

Kissing you my loveliest and dearest child,
Father,

Original written in English.

Marx, March 3, 1946

My dear Laluniu,

Today I received a postcard from you dated January 22, Informing us that you sent again a package. From the torrent of packages you are sending us, we got only few. We hope to be leaving soon, so why do you go to all that trouble and expenses? Our needs are not that great. When we eventually do get to Krakow, then we will need more things, and I think that there we will receive if not all, then at least most of the packages sent to us. Here so far we got two packages with clothing and two packages with matza.

Two transports left for Poland already. We are waiting anxiously for our turn to come – hopefully in the next days or weeks. My love to both of you,

Father

Translated from Polish by S. R.

Marx, March 19, 1946

Lalunlu mine,

The so anxiously awaited letter from you came today. You begun to write on December 20, and finished on January 1. My precious child! You complain about the longing that torments you – I must tell you that I feel the same way, and I control myself with all my might. Sometimes it seems to me that I am losing my mind. What makes the situation even more difficult is that since a year I'm trying to leave for Poland and from there to follow you – but to no avail. Some people returned to Poland already, but those were the lucky holders of Soviet passports. Those documents allowed them to travel freely to Lwow, and from there to Krakow. All of those that were deported to Yakutenland were forced to accept stateless passports, and with those could not move from one place to another. Now you understand why we are stuck here. I appealed a number of times to the Polish Embassy in Moscow and to Premier Morawski and the Ministry of Commerce in Warsaw, and have yet to hear from any of them. I even offered to pay my own expenses, all to naught.

At present we lead the tragic existence of people without a country. Those that voluntarily exchanged the Polish passports for the Soviet ones have received Polish visas without any trouble and are expecting to be leaving on March 27. The bureaucrats tell us to be prepared for the possibility that our visas may come at the last moment, and thus we live with tension, not knowing whether the departure will be in a few days, weeks, months, or never.

I hope that at the end we will leave and a new era will begin. We will be re-living symbolically what you suffered during the war. I dread the moment we will pass the border and even before. Sambor, where so many of our beloved lived, is not part of the U.S.S.R. Therefore, I am greatly annoyed when you worry so much about us. What is to worry about, we are the ones that remained alive, thank God

We received another three packages and an announcement that one more is on the way. A pity that you send us so many. It must have cost you so much effort and money, and you work so hard.

When I reach Krakow, I hope to write you a long letter with all the details that interest you. At the same time I am sending a separate letter to Mamusia. I embrace you with love,

Your father

Not much space left to write. You should not worry about us. We are well off, have enough heating wood and don't suffer from cold. I kiss you both.

Dina

My children send their love.
Translated from Polish.

Marx March 28, 1946
My dearest and most precious Lala and Chacia,

The day before yesterday, I wrote a long letter to Mamusia, today I am happy to inform both of you that we are overjoyed. The third package of matza has arrived, as well as four other packages.

284

The repatriation has officially begun, but it is over a month that our departure is being postponed from day to day. I hope that the rest of the packages sent to Marx will reach us here. I really do not understand why you went to the trouble and such great expense when you knew already in January that we will be leaving Marx. We live with the illusion that we will be returning to our apartments and find all our things there. If not, then I am confident that we will overcome all difficulties. It really is a pity that material things take up so much of our thoughts.

I wish you a nice holiday,
your Wolf

Translated from Yiddish by S. R.

Marx, April 13, 1946
Saturday evening

My dear Laluniu,

It is for the seventh time that we stand before the eve of the holiday of Redemption and prepare for a seder that we will celebrate so far apart from each other. We never imagined that a whole year after the end of the war would pass and we would still be so far from our dream of sitting together at one table. This holiday coincides with spring-time, when the sun shines brighter, warming and awakening nature. The sun rays, coming after a long and hard winter, bring hope of renewal to all men. To all, but the Jewish people, whose wounded soul hurts and hurts. Nothing can put the torn shreds of the Jewish heart together. Nations of the world persecuted us throughout millenia, but what happened in our times defies human understanding.

Is this the way nations repay the Jews for bringing the idea and belief in one God? Or is it a compensation for the contributions in science, technology, art, music, and general knowledge Jews made in every country they lived?

Germany waged a war against the entire world. The same Germany that counted among their citizens Jewish scientists like Einstein, Ehrlich, Zondek, and many others, that brought glory to the German science. It was thanks to Jews like [Walther Rathenau, who as Minister of Reconstruction in 1922 secured from the Allies a reduction in Germany's war reparations, that Germany rose after the defeat of World War 1. Why, why did they have to choose Jews, gather them from the farthest corners of the continent, and destroy in most bestial ways?

It is with a heart full of bitterness and disappointment that I appraise all institutions of higher learning. All those universities, with their well-equipped laboratories, staffed with Jewish talent, contributed and laid foundations to the most advanced technological innovations, without imbuing any moral values in their students. Before the great advancement of science took place killing one Jew required one bullet. The new technology permitted [anti-Semites] to kill thousands at once, without wasting one bullet. Just a little can of cyclon gas did it. That much for what the enlightened secularists so pompously call progress.

And what about the nations of the world that collaborated with the Nazis? And those who closed their gates to the fleeing Jews? And those who acquiesced by indifference and those who actively participated and denounced innocent people?

No wonder that the wounded Jewish heart rebels against the people whose hands are stained with the blood of our innocents. Bewildered people asked God how could He let it happen? This question has no logical foundation. All horrors and sufferings that became our lot came by the hands of men, members of the most enlightened nation in the world. Culture that denies the one and only God does not contain any moral basis.

As every discipline has individuals whose genius contributes to its growth, religious faith is enriched by few chosen, who are blessed with the understanding of the uniqueness of God, and the ability to expound on His Commandments. Talmud tells us that a time will come when the world will be nearing its end, and one Jew will be left for every settlement, and two of every family. Tragically, it has become true in our day. Afterwards will come Redemption and liberation of the Jewish nation. Having witnessed unbelievable technological achievements of men, should we doubt God's ability to fulfill His promise?

[The rest of the letter is missing.]
Translated from Polish by S. R.

34 · No home to go back to

My father selflessness and devotion to his community is best illustrated by an incident after his return to Poland from the U.S.S.R. It was spring of 1946. The survivors from Hitler's and Stalin's concentration camps and deportations were returning to their homelands. It was midnight already when the train carrying a group of Polish Jews from Saratow, stopped in Krakow. My father, my two brothers, and father's ward, the war widow Dina Anisfeld and her three children – Moshe eleven years old, Braha nine, and Rachel six got off the train. After an uninterrupted trip in a freight train, which took ten days, they were tired, hungry, dirty, and insecure. The children were sleepy, and they were crying. Father held his emotions in tight grip: "Don't worry children. Uncle Wolf has a key to his house, and he is taking you home."

Having very little luggage, they were all able to squeeze into one buggy.

"Where to?" asked the sleepy coachman.

"Bonifraterska One" answered father, his voice choked by emotion. The streets were dark and deserted, and the trip did not last long.

"Who are you visiting so late in the night?" asked the driver. "Seems no one is expecting you. All the windows are dark."

"This is my house," Father said, tears streaming down his cheeks.

"Your house?" The man looked at Father's tattered clothing, said mockingly. "Maybe it is my house?"

Father took a key out of his pocket, turned it in the lock, and opened the gate. "Come in, *shefaloch* (little lambs). We are home!" The startled coachman scratched his head and muttered under his breath, "Some house owner," swished the whip over the horse's head and the old buggy rolled away into the night.

"Imagine, they never changed the locks." With a trembling hand Father fitted the key, but before he had time to turn it around, the door opened. Blocking the entrance stood a tall man.

"Who do you think you are daring to enter my house in the middle of the night?" he demanded in a loud voice.

"I am Wolf Landerer, and this is my house and my apartment. Those are my sons, Berl and Moshe, and this is my sister-in-law, Mrs. Anisfeld, and her children. Who are you and what are you doing in my apartment?"

"Your apartment? Your house? Where have you been? Don't you know that in socialist Poland there are no home owners? I am Dr. Merz and this apartment was given to me by the government of the People's Republic of Poland. Stop harassing me or I will call the *milicja*, and they will know how to deal with imposters like you."

As it turned out, the apartment had been divided in two. In one part Dr. Merz had living quarters and his office, in the other part, the Nastaleks, our former superintendent's family, was allowed to move in. The frightened children were crying. Dina, who only recently found out that she had no husband and no place she could call her own, was sobbing disconsolately. The commotion woke up Maria Nastalek. When she saw my father, she crossed herself and burst out in tears. "Mister owner, our Mister Landerer!" She was beside herself with joy and turned defiantly toward the doctor. "Mister Landerer came back, and he is my boss!"

"Then she went to call her husband and son: "Antoni! Edek! Get up! Look who is here!"

The Nastaleks took them in. They themselves bedded down on the floor and gave their beds over to my father and Dina with the children. They stayed with the Nastaleks for days, till they found an apartment in the Kazimierz section. All of the returning Jews, a pitiful few, congregated in their old neighborhood.

Soon after Father arrived in Krakow, came the pogrom in Kielce, where 42 Jews were murdered by Poles. Lesser incidents followed. Repatriates were made to understand that their former homeland could only be a transit stop for them. It was time for Father to come to terms with reality.

He had lost a daughter, a twenty-year-old girl, and he didn't even know how and where she had died. Moreover, he, wealthy, charitable

288

Wolf Landerer, had become a pauper. At the age of fifty-four, he had to start rebuilding his life.

First something had to be done about Dina and her children, alone and unprotected. She had not only lost a husband but her eight brothers and a beloved sister as well. She could not stay in Poland, with native anti-Semites ready to take up where the defeated invaders had left off. She was expedited to Kassel in West Germany, where displaced people were under the protection of UNRRA.

Next, he tried to renew his business contacts and collect some old debts. Some money was coming to him from Argolanda, for past commissions. But his friend Schroeder was dead, and the new management claimed that they had suffered losses in Poland which they had to cover by impounding Father's commission. The land was in disarray, and the process of socialization of private enterprise had begun. His one piece of luck was that he succeeded in selling the house in Krakow for the "large" sum of $1,500 and some land holdings he had, a most valuable property in the past, for an equally ridiculous amount.

At the same time Father became one of the moving forces in the temporary Jewish community. He was instrumental in the reopening of the ritual bath, the mikvah, the use of which is fundamental in religious observances. But most characteristic of him and most moving was the letter he wrote to a young woman who gave birth to a baby boy and adamantly refused to have the child circumcised according to religious law.

My father was at his best when he could act on a personal level. At the behest of the young woman's in-laws, he wrote her a letter which I present here in a shortened form:

Dear Mrs. T.

I assume that my letter surprised you and probably left you wondering that nowadays, when everyone is swamped with his own troubles, someone should take an interest in other people's problems. As for myself, unfortunately, I wasn't spared either, but I feel that the common tragedy of our People brought us, the survivors, closer to each other. One Jew's pain touches everyone in our small community.

First, let me congratulate you on the birth of your son. I heard that you refuse the circumcision, wishing with this act of defiance to express your bitterness toward God. I understand your pain and hurt. We all suffered. All Jewish hearts are bleeding. The tragedy that has befallen us has no comparison in the history of mankind. I feel with you, and I weep with you. But is putting the blame on God, being angry at Him, the right way to protest? Would the Jewish tragedy have come as a result of uncontrollable forces of nature, a gigantic volcanic eruption, a deluge or conflagration started by fiery lightening, then maybe your action could be forgiven and understood. But everything that happened to us during the last five years was caused by men, members of the most civilized and enlightened nation on earth.

When God created man, He endowed him with free will. Thus nations were at liberty to accept or reject the Torah. Now we see with what they replaced it. At present England, called "The bearer of culture among nations," refuses to let the tragic remnants of European Jewry reunite in their historical land. It is with deep pain and shame that I realize how many of our own people, impressed by the false gods of the so-called progress, are abandoning the traditional way of life of their fathers. One cannot blame God for man's actions! The understanding of God's mind however is beyond human comprehension. One would have to have faith and trust in the Creator. I truly do believe that there is reason and justice in all His ways.

What is the logic, if I may ask you, behind your decision to refuse the Child's circumcision? Your husband, his parents, especially his mother who is a loving mother to you, should they be condemned to the curse of the moment this child was born? The hurt, pain, and shame caused by the exclusion of their own flesh and blood from the Covenant of Abraham our forefather, is hard to describe. Could you imagine your son's reaction, his embarrassment and bitterness, when he realizes that he is different from other Jewish boys? How will he feel when he finds out that this was his own mother's doing?

I implore you, in honor of the memory of your own martyred parents, stop fighting the phantoms of the past, you are a daughter of People with a great and proud tradition. Don't desecrate their memory!

I hope that my plea, straight from a caring friend's heart, will be well received. I took the liberty to write to you because of the ties of friendship with your late parents, and your in-laws, may they live and be well. To be witness to their anguish is more than I can bear.

I conclude with the hope that you understand that the well-being of you, your family, and the newborn child is foremost on my mind. In anticipation of an invitation to a Brith-Mila I remain yours truly.

Shalom,
Wolf Landerer

A few days later came an invitation to the Brith-Mila, subsequently celebrated by the entire group of repatriates.

In 1947 my father and one of my brothers joined Mother and me in Tel Aviv. My oldest brother, Benek, married a Krakow girl whom he met in Siberia, and they together with his wife's family, moved to Antwerp, Belgium. In a way, we were astonishingly lucky – five out of six of us had survived.

But Uncle Haskel was not so fortunate. Full of hope and his usual verve, he returned to Krakow with his Russian fiddle under his arm. On the train carrying him home, he practiced his wife's and daughter's favorite melodies. He heard scary rumors of what had happened to Krakow Jews, but he tried not to believe them. Such things could not have happened to his lovely wife, to his beautiful Eva, just fourteen when he last saw her.

No one was waiting for him in Krakow. But through the services of the Joint Distribution Committee, he found out that his son Bubek had survived and was then living in a displaced persons camp. Haskel left Poland and went in search of the boy, and in time, they had a tearful reunion.

Separated again when Bubek sailed for Palestine, they were once more victimized by a cruel fate. Bubek's ship was intercepted by the British, and he was sent to Cyprus, where he found himself behind barbed wire for the second time in his life. After the State of Israel was established in 1948, he was allowed to continue on to Tel Aviv, and Haskel joined him there three years later.

Haskel never regained his zest for life. Music could not fill the emptiness left behind by the loss of Sala and Eve, and he gave up trying to rebuild his life. Inconsolable, he died at the age of fifty-eight, a broken and bitter man.

35 · Eulogy

Before I leave I must pause here to remember those of the numberless dead who were particularly precious to me, because they are gone, and there is *nothing* left of them except the memory. The overwhelming tragedy of the Holocaust is the totality of the destruction it caused. It left no trace of the past and no hope for the future. It wiped out not just lives but a way of life, a tradition, and a thousand years of the history of Polish Jewry.

First among my dead is my sister Lela. The pain of losing an older sister cannot be conveyed in words. Only a woman who had a sister close in age and lost her young could understand the magnitude of my loss and pain.

Lela was everything I wanted to be and some more. She had a brilliant mind that established a high standard for all her performances. She was ambitious, hardworking, courageous, loyal, loving, charitable, and sharing. When the first group of Jews to be expelled from Germany, the "Zbaszyn Group," arrived in Krakow in the fall of 1938, she sent to the Kahal an anonymous donation of the first money she had ever earned by giving private lessons in math.

The same standards she set for herself she expected from everybody, especially from me, her younger sister, but at the same time she was tolerant, protective, and understanding of my shortcomings.

Her tragic death created a void in my life that nothing and nobody can ever fill. I will never stop missing her, I will never stop mourning her!

My Aunt Sala, the wife of Haskel Landerer, and their daughter Eva, were part of my everyday life. Eva's parents were ten years younger than my own and Eva, their oldest, was exactly my age. I loved this young family and their house, always full of music, laughter, and young people, where I spent most of the days I was free from school.

My cousin Eva was a beautiful girl. As musical as her father, she was a promising piano student, a good skier, and great fun to be with.

If there ever was a prototype for the meaning of the word "lady," then my Aunt Sala was it. We lived together for over three of the most difficult years imaginable, shared beds, food, all chores, and not even once was there a loud word spoken or an argument between the two sisters-in-law, my mother and Aunt Sala. They complemented each other, and during these hard years a bond was formed among us all that only death could have cut – as it did.

My wonderful Aunt Sala "went with the big transport." This was the euphemism used during the war for the disappearance of people taken away for extermination.

And together with her mother went Eva, beautiful Eva with waistlong ash-blond hair, the largest gray eyes I have ever seen, and long fingers always tapping imaginable piano keys. And she was only eighteen years old.

How can I ever forget my Uncle Hirsh, the first one of the family to "go with the transport." I was told recently by my cousin Aron that, when Hirsh and his family reached the train station, the entire transport was segregated, all young, able-bodied men being separated from the rest. Considered by the Germans as potential slave laborers, they might have had a chance for survival, but Hirsh – who was by no means an old man – refused to accept this chance and returned to the group where his wife and children were standing. This is the last that is known about Hirsh to us, the few survivors of the large Horowitz family.

The abyss of suffering that Ghetto Tarnow had become swallowed another one of my closest family, my cousin Esther Freifeld, the younger daughter of my Aunt Ruchcia Beer, lovely Escia, considered the most beautiful girl in the entire Myslenice district, married Saul Freifeld from Krakow two years before the war. In 1942 they moved to Tarnow, where she perished during the second Action. Escia and her two year old Idus (Yehuda) were murdered during the second "Action," and her husband Saul died in a concentration camp in Germany. Esther's oldest brother Josek was with them in Tarnow; how he met death I do not know.

And Rochma? Iciu Weinberger's fiance who never became a bride?

Once upon a time in the not distant time, in the town of Nowy Sacz high up in the Karpathian Mountains, there lived a girl, and Rochma Klagsblad was her name. The details of her martyrdom are not known to me. I can only attest that she existed, and loved, and hoped, and wanted to live. Would anyone care to remember her name?

Reminiscing about my family's Nowy Sacz martyrs, I cannot omit my Uncle Haim Horowitz, one of my mother's younger brothers. Having been refused a permit to remain in Ghetto Krakow, he joined his wife's family in Nowy Sacz. This was the last trip this young family took together. What kind of torture cut short their young lives I do not know, because I have never met a Nowy Sacz survivor – if there are any. But I would like to go back to my good memories about them.

How proud they all were of their Haim, the public spaker. How did they enjoy talking about the day when Haim spoke during the Third of May celebration, a major national holiday in prewar Poland. The entire adult population of Myslenice crowded the town's main square where all government buildings were located. Speakers appeared on the balcony of the main district building. Haim Horowitz, twenty-one years old at that time, was one of the featured speakers. The seemingly unworldly yeshiva boy spoke so well that the enthusiastic crowd did not want to let him go, and when after a prolonged applause the next speaker, the esteemed *starosta* (head of the district) appeared, the crowd begun to shout: "Horowitz! Horowitz!" and kept it on for a long time. It has to be emphasized that Myslenice was one of the most anti-Semitic towns in Poland.

In addition to his faultless command of the Polish language and oratory gifts, he was a Jewish scholar, known to spend entire nights studying Talmud.

His wife Sala was a lovely woman, who, with her gentle ways quickly won her husband's family love. When Itzek Horowitz, Haim's brother, was brought to Krakow for cancer surgery, he wanted to stay only with Haim and Sala, who opened their home and hearts to him. Their love, devotion, and kindness eased the sick man's sufferings.

Haim and Sala Horowitz had three children, two boys, Hasiu and Monius, and a daughter, Rechusia. During the first year of the war, after the schools were forbidden to Jewish children, I taught the two boys and got to know them well. The oldest, Hasiu, was amazing. His quick mind absorbed knowledge like a dry sponge soaking up water. As young and inexperienced as I was, I sensed that my little cousin was unusually talented, especially in composition. His little essays were circulated among the proud family. Monius was three years younger, and the instruction was only on a second-grade level, but he was an outstanding student as well. Rechusia was born right at the beginning of the war, and in no time became the pet of the entire family. Even in our one room in Tarnow her photos were proudly displayed.

They all, of course, vanished when Ghetto Nowy Sacz was liquidated. All that is left to me when I think of them is a dull, persistent ache in my heart.

Not much is left to tell about the rest of the Horowitzes. My Aunt Bala with her daughter Rachela perished in Auschwitz. I have already described how my Uncle Josiu survived two years in Auschwitz and three months in Gleiwitz, then was sent to Theresienstadt, where he lived to be liberated by the Russians. Unfortunately, after the liberation his wasted body succumbed to the dreaded typhus, so that he was as much a martyr to Nazi atrocity as the others.

Leibus, the next in line after my mother, his wife, and their three handsome boys who grew up on the estate and loved the land and life close to nature vanished into the silence. Leibus Horowitz, the family *illui* (genius), who knew by heart entire sections of Taimud and the Book of *Zohar* (kabbala), whose greatest ambition was that his sons become scholars. My uncle Leibus, who sent us a letter to Ghetto Bochnia telling us not to worry, not to lose heart and hope. "I have buried gold, dollars, jewels, hidden hides, textiles, everything to provide for the future of us all." My uncle Leibus with the buried treasure that would have taken care of all our needs, he is gone, and his family with him. We don't even know when or how it happened. Since there is no one to tell about their last moments, remembering them is my sacred duty.

Wolf, – called by all Wolvek, to distinguished him from my father, the other Wolf in the family – my uncle Wolvek, his scholarly wife, Miriam, who was so well versed in the German classics and the Bible with commentaries, their daughter Rachela, and their three boys, were among Limanowa's martyrs.

Yankel, Wolvek's twin, lived in Chrzanow. He used to come to us often and bring with him his daughter Recha, who was one year older than myself. Recha Chrzanowska, as she was called in order not to be mistaken with the other Rechas, was very musical and studied the piano. During the war, while we were already in Chrzanow, Recha died of a disease whose nature was not known to us. Her parents were devastated and stopped writing altogether but through a Chrzanow girl in Tarnow, we heard that Recha Horowitz had died, and all that was left of her was the memory of fingers on the keyboard. Yankel Horowitz, his wife Freida, and their younger son Iciu perished with the rest of Chrzanow's Jewry.

My Uncle Itzek Horowitz, whose red hair belled his gentle disposition, lived in Jaworzno, about an hour by train from Krakow, unassuming and rather shy – unusual traits for a member of the exuberant Horowitz clan – he did not visit us often. I remember him best from the time he was sick with cancer, and Reeva and I went to the hospital to visit him on Shabbat. The hospital of the Merciful Sisters was a private institution very far from where we lived, but we could not ride on Shabbat, and the walk was too difficult for our mothers.

It was a warm spring day, and he was covered with a light sheet only. While we were talking, he moved and the sheet slipped off a bit, baring one leg from the knee down. It looked like part of a skeleton, and it made me realize how sick my uncle was. But he was happy to see us and wanted us to stay till the end of the visiting hours.

From the hospital he went back to Sala and Haim. A few weeks later he was taken home, and shortly after they all left for Jaworzno to attend the funeral and sit *shibah* at the home of their deceased brother.

His wife and son Moshe perished in Jaworzno. I have already described how Szaye, the youngest of the brothers, died in Gleiwitz the night after he met his oldest brother. And his wife Rozia, our golden princess, on whom life was always smiling? Were her children torn away from her? Was Vigdus, that exquisite child of love, made to face his executioners all by himself, and he only seven years old? Or was he permitted to hold the hand of his baby brother Talus? When and where did they fall, those two unknown soldiers killed in the war waged by the mighty German Reich against Jewish children? Were they made to face the firing squad while clutching their toys and crying for their mommy? Or were they blindfolded or made to look at what they could not comprehend?

My Aunt Rozia, did she live to mourn her children? Was she all alone with that nightmare? Even Satan himself could not devise a more horrendous torture!

I could see them all, the children from my family. The Horowitzes, the Landerers, the Weinbergers, the Balkens, and every other Jewish child whose name is a million! One million young lives, each one a world of love, hope and promise wiped out in the name of an ideology gone mad. What is left is a procession of children's ghosts hovering all over Europe and crying out to us: REMEMBER!

And I do remember.

I remember Avroom Landerer, Cyla, Gusta, and Lulek, their American visas and dreams of a new life all gone up in the flames of Ghetto Przemysl.

I remember David Landerer and Thilla and Sala and Benek. Were the brothers taken away together, with their families? Were they spared the cattle train transports and the agony of the crematoria? Who knows? Those were times when death by a bullet was in the realm of wishful thinking.

I remember my father's oldest sister, Haya Goldwasser, whose husband was sent to Auschwitz via Tarnow's prison. I remember her daughter Dorcia and her letters begging us not to forget her father in prison – as if we could! Her two married daughters with their husbands and Haya's four blond grandchildren, her daughter Henia and son Benek – I don't even know when, where, and how they all met their end. They were all in Makow when last we heard, but the Germans often transferred people from one ghetto to another, and we lost contact after our arrival in Bochnia. They are gone, that's all I know.

I remember my Aunt Ryfka Balken, who always made me laugh, and her husband, quiet, gentle Szymon Balken, who used to take the kids on long hikes in the country. And their two boys, the black Arek as opposed to the fat Arek, and Betek, my pal during the summer vacations.

I remember Aunt Blimcia with special pain. There was a profound parallel between her name, Little Flower, and her destiny. By carrying the promise of fruit and continuity, every flower reflects the universal design of life. The plant does not disappear when its flowers and leaves are blown off by violent elements, because its roots remain in the ground. If by chance or design the roots are destroyed, it is still possible to hope that some scattered seeds will put down roots in the new soil. But the Holocaust pulled up this gentle, loving woman by the roots and destroyed her seed as well.

One of her sons died of consumption in Rzeszow concentration camp. The other vanished when that hellhole was liquidated, and the details of his martyrdom are not known. Moniek was seventeen years old when his mother saw him last.

And her daughters? Beautiful, brilliant Recha with the chestnut hair and dimpled smile, all goodness and kind heart. Reeva, my special friend, who watched the changing Vistula with me from their apartment window, freckled, earnest, so certain that she could not measure up to her dazzling siblings. Long-legged Hinda, Professor *Mucha*, who read her way through the library too soon, and Baby Dina in hand-me-down clothes.

Was Blimcia forced to witness their martyrdom?

And Meir-Halm, her husband, kindly and pious. When did she see him last? Did they enter the gas chamber together, stripped naked, deprived of human dignity?

All I know for certain is that the Weinbergers are gone. That wonderful family, those people whose lives were as pure, as good, as just as their deaths were ghastly, cruel, and bestial.

I remember my grandmother, Feiga Landerer, and her indomitable spirit. The small dark figure, vain of having no gray hair under her sedate wig, making cookies and sourballs and urging them on her reluctant grandchildren, emptying the koshering pail – though she'd promised not to – and playing tricks on Aunt Sala and curing the girl the doctors had not helped. At the age of seventy-five, she was murdered in Ghetto Sambor. Was she wearing, I have often wondered, one of her sombre old-fashioned dresses with a little round collar?

And I remember all the others, youngsters and adults, second and third cousins, and the cousins of the cousins, and their aunts and uncles, and the storekeepers, the traders, the porters, the *belfers*, the people on the streets and all the inhabitants of the Jewish sections, all

298

those who were part of our world. They were murdered by the German Nazis.

On Yom Kippur, the Day of Remembrance, I light a candle and recite a prayer for the eternal peace of each beloved soul. If it were possible to build a pyre out of pain and despair, then I would erect a giant one and light it and let it burn, for the whole world to see. It would mourn not just these people and the millions of others who went to their deaths in the murder camps but the entire world we lived in, which was murdered, too. A way of life and love and tenderness passed into nothingness, gone up in the smoke of the crematoria.

The smoke was blown away long ago. The wind scattered the ashes, and all that was left to us, pathetic survivors, are our bitter memories that will live as long as we do. And then? Who will tell this story?

This is why I wrote this book.